THOMAS HUX

High Street,

POLITICAL THOUGHT

Political Thought is about the State, its structure, its nature and its purpose. Its concern is with nothing less than the moral phenomena of human behaviour in society. It seeks not so much an explanation of the existence of the State as a justification of its continuance. The intention of this book is to provide for the beginner a comprehensive introduction to this most important subject.

This is a book for discussion, study and reflection; the issues are fairly and succinctly put with a wealth of apt and fluent quotation.

Higher Education Journal

TEACH YOURSELF BOOKS

POLITICAL
THOUGHT

C. L. WAYPER
M.A., Ph.D.

TEACH YOURSELF BOOKS

ST PAUL'S HOUSE WARWICK LANE LONDON EC4

First Printed 1954
This Impression 1971

ISBN 0 340 05691 6

PRINTED AND BOUND IN ENGLAND
FOR THE ENGLISH UNIVERSITIES PRESS LTD
BY HAZELL WATSON AND VINEY LTD, AYLESBURY

CONTENTS

CHAPTER IV

CHAPTER V

INTRODUCTION
(Political Thought—What it is and Why it Matters)

POLITICAL Thought is thought about the State, its structure, its nature, and its purpose. Its concern is with nothing less than "the moral phenomena of human behaviour in society." It seeks not so much an explanation of the existence of the State as a justification of its continuance. What is the State and why should I obey it? What are the proper limits of its authority and when may I refuse to obey it? How is the authority of the State with which I cannot dispense to be made compatible with the liberty without which I am less than a man? These are the questions which political thought is for ever striving to answer.

To these questions it can never give definite, once-and-for-all answers that will convince everyone. For it is so difficult to separate the purpose of political life from the purpose of life itself that the answers we give to these questions, or political theory, in the last analysis depends upon our conceptions of right and wrong. And because it is thus a branch of ethical theory it can never convince all, for there has always been and presumably always will be fundamental disagreement over first principles.

Hence it is better to speak of political thought than of political science. There was deep wisdom in Maitland's comment: "When I see a good set of examination questions headed by the words 'Political Science,' I regret not the questions but the title." For science demands general laws by the aid of which we can reach exact results. Yet the student of politics seeking such laws would be like the alchemist vainly searching for the elixir that would turn everything into gold. For as Graham Wallas said: "He cannot after twenty generations of education or breeding render even two human beings sufficiently like each other for him to prophesy with any approach to certainty that they will behave alike under like circumstances." We must say, then, with Burke that there is no science of politics any more than there is a science of æsthetics, for "the lines of politics are not like the lines of mathematics. They are broad and deep as well as long. They admit of exceptions; they demand modifications. No lines can be laid down for civil or political wisdom. They are a matter incapable of exact definition."

But if, to quote Sir Ernest Barker, "each professor of political thought is apt to feel about all the other professors, if not about himself, that they argue from questionable axioms, by a still more questionable process of logic to conclusions that are unquestionably wrong," what, it may well be asked, is the value of political thought? Answers of an extreme nature have frequently been given to that question. One is that it has no value, that it is arid and abstract, that as Bacon says, "like a virgin consecrated to God, it is barren." It is, it is maintained, a convincing illustration of that peculiarity of philosophers which Berkeley noticed, their habit of first kicking up a dust and then complaining that they cannot see. It is, as Burke tells us, "the great Serbonian bog 'twixt Dalmatia and Mount Cassius old, where armies whole have sunk." Another is that it is damnably dangerous, dealing darkness and devoted like the devil to disaster. The words of the Old Testament preacher, "In the day of prosperity rejoice, and in the day of adversity consider," have been interpreted to mean that consideration is either the prelude to or the proof of adversity. "Happy is the nation which has no political philosophy," Leslie Stephen wrote, "for such a philosophy is generally the offspring of a recent, or the symptom of an approaching, revolution." "One sure symptom of an ill-conducted state is the propensity of people to resort to theories," said Burke; and Hegel added that "the owl of Minerva takes flight as darkness falls." Men of the camp and cabinet agreed with men of the cloister. Napoleon and Metternich imputed the disasters of the age to the currency of too facile generalisations in political philosophy, and, like their 20th-century totalitarian successors, drew the conclusion that an open season should be declared on owls. Yet a third answer to the question what is the value of political thought is that it is the distilled wisdom of the ages which one has only to imbibe sufficiently to be translated into a rosier world where men stumble not and hangovers are unknown.

A less extreme answer to the question why should we study political thought is, however, possible. Reasonable students of political thought who neither believe that they are dealing with dynamite nor disturbing the dust will not set their sights too high. They will not expect to graduate automatically in wisdom, to lay bare in solitude all the secrets of political power, and to emerge from the study to handle the reins of authority, not with the fumbling touch of the amateur but with the assurance and skill of the master. They will know that philosophers, as history shows, have revealed as little aptitude for kingship as kings have for philosophy. But to shun absurd pretension is not to admit insignificance, and no one need apologise for indulgence in the study of man in his social and political relations. And if that study is not necessarily a guarantee of wisdom, it might at least be expected to be some protection against folly. There is no sovereign inoculation against nonsense, for men, as Hobbes saw, cling to their privilege of absurdity. Nevertheless, the student of political thought has met and seen exposed the specious solution, has encountered and been made to see in its true light the claptrap, knows the terrible power of words to cloak reality, and is aware of the duty that lies upon him of penetrating to that reality in spite of the torrent of words which may drum on his ears and drum up his emotions. "Do you not feel sovereignty coursing through your veins?" a French Revolutionary orator asked his hearers. No doubt many of them thought that they did, but the student of political thought might have been expected to content himself with Harvey's theory of the circulation of the blood. "We don't want higher bread prices, we don't want the same bread prices, we don't want lower bread prices," the Nazi orator raved, and his audience agreed with him that National-Socialist bread prices represented all their longing. Again a student of political thought might be expected to have been at once less hard to please and more discriminating. For he would have learned to beware of "things that featly blear our eyes," would be aware with Thucydides of "the use of fair phrases to arrive at guilty ends." Moreover, the very harshness of the 20th century will confirm for him the truth of Aristotle's remark that the political art is the most important of all arts, and he cannot therefore believe that its study will be the least significant of studies. Rather will he turn with renewed interest to the masters, eagerly conscious of the fact that to go to school with the great is never an experience to be avoided but a privilege to be sought.

Answers to the question : "What is the State and why do men

obey it?" have been of two kinds. One is that the State is an organism of which men themselves are parts and which is therefore greater than they are. It is real and they are merely abstractions. The other is that it is a machine which men create for their own purposes and which is therefore no other than they are. They are real and it is merely a device. Both views are dealt with in this book. At different periods in history, now the one, now the other has been generally accepted. The idea of the State as an organism was hit upon by the Greeks. By the Stoics it was applied to humanity as a whole. It was then taken over by Christianity, and throughout the Middle Ages reigned supreme. It was challenged at the time of the scientific revolution of the 17th century, which led to the development of the "mechanistic" view of the State. This view was maintained throughout the Enlightenment of the 18th century, to be rejected again by Rousseau and by the German Romantics, who stressed the "organic" view as against the "bloodless" and "soulless" mechanistic doctrine. Once again came the swing of the pendulum, if for no other reason than that political and ecclesiastical reactionaries, such as Adam Müller and de Maistre, so enthusiastically embraced the organic doctrine in the hope of using it to repress the new liberal forces which they so much disliked. The mechanistic view yet again came into favour, only to be strongly attacked by the organic view strengthened by 19th-century biological theories and by 20th-century totalitarian practices. Both views still persist and still contend for domination over the minds of men.

This division of political thinkers into upholders of the organic and mechanistic views of the State is not, however, the only possible classification of such thinkers. A further classification may prove yet more helpful, one which stresses the difference as well as acknowledges the similarities between Aristotle and Hegel, and Plato and Rousseau. This would allot political thinkers to three different traditions. The first is the Rational-Natural tradition. According to this, Society and the State can be understood only when they are related to an absolute standard, which exists in nature and which is therefore outside human control, but which, nevertheless, can be known by men through the use of their Reason. Society, according to this tradition, must copy the pattern offered by nature which Reason has apprehended, and if we want to know whether laws and institutions are good, we have only to ask if they are close copies of the existing natural standards. The second is the tradition of Will and Artifice. According to this, Society and the State are artificial and not natural. They are genuinely free creations of man and not a copying of something that already exists in nature. Therefore, according to this tradition, it is not the Reason of man but the Will of man that is required to produce the State, and human will has freedom to alter society. The third is the tradition of Historical Coherence. According to this, both of the other traditions are defective. Since natural laws have to be changed to suit civil society, the Rational-Natural tradition, it maintains, is really neither rational nor natural. And since man's will is always limited by the will of others and by what has been willed previously, the tradition of will and artifice, it declares, attributes too much importance both to will and artifice. Hence the tradition of Historical Coherence attempts to combine the earlier traditions, to fuse Reason and Will as in Rousseau's "General Will" and Hegel's "Rational Will." It emphasises the importance of historical growth and denies that absolute standards exist. Goodness and justice, it avers, consist of the coherence of the part with the whole, and if we want to know what is goodness we must seek conformity not with the will and desire of society at any given moment, but with the standard of coherence in that society as it has developed historically over the years. The State, according to this tradition, is not a copy of the natural world. But to some extent it can be seen as natural because it is the result of an historical evolution that can be thought of as part of nature. To some extent, however, it can be regarded as artificial, for it is the result of men not following but transforming nature. All believers in the State as a machine belong to the Will and Artifice tradition. Believers in the State as an organism may belong either to the Rational-Natural tradition or to the tradition of Historical Coherence.

In terms of this triple division, this book begins with an examination of the Rational-Natural tradition of the Greeks. It passes to the Will and Artifice tradition of the 17th century and on to the tradition of Historical Coherence of the 18th and 19th centuries. It moves to the consideration of a political thought that is essentially hybrid, of the thinking of the Communists, beginning with Marx, who belonged to the tradition of Will and Artifice to which the State is a machine, and ending with Stalin, who would seem to be most at home in the tradition of Historical Coherence according to which the State is an organism. The book concludes with a brief discussion of the possibility of the peaceful co-existence of the varying views of the State thus outlined.

CHAPTER I

HOW IT ALL BEGAN

(THE GREEKS, PLATO, ARISTOTLE, AND THE ORGANIC VIEW OF THE STATE)

THE GREEKS

The Debt of Political Thought to the Greeks

POLITICAL Thought, as we know it in the West, was the invention of the Greeks. Before the Greeks governments and subjects had of course existed, but hardly politics as we understand them. Not all Eastern despots devoted themselves, as did the Burmese kings, to those great tasks of true kingship—building pagodas, collecting vassals' daughters, and raiding their neighbours for white elephants, occupations little calculated to produce great political thought. Not all Eastern rulers and thinkers have been indifferent to the welfare of society just as not all Western rulers and thinkers have been concerned with it. One of the earliest of all legal codes resulted from the determination of Hammurabi, god-king of Babylon, to "uphold justice in the land." Ancient India speculated much on the function of kingship and the proper education of kings, even suggesting that they should, as it were, work in the mills before taking over the management. Chinese thought about man and society was as profound and as subtle as any such thinking in the West.

But Eastern thought was thoroughly authoritarian. The laws of Hammurabi were the laws of God, to be obeyed, and not questioned by mortal men. Similarly the justice sought by old Testament Jews was the justice of Jehovah, not the justice of Man. Indian and Chinese thought, while more secular, was not less authoritarian. Indian thinking accepted only the possibility of absolute monarchy and no one has ever insisted more than did Confucius on the necessity of establishing a universal orthodoxy. He justified, for instance, the execution of Shao-cheng Mou: "His dwelling serves as a gathering place for his disciples, forming a party; his theories serve to beautify unorthodoxy and please the multitude; his stubborn arguments are sufficient to upset the right and constitute a new and independent theory—he is thus a villain among men and must be eliminated." "He who is not in office," he taught, "has no concern for administrative duties." Hence there developed that traditional Chinese readiness to leave politics to the Superior Men who were Confucius's ideal. And we can read of the general criticism directed against a chance traveller who dared to mention politics after dinner at the inn— "the mandarins have to attend to affairs of State; they are paid for it. Let them earn their money then. But don't let us torment ourselves about what does not concern us. We should be great fools to want to do political business for nothing." No Greek could have said that, and it is not surprising that Chinese political thought, profound as it is, has a passivity which is alien to the West. It is this element of passivity that is so characteristic of Eastern thought. An idea, however exalted, of the public good is not sufficient for the development of political thought as the West understands it. Freedom to discuss it, and eagerness to discuss it and to apply it, are also essentials, and it was left to the Greeks to combine the three.

Greek Characteristics

Indeed, in all that is required for the development of political thought the Greeks were both first and supreme. "You Greeks are always boys; there is not an old man among you; you are young in your souls" said the Egyptian priest in Plato's *Timæus*. He was right. They never lost the boy's insatiable curiosity. They were a race of seekers after unknown truths. Thales, Anaximander, Pythagoras, Heraclitus, Parmenides, Zeno, all speculated about the origin and nature of the universe. Xenophon wanted to know why there were fossils in the Sicilian rocks. Herodotus wanted to know about soils and climates and customs, and about everything under the sun. "All men want to know," said Aristotle, and he added, "the feeling of wonder makes the true philosopher, for this is the only source of philosophy." For ages before the Greeks men had successfully curbed the longing to know which Aristotle ascribes to all men. But what he wrote was true of all Greeks, and it is because it is that Greece is one of the mainsprings of Western civilisation.

To great curiosity, the Greeks allied great faith in reason. They believed that life and the world were rational and that the laws that governed them might be apprehended by man. They were the first to call the Universe a "cosmos," an "order," and so ruled by law. Homer sees behind the gods an order to which even they must conform, and it is because the Greek tragedians shared his view that Whitehead called them the true founders of scientific thinking. No people was ever better at disentangling the essential from the accidental, for it was the law rather than any particular application of it that might be to their immediate advantage that fascinated them. Indeed, there is a Pythagorean proverb: "A new diagram, that means a step forward, but we do not draw it to make a threepence." And no people was ever better at seeing the universal in the particular, as the speeches with which Thucydides studs his History show.

Their attachment to intellectual truth was as great as their curiosity and their faith in reason. In ordinary life they never felt it necessary to tell the truth if it appeared to them that a lie would do better. To win a momentary advantage they might hope to deceive others. But in all that mattered in life they never sought to deceive themselves. They insisted on the real explanation even if it was unpleasant. And they would have said with Phædra in Euripides' *Hippolytus*:

> *"This is the truth I saw then, and see still,*
> *Nor is there any magic that can stain*
> *The white truth for me, or make me blind again."*

They had a great instinct for criticism. "The unexamined life," said Socrates, "is unlivable for a real human being." Not till the Stoics did they produce a philosophy based on obedience. They had a passion for analysis and a hatred of woolly thinking. They liked exact definition, even though they made Socrates drink the hemlock. Aristophanes laughs at "that native way of ours, that 'just what mean you?' that always pops out"; but it is doubtful if he thought it such a bad way at that.

Their great instinct for criticism of everything, including themselves, was inseparable from their great faith in rational discussion. "The great impediment to action is, in our opinion, not discussion, but the want of that knowledge which is gained by discussion preparatory to action," Pericles said, and those words that he uses of the Athenians can in some measure apply to all Greeks. "No greater calamity could come upon a people than the privation of free speech," Demosthenes says, and Euripides proclaims:

> "This is true liberty, when free-born men,
>   Having to advise the public, may speak free."

Such was their faith in rational discussion that Aristotle can say: "the many of whom each individual is but an ordinary person, when they meet together may very likely be better than the few good, if regarded not individually but collectively"; and never fear the irrational behaviour of the crowd. Indeed, it can even be argued that Rhetoric—the characteristic invention of an argumentative people—was their most typical art. Certainly not the least of what we owe to them can be ascribed to their great regard for intellectual truth, their great clarity and steadiness of vision, their great instinct for criticism and their great enthusiasm for rational discussion.

Above all, they were great humanists. Cicero was justified in telling his son who was starting for Athens: "You are going to visit men who are supremely men." Man is the centre of their thoughts, as their religion so clearly shows. "One is the race of gods and men," says Pindar—a view which exalts men as much as it reduces gods. Their sculpture and painting concentrated on the problem of depicting the human form. The inexhaustible theme of their poetry from Homer onwards is man. Their philosophy very typically moved from the problem of the cosmos to the problem of man. "The noblest of all investigations is the study of what man should be and what he should pursue," Socrates maintained, and Plato and Aristotle agreed with him. In all Greek literature there is nothing more Greek than Sophocles' noble line: " A wondrous thing is man—none more wondrous." "Other nations," it has been well said, "made gods, kings, spirits; the Greeks alone made men."

With their great interest in man they could not but be great individualists. Indeed, for evil as well as for good, no greater individualists have ever lived. The right to think their own thoughts, the right to speak them publicly, the right to act according to conscience so far as the welfare of others allows, were for them the most precious of rights. In the end individualism destroyed them. Yet their discovery of the individual, their realisation that a man's chief contribution to national life is his personality developed to the highest degree, is perhaps their supreme gift to the generations that came after them.

But if they were great individualists they were keenly aware of the importance of society, and if they refused to be stifled by tradition they were not indifferent to it. In their regard for the "nomoi," the old laws, and in their reluctance to countenance any changes in them they were a veritable race of Burkes. Had they been less interested in the individual or less concerned with the community, their fascination for us would have been much less than it is. Others have been great individualists or great believers in the State. No people has ever joined as they did such keen regard for the individual and such deep concern for the State. It is as much because of this as because of their eager curiosity, their passionate belief in reason, their scientific spirit, their fresh, critical outlook, and their humanism that the Greeks have continued to be the inspiration of so many succeeding generations.

The Language

If these were the qualities that made the Greeks the masters of political thought, they were fortunate in that in their language they had the perfect vehicle for the expression of these qualities. Greek is the finest of all languages in which to express abstract terms, for it is at once the clearest, the most flexible, and the most subtle instrument of expression ever devised. Whereas English would have to content itself with a series of consecutive sentences, Greek groups ideas into one long period, so intelligibly and with such complete command of structure that it seems almost architectural in character. A Greek sentence, said the disgruntled schoolboy, is like nothing so much as a lot of little pieces of string, all tied together in one enormous knot. That very tying together helped the Greek to his exact grasp of logical relationships and to his unique clarity of thought. Greek is clear and exact; it is direct, vigorous and simple; it expresses in the briefest possible way the fundamentals of anything with which it is dealing. Yet it is so subtle that it has many shades of meaning as yet untranslated. No one could say of the Greeks, as Lowell said of the Germans, that they used "fog as an illuminating medium." For their language is unkind to the traffickers in nonsense, as French was unkind to the propagandist of the Croix de Feu and German kind to Nazi ravings. When we add for good measure that Greek is a tongue of outstanding delicacy and beauty of sound, we will not be tempted, in speaking of the qualities of the Greek spirit, to forget the language which expressed it and preserved it, and which, it is fair to add, played its part in forming it as well.

The Polis

Brilliant in spirit and fortunate in language, the Greeks, by accident or by some singularly gracious gift of the gods, hit upon that organisation of life which focused as nothing else could have done their great energy, and allowed them to make the most of their great gifts. That organisation was what the Greeks knew as the Polis, a term for which there is no exact translation but which we render most inadequately as the City State. It was much more than we mean by a city and a great deal more than we understand by a State.

The Polis was, of course, inseparable from the City. France, not Paris, is the State. But Athens, not Attica, was the Polis. It was small—about the size of a small English county. Only three Poleis had more than 20,000 citizens—Athens and Syracuse and Acragas. Poleis of 10,000 citizens were not numerous. Rich and important, Ægina never had more than 2,500 citizens. In some districts there were as many as four Poleis in an area eight by twelve miles. Aristotle analysed the constitutions of 158 Poleis—and we may be sure that there were at least ten times as many. All kept their populations restricted. Hesiod even appealed for the single-child family, and public opinion never frowned upon abortion, infanticide, exposure and homosexuality. Nor was it consciousness of the niggardliness of nature alone that made the Greeks deplore large populations. They desired to live "in the leisure of free and abstemious men"; and they wanted a sufficient number of citizens to make cultural life feasible, but not too many to make direct participation in government impossible. They strongly agreed with Aristotle that "ten men are too few for a city; a hundred thousand are too many."

Above all, the Polis was free. Its liberty was the breath of life to the Greeks. The Melians, saying in the face of overwhelming Athenian might : "it were surely great baseness and cowardice in us who are still free not to try everything that can be tried before submitting to your yoke," were typically Greek. So were the two Spartans who offered their lives to the Persian king in palliation of the execution of the two Persian envoys at Sparta, saying, "you have never tasted liberty . . . if you had you would urge us to fight for it, not from afar with javelins, but with axes at close quarters." It is, indeed, because the sovereignty of the Polis was so fundamental to it that the Greeks never formed a nation—the very idea of the Polis being as much opposed to it as the idea of caste in India. The better is the enemy of the good, and in all that makes life thrilling and whole the Greek was convinced that he had the best.

Its size and sovereignty made the Polis the most intimate and intense form of political grouping that has ever existed. Its impact upon its citizens was much more direct than the impact of a great modern State can ever hope to be. This is obviously so in a democratic Polis where the citizen was a member of the Sovereign Assembly, where he might be chosen by lot to be the Chancellor of the Exchequer, where he could reckon on holding office every so often, where he might find himself in command of a campaign as one Athenian leather-merchant did after expressing trenchant criticism of the conduct of operations. But it is no less true of the non-democratic Poleis. There the citizen's sense of belonging to the Polis, of being a member not a subject of it, was as acute. There his sense of living in immediate contact with it was as strong. There his devotion to it was as ardent —in its way Simonides' epitaph on the Spartan dead at Thermopylæ, "Go, stranger, tell the Lacedæmonians that we lie here obedient to their commands," is as eloquent as the famous Funeral Oration of Pericles. To the Greek, therefore, the Polis had a much more concrete meaning than the State has for us. In it things that appear to us abstract and wearisome necessities were vivid and immediate, so that even the paying of income tax became less objectionable because less remote. Rich men in the Polis were not required to pay supertax but were expected to produce a play, or to commission a warship, and however strong their reluctance to part with money may have been, it is not unreasonable to believe that they felt more satisfaction in contemplating the plays they had produced or the warships they had fitted out than those who pay surtax today do in contemplating their tax returns.

As a result of this intimacy and directness, the Polis had a much fuller meaning for the Greek than the State has for us. He identified it with all human values. It was so much a part of

his life that it was impossible to think of him apart from it, so
that the Greeks never found it sufficient to know a man's name
and his father's but always required the name of his Polis as
well. The Polis was so much a part of his life that it was impossible to think of it apart from him, so that the Greeks did not
speak of Athens, Sparta, or Melos, but always of the Athenians,
the Lacedæmonians, and the Melians. No Greek belief was
stronger than that it is only in the Polis that men worthy of the
name can live. Indeed, the Greek word "to live" means also "to
take part in communal life." (It is interesting to note in the
modern Greek word "politeuma," which means culture, perhaps
the last trace of this old conjunction of life and politics.) And
the name they gave to a man uninterested in the Polis was
"idiotes"—from which comes our word "idiot." For life to be
worth living must have meaning, and only in the Polis, they
were sure, did it acquire meaning. The life of the Polis, they
believed, was essential to the whole man. When Aristotle said
that man is a political animal, he meant that it is the characteristic of man to live in a Polis; and if he does not, he is not
truly man. The Polis alone made the good life possible and was
therefore the greatest education in virtue that man could ever
know. This is what Simonides meant when he said : "The Polis
teaches the man." It was Church, University, State all in one.
There where the Polis was not, slavery and barbarism reigned;
here where it added colour and passion and intensity to life, man
could alone fulfil his nature.

From life so intensely lived and sovereignty so ardently cherished sprang rivalry and bitter enmity both within and without
the Polis. "Stasis," or virulent faction, was its great internal problem, so that revolutions were as frequent as in our lifetime they
have been in South America—and much more significant. War
was its great external problem, so that no civilisation, perhaps
not even our own, great as is its claim in this respect, has shown
more conclusively than the Greek how wolfish man can be to
man. Yet the very defects of the Polis were an added stimulation
to the Greeks. The knowledge that any action of his Polis today might lead to defeat in war and to enslavement or death tomorrow; and the very rapidity of the constitutional changes that
took place before his eyes quickened his interest in political life.
And if in a world of antagonistic Poleis death was never far
away, there was also glory in it—as the Blackfoot chief said

when, from the peace of the reservation, he sighed for the days of tribal warfare. If in spite of the smallness of the Polis there was never anything parish pump about the mentality of the Greeks, that was not least because the decisions they were constantly called upon to take were not parish-pump decisions.

The Variety of their Political Thought

Such a vivid and intense life in the Polis, such a concentrated experience of political change, when allied to the great intellectual virtues of the Greeks, could not but produce great political thought. Hence it is fitting that we pay our tribute to them whenever we use the word "political," a derivation from the Polis, for whatever else of the Polis has vanished from the memory of man, politics and political thinking remain as its undying legacy to all future ages.

In their political thought they could not of course step outside their age any more than we can step outside ours. And it may be suggested that if the Polis did so much to make possible their political thought, it also did something to limit it. Only with the Stoics, who were not the truest of Greeks, did ideas of the Cosmopolis or World-State emerge. Yet only in minor ways can it be said that Greek political thinking was restricted by the Polis. Indeed, it would be truer to say that it was coloured by it rather than confined by it. For the Greeks found all the main answers that have been given to the question why should men obey the State.

We will find in them the view we associate with Marx that class determines the form of the State and that class is itself determined by economic interests. Plato tells us that "any city, however small, is in fact divided into two, one the city of the poor, the other of the rich." Aristotle likewise says that the economic structure of the State will condition its nature. Here, too, we will find the view of the State as a machine, a product of man's will for his own convenience, "a guarantor of men's rights against one another" as the Sophist Lycophron, whom Aristotle attacked, maintained. Incidentally, there is also here the view of the State as contract. Glaucon, in the *Republic*, speaks of "the common view" that men "make a compact of mutual abstinence from injustice"—a view which the Epicureans shared. Here is the view of the State as force. Thrasymachus, in the *Republic*, says that "Justice is simply the interest of the stronger." The Athenian ambassadors, in Thucydides, tell the Melians: "You know as well as we do that right, as the world goes, is only in question between equals in power, while the strong do what they can and the weak suffer what they must," and add, "of the gods we believe, and of men we know, that by a necessary law of their nature they rule wherever they can." Here is the view of the State as will. Aristotle says of the Politeia: "Its intrinsic strength should be derived from the fact not that a majority are in favour of its continuance (that might well be the case even with a poor constitution) but rather that there is no single section in all the State which would favour a change to a different constitution." In the belief of the Epicureans that the State exists to secure the largest possible private good which is identified with pleasure, we can see a foreshadowing of the Utilitarian State. And is it fanciful to see something of Rousseau's distinction between the General Will and the Will of All in the distinction the Greek drew between the Nomoi and the possibly transitory expressions of the popular will, or in Aristotle's insistence that that form of government is good which acts in the interests of the whole and bad which acts in its own interests?

But, above all, we will find in the Greeks the view of the State as an organism, as a whole which is more important than its parts. With Plato we have the typically organic view that the happiness of the State is not the same as the sum of the different happinesses of its members: "Our duty as regards happiness is to see if our State as a whole enjoys it, persuading or compelling these our auxiliaries and guardians to study only how to make themselves the best possible workmen at their own occupation, and treating all the rest in like manner, and thus, while the whole city grows and becomes prosperously organised, permitting each class to partake of as much happiness as the nature of the case allows to it." For Plato, the State is happy if it conforms to an absolute standard which is to be found in nature by the use of man's reason. The extent to which any given State does so conform, and not the happiness of individual citizens, is the criterion whereby we must judge of the happiness of States. To Aristotle, too, though he will not admit any more than will Plato that it is an organism beyond the capacity of man to influence, the State is still an organism, the whole greater than the part. "The Polis is prior in the order of nature to the family and the individual. The reason for this is that the whole is necessarily prior to the part." The idea of the whole must first be there before the part can be understood. It is this view of the State as an organism, this that has been termed the Rational-Natural view of the State, that is the greatest and most typical Greek contribution to political thought. It is this that will now be examined in the work of Plato, still the acknowledged master of political thought.

PLATO, 427–347 B.C.

His Life and Writings

Plato was born in Athens in 427 B.C., one year after the death of Pericles, and he died there in 347 B.C., ten years before the battle of Chæronea which gave Philip of Macedon the mastery of the Greek world. The Athens into which he was born was still the greatest of Greek "Poleis," "the educator of Hellas." Sophocles was then at the height of his powers; Aristophanes was beginning to entrance the Demos; the Parthenon had been finished but ten years before. But it was in an Athens from which virtue was passing that he grew up, an Athens strained in the Peloponnesian War, an Athens where democracy was beginning to pass into those extremist forms which he so mercilessly satirised. He was a schoolboy when the great expedition sailed to disaster at Syracuse; he was a young man of twenty-three when defeat ended the war and the democracy in Athens fell.

Born into a family which on both sides was one of the most distinguished in Athens, as old-established and as prominent politically as the Cecils in England, reared in the household of his stepfather who was one of the leading figures in Periclean Athens, Plato might seem predestined for an active life in the service of his State. So he thought himself. "When I was a young man," he says in the Seventh Letter, which was written towards the end of his life, "I felt as many young men do: I thought that the very moment I attained my majority I should engage in public affairs." The opportunity soon presented itself. A revolution overthrew the democracy in Athens and established the rule of the Thirty. Among them were Plato's kinsmen, and they asked him to join them, thinking, in his own words, that "politics and I were a fit match." But their behaviour was such, he writes, that "my blood boiled at it," for "as I looked I saw those men in a short time make the former democratic government seem like a golden age." Another revolution soon brought the democrats to power, and although at first they won Plato's respect by their "considerable leniency," they nevertheless committed the act which decisively drove him from active political life. They executed his friend Socrates on a charge of corrupting the youth of Athens.

Socrates, whom the Oracle at Delphi had pronounced to be the wisest of mankind, was regarded by Plato as the best of men. As we see from Plato's Dialogues, on all those who loved him his personality had an extraordinarily powerful effect. "When I hear him," Alcibiades says in the Symposium, "my heart leaps in me more than that of the Corybantes; my tears flow at his words, and I see many others that feel just as I do. . . . And with this man alone I have an experience which no one would believe was possible for me—the sense of shame. He is the only one that provokes it. For I know in my own heart that I cannot gainsay that I ought to do as he bids me and that when I leave him it is my vice to yield to the favours of the many. . . . Often I would be glad if I should not see him again in this world, but if this should happen I know well that I should be more miserable than ever; the truth is, I do not know what to do with him." Questioning all whom he could induce to listen to him so that he might arrive at truth, and incidentally exposing the pretensions and revealing the inadequacies of those who claimed to have found it, Socrates was the gadfly of Athens. Meno varied the image and told him: "Not only in shape but in everything else too you are exactly like that flat sea fish, the sting ray. It, too, numbs with its shock whoever comes near it and touches it, and that is just what you have done to me now, I think."

But men will not always reconcile themselves to continual stinging, and Socrates' condemnation, however much to be regretted, is not altogether surprising. His death was perhaps the most important event in Plato's life, turning him from politics to philosophy. Henceforward, he tells us: "I was compelled to say, in praising true philosophy, that it was from it alone that one was able to discern all true justice, public and private. And so I said that the nations of men will never cease from trouble until either the true and genuine breed of philosophers shall come to political office or until that of the rulers in the states shall by some divine ordinance take to the true pursuit of philosophy."

In his wretchedness Plato left Athens for nearly twelve years, travelling to Megara, Cyrene, Italy, and perhaps Egypt, and establishing that connection with Sicily which gave him later in life the chance, however slender, of making a King a Philosopher and thereby of translating his ideas into practice. He returned to Athens in 387 B.C., and, in a grove outside the city, founded the Academy, over the door of which it is said ran the inscription: "No one without a knowledge of mathematics may enter here." In this insistence on the discipline of exact study Plato's Academy can be called the first of Western universities. It might be regarded as the first of Western universities in this, too, that it hoped to provide men who, nurtured by their academic training, would become leaders of their communities, lawgivers and statesmen. It would have been unnatural in the extreme for a Greek to neglect the State, and Plato had behind him a family tradition of service to remind him of the philosopher's duty to society. Thus, very typically, he can write in the *Republic* that the philosopher cannot count his the greatest of achievements "if he does not find a state that fits him: for in the state that fits him he himself will attain greater proportions and along with his private salvation will save the community as well."

It was in this spirit that members of the Academy legislated for various States. And it was in this spirit that Plato himself answered the call when it came to him from Syracuse to help in the fashioning of the Philosopher King. In this luxury-loving Sicilian city, in which he had previously experienced a life that "consisted of a vast amount of eating Italiate and Sicilian cooking, stuffing oneself twice a day and never sleeping a single night alone, together with all the usual practices which go with this sort of life," he had unpromising material. There were, moreover, other difficulties which should have been obvious, but which he had insufficiently foreseen. On his first visit to Sicily he had become friendly with Dion, a young man of whose character and ability he thought very highly and who eagerly embraced his philosophy. It was Dion who, now very influential at the court of the young Dionysius II, urged Plato in 367 to come to Sicily to help him be the philosophic adviser of the new prince. But Dion's very presence proved embarrassing as perhaps not unnaturally it gave rise to the suspicion that there might be plans not only for turning a King into a Philosopher, but conceivably also as an alternative for turning a Philosopher into a King. Moreover, Plato sadly underestimated the difficulty of persuading a young despot with a war on his hands to devote the time to and develop the taste for mathematics. Plato still, however, cherished the hope "that he might come to desire the life of philosophy," though not even his patience and optimism could have allowed him to regard the banishment of Dion, the sequestering of his estates, and the forced marriage of his wife to another man, as the first tottering steps of a beginner in philosophy. He left Sicily having accomplished nothing —unless we except that message of apology which he was to carry to Dion wherein Dionysius urged that Dion should regard banishment not as a punishment but as a holiday abroad, thoughtfully, however, forbearing to add that he should look upon the loss of his lands and of his wife as a happy release from the cares of property and the thraldom of wedlock.

In spite of that experience, Plato returned to Sicily, only to find that Dionysius's aversion for mathematics was if anything greater. Grateful to escape with his life, Plato made no further excursions into politics, though when a very old man he was asked to go again to Sicily to straighten out the chaos into which that country was now plunged. Even more striking than the fact that so old a man was asked to tackle again what he had previously tried and failed to do was the marked tone of regret that characterises his refusal. Clearly we must say that the Sicilian episodes show Plato as blind to the realities of power, and as too ready to allow himself to be deceived into thinking that perhaps there was a chance when reason and experience alike denied it. Yet the justification of his actions that he gives in the *Seventh Letter* is very revealing—and very Greek. "And chiefly," he writes, "I was urged by a sense of shame in my own eyes that I should not always seem to myself a kind of argument pure and simple, never willing to set my hand to anything that was an action."

Plato failed, then, to find a state that fitted him, and according to his own view his achievement thus fell short of the highest. Nevertheless, it was very great. In his lifetime he was renowned not only for his work in the Academy but for his writings. This perhaps is paradoxical as he himself was contemptuous of books—reflecting in that the attitude of his civilisation, the Greek being a seeing and hearing rather than a reading public. Moreover, he tells us in the *Seventh Letter* that he has never put his philosophy into writing and never will. Yet if he never produced a final system of philosophy, he conveyed enough in what he did produce, and that so brilliantly, to win him a lasting reputation. For his mastery of words was such as to fascinate that race whose ideal was that of Achilles—to be a speaker of words as well as a doer of deeds. He was a supreme poet—his epitaph on the Eritrean exiles in Persia is as beautiful as anything in Greek poetry. He was a superb dramatist, with a sure grasp of form and movement, an unfailing command of vivid detail and gripping situation. And he found that form for his writings which gave fullest play to his great literary gifts. He wrote in dialogue form, generally representing Socrates as his chief speaker. His Dialogues were the artistic presentation of political and philosophical problems, and were instinct with life. We are given a fascinating glimpse of a slave hunt in the *Protagoras,* and are shown the absurdity of Protagoras pacing the courtyard while his disciples fall over themselves so as not to get in front of him when he turns to retrace his steps. Or we are made vividly aware in the *Republic* of the uncouth mannerisms of Thrasymachus. For Plato is intensely preoccupied with life, to a degree quite inconsistent with his own theory that the true philosopher does not think about people but meditates on abstract reality. In practice he is as much in love with the conversation of "people in the city" as Socrates had been, and his Dialogues show it, whether they be pure comedy as in *Euthydemus* or tragedy as in the *Phædo.* Hence they live and move and enthral as do few philosophical works.

It is worth emphasising that they were not of course intended to be exhaustive treatises, compelling acquiescence by the very power of their logic, as Aristotle sought to make his works. They were rather designed to give flashes of illumination, to make the reader imaginatively understand a particular approach, to give no more than indirect indications of the approach to the good life. They were not so much philosophy as the stuff of which philosophy is made. By 362, when he returned from his last visit to Sicily, Plato had written the following Dialogues: *Crito, Apology, Euthyphro, Laches, Lysis, Charmides, Phædo, Georgias, Meno, Protagoras, Phædrus, Symposium, Euthydemus,* and *Republic*. In his later years he wrote the *Theateus, Parmenides, Philebus, Sophist, Statesman, Timæus, Laws,* and the half-finished *Critias*. Of these the greatest is the *Republic*, which is also the greatest book in the history of Political Thought. It is mainly from the *Republic* that the following account of his political thought is given.

His Political Philosophy—The Human Predicament

In his contemporary world Plato saw "stasis" everywhere--cities so divided that their citizens stood "in the state and posture of gladiators" against one another. He saw unrighteousness rampant and injustice enthroned. He saw ignorance supreme and parading up and down in the guise of knowledge. And he saw everywhere, too, the predicament in which men found themselves. Doing what their natures suggested to them, they found not what they sought, but turmoil and strife and agony and death. This was so because to be mistaken seemed part of their very natures. They desired, as all men must, "the good for man"; "that which would make any man's life happy," "that without which man can never know peace." But they looked for it in the wrong places. They sought it in pleasures, in health, in long life, in wealth, in power. They chose evil because they thought that would be a good for them. And they were not corrected by those who led them. Even the best of these were unhelpful. Themistocles and Pericles were accounted great statesmen, but they failed to make their people "better and gentler." Moreover, at the end their people disgraced them, and their very ingratitude was a proof of the failure of government, of the poverty of statesmanship. For what sort of teamster would we call him who undertook to train a team of horses and ended by having them run away and throw him? In fact, the very leaders made matters worse. They directed attention precisely to those wrong things to which man anyhow was so likely to be attracted. They confirmed him in his mistakes. Pericles filled the city with "harbours and dockyards and walls and such trash," not with good men. All goods are of two kinds : unlimited, as for instance Beauty and Wisdom; and limited, as for instance Power and Wealth. Beauty and Wisdom are unlimited because my possession of them in no sense diminishes yours or is diminished by yours. My appreciation of art does not preclude your appreciation, and is in no way lessened by yours. Power and Wealth are limited because my possession of them very much diminishes yours or is diminished by yours. My desire for power undoubtedly precludes yours and my hopes of gaining it are greatly lessened by yours. Unlimited goods, because they are unlimited, cannot cause strife. But limited goods, because they are limited, must always cause strife. If we yearn for Power or Wealth our struggle will be protracted and bitter precisely because they are limited, whereas Wisdom and Art are not. It was to the limited goods that Pericles directed the attention of his people, and it was from this pursuit of the limited goods that sprang all the troubles that plagued the race of men.

The root cause, then, of men's troubles is that they are led by ignorant men who pretend to knowledge but who are in fact as ignorant as themselves. They are led by those who do not know where they are going. At best those leaders have formed opinions about things which not surprisingly are unsound. They are like men who, sitting bound in an underground cave with a fire burning behind them by the light of which shadows of people walking about outside are cast on the wall in front of them, have earned a certain distinction for remembering which shadows came first, which last and which together, and for guessing which were coming next. They are like the keeper of the great strong beast, who has learned all its moods and passions, how to approach him and how to touch him, when he is most savage and when most gentle, what makes him the one and the other and the sounds that he makes to express each, and who finally calls his knowledge wisdom and constructs it as a system or an art. They are like sailors on a ship who argue about their course and clamour to be the steersman while the true navigator is bound to the mast and called a useless, stargazing fool. This is the predicament of men, that they constantly mistake their good and that their mistakes go uncorrected and are even made worse by their leaders. And from this predicament they will never escape until they realise that power is in the hands of the ignorant, that power in the hands of the ignorant is poison, that ignorance and opinion must give way to knowledge, that there are indeed those who do not merely have opinions about things but who know, and who are capable of exercising power, even if at the moment they do not, and that it is into their hands, however reluctant they may be, that power must be placed.

The Existence of the Good

The early Greek philosophers were particularly concerned with two outstanding problems—the problem of Variety and the problem of Change. The variety that they saw was such that the world seemed unintelligible, and they felt impelled to try to reduce all the varieties to one substance, to "find the one in the many." Some thought that one substance was water, some air, or fire, or earth. For Anaximander it was the infinite; for Pythagoras number. The definitions of the one substance differed, but there was general agreement that, whatever it was it was divine. The change that they noticed constantly taking place seemed to them a particular form of the problem of Variety. The idea of change, they concluded, assumes the idea of permanence, since however much an object changes there must be some part of it that does not or we would be compelled to speak not of a changed, but of an entirely new object. What does not change, they said, must be the permanent character of the object. Triangles, for instance, change, but the quality of triangularity is permanent. Geometrical character, in this case, was the permanent quality that did not change. Further, they believed that there could be "doxa" or empirical observation about the changing, but that "Episteme"—or real knowledge—could be had only about that which was permanent. Heraclitus, who maintained that all things change, that the world is in a state of permanent flux, that "we cannot step twice into the same river," added the further idea that natural law was the permanent character of all things; that is, that there was a natural order in the world ordained by God.

It was against this common background of philosophical speculation that Plato worked out his Theory of Ideas. He also saw in the actual world constant flux, a perpetual flow of ever-changing appearances. He also sought to make the world intelligible by finding the permanent in the changing. The permanent character of anything he calls the Idea, or as some who are dissatisfied with this translation prefer to call it the Form. If we use the word Idea it is as well to remind ourselves that Plato did not mean by it as we do a thought existing in the mind, for such a thought, he would maintain, is as transitory as any event in the outside world. An Idea in Plato's sense is not part of the world of time and space. It is eternal, it is the final and inde pendent reality. Because it is eternal it must be different from the object in which it appears. The Idea of a horse will be different from any particular horse. The Idea of a Polis must be different from any particular instance of a Polis. But although it is different from the things in which it appears, it cannot exist without those things. There could not be an Idea of a horse if no horse existed. Hence Plato's Ideas are not to be regarded as transcendent. They could not exist in an ethereal world of their own. They are, on the contrary, immanent in the transitory nature of things, as the Idea of a horse is immanent in horses. An Idea, then, is eternal though it can only exist in time. It is permanent though it is not separate from the world of change. It is in fact the law according to which a thing behaves, for that is permanent and does not change with the changing thing, that is not separate from the thing but is nevertheless distinguishable from it.

The Idea, then, is what makes things what they are. All horses in the world, however much they differ, have one quality in common—that quality by reason of which they are horses, or horsiness. We recognise them as horses because they "partake" of this quality, horsiness. The Idea of Horsiness is thus the source of the common quality that all horses possess. It is also a perfect example of a horse. In some degree all actual horses are imperfect—in the Idea of a horse is no imperfection. Consequently if we want to know what is a good horse, we must discover how closely it approximates to the Idea of a Horse. Moreover, the Idea is an end as well as a source. Only metaphorically can one say that all horses strive to become more and more like the idea of a horse. But artists strive to make their art more and more like that Idea of Beauty, by virtue of which all things that "partake" of it are beautiful. And citizens should seek to make their Polis more and more like that Idea of the Polis which is laid up in heaven.

The world of Ideas is, Plato maintains, the real world: the familiar world is a world of shadows. Of course we believe our own everyday world to be the only real world, for we are like the prisoners in the cave who have never seen the light and of whom it must be said: "Then surely such persons would hold the shadows of those manufactured articles to be the only realities." Our dimness of vision is to be deplored, but the fact of the existence of this real world of archetypes in which there is a model of each class of things is not to be denied. Moreover, Plato urges, if we were not so blind we would see that beyond these Ideas, these models, these archetypes, there is the Idea of all Ideas, the model of all models, the prototype of all archetypes— the Idea of the Good, the final and independent reality existing "itself by itself." This Idea is the source of all goodness. It is that by virtue of participation in which men are good.

It is impossible to have certain knowledge of things that are constantly changing. We can merely form opinions about them. Only of the permanent, of the Idea, of the law, can we have genuine infallible knowledge. Hence, Plato concludes, the good exists, whatever men may think about it. And because it exists they have at least the hope of escaping from their predicament. That they were unable to do, so long as they had only opinion to go by. For there was nothing to choose between the many opinions that men had formed about the good life. They were all mistaken and all misleading. But if men can comprehend the Idea of the Good, they will have laid hold of truth, they will have passed from mere opinion which confirmed them in evil to knowledge which will draw them irresistibly to good, and only in following after good will they find respite from their many afflictions.

The Soul and the Possibility of Knowledge

Plato has so far told us that the Good exists, and that only of it can there be true knowledge. But he has not shown us how men can acquire that knowledge. This he now proceeds to do by elaborating that doctrine of the Soul with which his doctrine of Ideas is inseparably connected.

The Body, he says, is not the whole of man. It is indeed his less important part. The most important part is his Soul which may truly be said to be divine. Plato is here of course using divine in the old Greek sense, something which is immortal in its own right, not because of any gift of the gods. Because the Soul is immortal it existed before it became incarnate, just as it will continue to exist after it leaves the body, which is its temporary dwelling-place. It's real home is its abode when not incarnate, and that is the higher world of Ideas. Before its incarnation it thus had knowledge of the Ideas among which it lived. And after its incarnation it is reminded of those Ideas through the senses when it sees those earthly things which "partake" of the Ideas. Hence the part played by the senses in the acquisition of true knowledge is very subordinate. It is only apparently through the senses that men learn truth. In fact, it is only because the Soul recollects what it has known in a previous life among the original models or archetypes or Ideas that men can have knowledge of these Ideas. These recollections of the Soul are the only genuine form of knowledge, and because men possess Souls they have therefore the possibility of arriving at it.

The Soul and its Thirst for the Good

Not all Souls, however, are capable of recollecting the Ideas they knew in their previous life. For not all Souls are pure—indeed, there is a good deal of alloy in the incarnate Soul. That Soul has three parts—Reason, which is located in the head; Courage or Spirit, which is located in the breast; and Desire, which is located in the belly. Of these, Reason is incomparably the most important, for it partakes of the eternal, it is "the most divine" in man; whereas Courage and Desire belong entirely to the world of time and space. It is Reason, therefore, which sees the truth and which directs the activity of the good Soul according to the vision which it has seen. It is Reason which is "the inward man," the rational element in us that is our real personality. Courage is, on the whole, obedient to the dictates of Reason and will help it to establish its ascendancy. But Desire is strong, wilful, contentious, turbulent, and chaotic. It is constantly in arms against Reason. And Reason like a charioteer who is driving two horses, one tractable and one wild, has ever to fight a great battle to discipline the unruly steed with the help of the horse that is broken to harness. That Soul, then, is good in which Reason predominates over Courage and Desire. Indeed, that Soul in which Reason existed alone would be the best copy of the Idea of man. In the world of men such a pure Soul is not to be found. But all Souls in which Reason is master are sufficiently sensitive to recollect the Ideas they knew in their former existence, and thus to give to men knowledge of the good.

But if not all Souls are capable of recollecting the Ideas they once knew, all Souls are driven by Eros, or passionate longing for a good not yet attained. That longing will drive the best of Souls, in which Reason commands, to know and to identify themselves with the Reality behind all Reality, the Idea behind all Ideas, the Idea of the Good. But even those corrupt Souls, in which Courage rules or Desire, will be driven by Eros to seek the good, although they will not themselves be aware of it. All they will themselves be aware of is that they are impelled to seek *a* good, that is, a good suited to themselves—a further distinction for the Spirited Soul or an added indulgence for the Pleasure-loving Soul. But although of themselves they will not understand it, they will be unable to enjoy the objects of their longing until Reason is in her rightful position of authority. For instance, a man of courage or spirit who sought satisfaction in the service of a Caligula would brutalise not fulfil himself. The very means whereby he sought to become the better man would ensure that he became the worse. Similarly the pleasure-loving man will fail to find the pleasures he seeks. For if the appetites are left to themselves either one will so tyrannise over the rest as to starve them, or each desire will so struggle with all that none will find satisfaction. Only when Reason commands will each receive its fair satisfaction.

Plato can even make an ironic joke to drive home the point that only under the guidance of Reason will the pleasure-loving Soul find its fulfilment—the tyrant, he calculates, has 729 times less pleasure than the philosophic man. Indeed, this is a point which Plato repeatedly stresses because, as he says in the *Laws*, it is not gods but men whom we have to lead into right living, and we must therefore allow for the universal desire of men for pleasurable existence. When Reason rules, all will enjoy the greatest share of goods appropriate to their nature. But when Reason rules, man is following the Idea of the Good. Therefore not only is it possible for men to acquire knowledge, but they have a passionate desire for it, an unquenchable thirst for the Good, although only a few of them can realise that this is indeed the case.

The State as the Means to the Good

The qualities of the Soul, says Plato, are innate and inherent. They are a matter of birth, and no two persons are born alike. Their due balance, however, is a matter of training and restraining. Men are not born with that balance: they must be disciplined into it and prevented from violating it. The force necessary to do this must be all-embracing and life-long, and can only be the State, whose true function is thus education in the widest sense of that term. Nothing is more typical of Plato than this insistence that it is the State that makes the man. It is constantly emerging in his writings. We see it in his view that every type of constitution produces its own type of man, or in his declaration that those who blame the Sophists for the degeneration of the young are themselves the greatest Sophists, for it is the influence of the State, not the teaching of private individuals, that educates men.

But it is not the State as it actually exists that can help men to achieve the due balance in their souls. For the actual State denies rather than fulfils men. In it the Rational Soul will be less good than it might be, and possibly even more evil than it might be expected to be. It will be less good because it will lack that society which is necessary for the full development of the philosophic nature, the State in which the Philosopher will attain "greater proportions." It might be more evil because in existing society the very vigour of the Rational Soul is an added danger to it. "We know it to be true," Plato writes, "of any seed or growing thing, whether plant or animal, that if it fails to find its proper nourishment or climate or soil, then the more vigorous it is the more it will lack the qualities it should possess. Evil is a worse enemy to the good than to the indifferent; so it is natural that bad conditions of nurture should be peculiarly uncongenial to the finest nature, and that it should come off worse under them than natures of an insignificant order. So is it, then, with the temperament we have postulated for the philosopher: given the right instruction, it must grow to the full flower of excellence; but if the plant is sown and reared in the wrong soil, it will develop every contrary defect, unless saved by some miracle." Similarly, in the actual State the Courageous or Spirited Soul will not develop as it should. For, as Sparta shows, it will become proud and ambitious, will admire duplicity and low cunning, will become mean and deceitful and a prey in secret to all the passions which in public it denies. Again, in the actual State the Appetitive or Desirous Soul will not get what it hopes for. In a State such as Athens it will apparently enjoy the maximum of freedom, for there even the horses and asses are gorged with freedom, and the citizens, constant only in inconstancy, living "from day to day in the gratification of the casual appetite," are everything by turns and nothing long. But all this is but the guarantee of such strife as will stunt even the Desirous Soul, the prelude to tyranny which will deny it the satisfactions for which it longs.

If we would avoid ill-fitting clothes, we must not cut our cloth from a poor pattern. If we want the balanced Soul, it is not the actual State that will help us to achieve it, but the good State that is modelled on the Idea of the Polis laid up in heaven. Only in the good State will the Rational Soul reveal its divine origin, and the Courageous and Desirous Souls fulfil themselves to the greatest extent that their natures will allow. And then it will be apparent that the State, albeit the good State, is the only means whereby men may achieve the Good.

The Organisation of the State to Ensure the Good

From all that Plato has told us the first characteristic of the good State will be immediately apparent. It must be properly led. Power must not be given to those who will abuse it either for their own selfish interests or in pursuit of a misconceived common good such as wealth or power, erroneously seen in terms of those unworthy ends which make most appeal to their own diseased souls. For wealth and power are limited goods, "goods that can be fought for," as Aristotle calls them, and the individual or the State that pursues them does so at the expense of others and so stirs up strife. Power must rather be given to those who will use it aright to turn men's souls to the pure light of truth. It must be given to philosophers, for as philosophy is, as Socrates called it, the art of the "tendance of the soul," so it must also be the art of the tendance of the State. As the safety of the ship depends upon the skilled pilot, so the welfare of the State depends upon the developed philosopher. For the good the philosopher pursues is unlimited, it is wisdom which is not sought at anyone's expense, and which therefore creates no contention. On the contrary, the greater the philosopher's wisdom, the better for everybody if they can take advantage of it by making him control the State. And in innumerable images, such as that of the Cave, of the Ship, of the Custody of the Beast, of the Cook and the Doctor, and in myths such as that of the races of Gold, Silver and Iron and of the Soul making its choice of a "demon" before incarnation, Plato seeks to drive home the absolute truth of his challenging assertion which is the central part of the *Republic*: "Until, then, philosophers are kings, or the kings and princes of this world have the spirit and power of philosophy, and political greatness and wisdom meet in one, and those commoner natures who follow either to the exclusion of the other are compelled to stand aside, cities will never cease from evil—no nor the human race, as I believe—and then only will our State have a possibility of life and behold the light of day."

Philosophic natures, Plato knows, are extremely rare. He frequently insists that no one can become a philosopher who does not have very specific natural gifts. And he knows, too, that such natures will be very reluctant to possess power. For politics are an affair of the twilight, they concern the relations of men in the dimness of the cave, and what man who has enjoyed the steady light of the sun would eagerly return to the flickering firelight of the cave? "The man whose mind is really set upon the things that are," he says, "has not leisure to look down at the concerns of men, and to fight with them, and fill himself with envy and bitterness." But because "the philosopher living in fellowship with what is divine and orderly grows himself orderly and divine as far as man is able," he must be made to leave "the isles of the blest" and return to the cave, to the world of shadows and half-truths and ordinary people. In the perfect social order he can be legitimately forced to assume authority, for in moulding others he is still further developing himself, and in service he is paying the rent that he owes to the State for his own development. Of course, as it is only in the perfect State that the philosopher could get the right education, so it is only in the perfect State that he would be fully responsible to the community. He will feel no gratitude to existing States, for if he has been fortunate enough to develop himself unspoiled, it was in spite and not because of them that he did so. Therefore in actual States philosophers are unlikely to engage in political activity, but will rather confine themselves to the life of privacy and contemplation : "staying quiet and doing their own work, as though standing behind a wall in a storm of wind-driven dust and sleet; when they see others infected by lawlessness, they are content if they can live out their life here pure of injustice and unholy acts, and say good-bye to it cheerfully and pleasantly, full of good hope."

The first characteristic, then, of the good State is that in it power will be given to those not who want it most but who desire it least, to the philosophers who will, nevertheless, exercise it best. Perhaps it should be added to relieve those who are oppressed by the prospect of the Professor in politics as, for instance, Bismarck was by Gladstone, that for Plato the "philosophos" was not what in any academic sense we might understand by a professor of philosophy today. He was a "kaloskagathos"—a gentleman, the finest product of "paideia," a lover of culture, the most highly educated and cultivated of personalities. His was the noblest of natures, the most rational of souls. He was quick to understand, eager to know, of great intellectual power, indifferent to external goods or to display, magnanimous, courageous, self-controlled, and a friend and kinsman of "truth and justice." "A love of truth and a hatred of falsehood that will not tolerate untruth in any form" was his master passion. Like Confucius's "Superior Man," with whom he had so much in common, he was one who would follow the "Kingly Way," cleaving to righteousness and forsaking wrong. And it should be noted as well that Plato thought of his philosopher-kings not as lawgivers but as administrators. He believed that there must always be an element in the State in which the founder's spirit lives on, but he did not anticipate the continuous emerging of the original creative gifts which the lawgiver-philosopher who founds the State must clearly possess. It is significant that in the *Republic* Socrates and his friends are portrayed as the engineers of the toy model of the State. "Let us convince, first and best, the guardians," they say. Before there is a philosopher-king there must be an original philosopher to make the copy of the Idea of the Polis that is laid up in heaven. The function of the philosopher-kings, then, is to keep the State as close as possible to the philosopher's sketch of the Ideal State. They must, for instance, watch against the coming into the State of undue wealth and poverty. They must see that the State does not grow too big. They must ensure that the different classes fulfil their functions, and, above all, they must make certain that no innovation in education is allowed in the State. But if the guardians are not autocratic lawgivers, their work, though it may seem negative in form, is positive enough in content. It is nothing less than to nourish and shape souls. To believe that legislation could help them in that would be to imagine that inadequate means can produce desired ends. Politicians and quacks may content themselves with curing symptoms and ignoring causes. True doctors cannot. The root of human trouble is defective education, and the cure for those troubles is education that is not defective. When men have this they will find that laws are not needed, for they will be just without them. And here the parallel between the thought of Plato and of Confucius may be noticed again. For Confucius also is sure that right training will do away with the need for constant legislation—indeed he states that when that is needed it will be ineffective, saying, "Where the Prince is virtuous laws are unnecessary; where the Prince is not virtuous laws are useless." Again, both Plato and Confucius are agreed about the importance of right customs. In the *Republic* Plato displays a respect for age, and insistence on piety towards parents, on proper hairdressing, clothing, footwear, and posture that Confucius would most cordially endorse.

The good State must not only be properly led, it must be properly defended. Therefore the second characteristic of the good State will be the presence below the guardians, in whose hands supreme power is concentrated, of a class of professional soldiers. Plato calls them guards, thus by implication restricting their function to defence. Courage is their main virtue. They must be keen to see, swift to catch, and strong to destroy the enemy. And like the watchdogs that they are they must combine two contradictory qualities—mildness to their friends and ferocity towards their enemies. Accustomed to warlike sights and sounds at an early age, taught to be indifferent to danger and contemptuous of death, they will be able "to see bloody slaughter" and yet hold their ground. They will be men of fine quality, and they will live with the best of men. But they will not themselves be the best of men. Theirs are the Spirited Souls which are attracted by honour. And they will not rule, but will obey the rulers whom they considerably outnumber.

The good State must also be properly fed. This is the task of the appetitive natures who long for material goods. The good State, therefore, will have as its third characteristic the existence of a class of producers below the philosopher-kings and the guards. This class includes not merely those who in Marxian terminology are the workers, but all property owners, business men and shopkeepers, farmers and craftsmen. All who produce wealth belong to it, and all the wealth of the community belongs to them. It will not, however, exhibit too great a disparity of wealth, for too great wealth and too great poverty would usher in the class war that had ruined so many Poleis. It will contain by far the majority of the community, but for all that Plato does not say much about it. He is, however, kinder to artisans than is Aristotle, for at least he allows them to be citizens. But at best they are second-class citizens, in every way passive objects of government. A good indication of the value Plato attached to them is his provision that a soldier who disgraces himself by showing cowardice should be degraded into their ranks. The normal Greek punishment for such an offence was loss of civil rights. This third class cannot claim a virtue special to itself, as wisdom is the virtue of the first and courage of the second. But it shares in a virtue which characterises the other classes as well —prudent self-control, which indeed it is specially important for it to have. Less noble than the guards, the producers will like them obey unquestioningly the commands of the guardians; like them they will have no part in politics. But they will be content because they will have the wealth that they desire, and they will be doing the job for which they are fitted.

Proper leadership, proper protection, proper provision are indispensable to the good State. But the State which has them may claim not only to be good but to be founded on human nature. For men are by nature divided into those who love Reason and who are fit to rule, those who love Honour and who are fit to fight, and those who love Pleasure and material goods and who are fit to work. Indeed, it is only because they have these attributes that the functions of the good State can be adequately discharged, for Plato is never in any doubt that the social order to be stable must reflect the constitution of human nature, must provide satisfaction for men's normal desires. The good State, therefore, accepts human nature as it is, and does not seek to convert all men to the ideal of one type. It drafts each to his proper place and seeks to make sure that he stays there. But if it is founded upon and accepts human nature, it also fulfils human nature. In it the guardians will have the satisfactions of knowledge, of contemplation of the Idea, and of developing themselves still further in moulding the character of others. In it the guards and the producers will find the fullest satisfaction of their desires made possible through the directing power of a Reason which the State provides for them because they cannot provide it for themselves. Hence though they still pursue limited ends which in their very nature lead to strife, this will not now result because Reason commands. Thus a greater share of the goods appropriate to the nature of each than is possible in any other State will be enjoyed by all in this good State which accepts human nature, builds upon human nature, and fulfils human nature.

Here in the good State is enshrined Plato's ideal of Human Excellence. He is a passionate specialist. He believes that everything in life has its own peculiar and special function to perform, and that it can only be used with excellence in that peculiar and special function. He believes also that every man has his predominant character and that there is no two-fold or manifold in man. It is clear that only in following his predominant character can man achieve excellence. Moreover, Human Excellence is equivalent to Justice. Knowing oneself, understanding one's own mixture of faculties, knowing the predominant one and following that, in fact doing the work for which one is best fitted, is minimum Justice. Doing that work "in a certain way," in such a way that each of the component elements within a man does its own work, in the way in which it would be done in the good State, is true Justice. Understandably, then, Plato dislikes democracy. For its ideal is not Human Excellence based on specialisation, but the denial of it based on the versatility which Pericles lauded in the Funeral Speech. And because it is this, it is Injustice projected into the political system. The Good State is thus the Just State, because it fulfils the idea of Human Excellence. It will also be the Efficient State, because in it everybody does only what he is best at. But we must be careful not to conclude, as has sometimes been done, that Plato confuses the Just State with the Efficient State. That would be to put the cart before the horse. For Plato the State is efficient because it is just, it is not just because it is efficient. In it the individual will be the just individual. In it will be the fullest harmonious co-operation of various elements which together form a whole. In it each of those elements, because it does what it is best at, makes for the best working of the whole. "The intention was," says Socrates, "that each individual should always be put to the use for which Nature intended him, one to one work, and then every man would do his own business, and be one and not many; and so the whole city would be one and not many." Thus whereas ignorance and stasis, the first leading to the second, characterise the actual State, specialisation and harmony, the first also leading to the second, characterise the good State in which men can live out their days in peace, contemplation, and happiness.

Convinced that the best should rule and that each should occupy the place and do the work for which he is best suited, Plato knows well enough that even the best fall from grace and that men show the greatest reluctance to remaining in their due places. Certain precautions, of an educational, social, biological, and religious kind, are, he feels, necessary to ensure that all, including the guardians, shall do as they must if the State is indeed to be the good State.

Of these the most important is the educational. There are no constitutional safeguards in Plato's *Republic* against the abuse of unlimited power. If those who possess power wish to misuse it, then, in Plato's view, irreparable damage to the State has already been done. Their minds must be so directed towards the good and so strengthened against evil that they will not wish to misuse it. Thus the only safeguard against the abuse of power worth anything at all lies in the character and minds of those who exercise it. Mr. Attlee, it might be noticed in passing, when he spoke the words that U.N.E.S.C.O. has taken as its slogan, "Since wars begin in the minds of men, it is in the minds of men that we must seek to prevent them," was being a good Platonist. To develop character and train the mind is the business of education, which becomes the most important function of the State. Because this is so, much of the *Republic* is devoted to the problems of education. About the art of government or legislation as we would understand it, nothing is said there. For politics in the modern sense of the word we look in vain. Instead we find a long discussion of poetry and music, which must seem to us excessive even though we remember Hitler's love of Wagner and suspect that there might, after all, be a connection between the "Ring of the Nibelungs" and the destruction into which Hitler dragged his country and Europe. Instead we find a long discussion about the value of abstract science and the principles of education, so that it is no exaggeration to say, as Rousseau did, that the *Republic* is not a political system but the finest treatise on education ever written.

It is typical of Plato that he makes no provision for the education of the lowest classes. They may be presumed to reap some incidental benefits from the care lavished on the education of others, but if so it is only incidental and unconsidered. For the guardians and the guards Plato prescribes a careful training through the emotions, by means of gymnastics, a rigorous physical training which included a knowledge of medicine and dieting, and music, a subtle shaping of the imagination through all the arts. From the earliest days, he maintains, children must be submitted to the moulding influence alone of all that is noble and good. It cannot be hoped that they will grow strong and straight if they are "reared amongst images of vice, as upon unwholesome pastures, culling much every day by little and little from many places and feeding upon it, until they insensibly accumulate a large mass of evil in their inmost souls." All baneful influences must be removed from them. Poets, for instance, who feel impelled to tell the story of Kronos eating his sons and daughters, to advertise the adulteries of Aphrodite, to amuse with amorous adventures of Zeus, king of gods and men, and his ingenuity in slipping away from his jealous consort, the ox-eyed Hera, must be forbidden the State. During their youth the guardians and guards will study mathematics, for this is a means of "purging and rekindling an organ of the soul which would otherwise be spoiled and blinded, an organ more worth saving than ten thousand eyes, for by it alone the truth is seen." But they will not confine themselves to that empirical observation which is good enough for shop-keeper, soldier, and sailor, for that will not "lead the soul to look upwards." They will rather study mathematics scientifically, for it is scientific study which makes "the natural intelligence useful instead of useless." Mathematics provide both a development of logical thinking, a mental gymnastic and an actual introduction to truth. Of course immature minds cannot open and grow under the influence of mathematics, as will more mature minds. But they can gain something, so long as it is remembered that they should not be forced to study, but introduced to it as to a game, and that athletic exercise in this period is of outstanding importance.

After selection, about the age of twenty, the more promising will undergo another course of education lasting ten years. This will comprise an intensified study of mathematics and of "dialectic." "Dialectic," as Plato originally used it, meant no more than oral discussion by question and answer. Then it came to mean the process by which man's mind tries to reach truth by means of question and answer, either by discussion with others or by "inner dialogue" with itself. Finally by dialectic Plato implied the living embodiment of truth itself. A dialectician, he says, is one who "can give account both to himself and others of the essential nature of any given thing." And in the ten years between twenty and thirty the main objective of education will be to "bring within the compass of a single survey the detached sciences in which they were educated as children so as to show the co-relation which exists between them, and the nature of real existence." A further selection is followed by another five years' study of dialectic, to see who is capable of freeing himself from sense perception and pressing on to true Being, of converting, as Plato says, the soul to reality.

But even now the education of the ruler is unfinished. After fifteen years' study of dialectic come fifteen years of practical experience, of schooling in action and further training in character. All along the pupils have been under the closest of supervision and at least since the beginning of their adult education exposed to special temptation, "tried more thoroughly than gold is tried in the fire," so that the incorruptibility and self-control of the future leaders can be established beyond all doubt. And in this final period of fifteen years' practical experience they are once again "put to the test to see whether they will continue steadfast notwithstanding every seduction, or whether possibly they may be a little shaken." In particular they will be watched to see that dialectic has not, as it were, turned sour in them. For young philosophers, like young puppies, like to tear things to pieces, and the speculative spirit which is desirable may become the spirit of revolution which is not.

Now, at the age of fifty, those who have stayed the course, who "through their whole life have done what they thought advantageous to the State and inflexibly refused to do what they thought the reverse," are "to be introduced to their final task, and must be constrained to lift up the eye of the soul, and fix it upon that which gives light to all things; and having surveyed the essence of good, they must take it as a pattern, to be copied in that work of regulating their country and their fellow-citizens and themselves, which is to occupy each in turn during the rest of life; and though they are to pass most of their time in philosophical pursuits, yet each when his turn comes is to devote himself to the hard duties of public life, and hold office for their country's sake, not as a desirable but as an unavoidable occupation." With the original material, "philosophical, high-spirited, swift-footed, and strong," thus perfected, the rulers will exercise power in the best interests of the whole, the ideal State will be realised, and its people, balanced in soul, will be just and happy.

The second of the precautions that Plato takes against the abuse of power and the tendency of men to lust after functions other than those for which they are naturally best suited is a social one. The guardians and the guards are to live a life very different from that of the producers, one in which they must forgo all that makes life for the ordinary man worth living. They are not to own any property, for from the union in the same hands of political and economic power have sprung so many of the troubles of the world. If there is not a complete divorce between ruling and owning, rulers will not rule for the good of all but will use their power to increase their wealth, and owners, who lack the qualifications necessary for the proper exercise of power, will seek to seize control of the State. Significantly enough, when Plato analyses the corruptions of the ideal State he traces them all to that degeneration of men which leads to the union of political and economic power. Everything, therefore, used by guardians and guards will be held in common. They will have no private homes, but will live a hard barrack-room existence, receiving that bare maintenance deemed necessary for soldiers on unending garrison duty. Theirs, moreover, is a thorough-going Communism which extends even to wives and children. The rulers mate for a season, but do not marry for life, and their children are taken from them and put into public nurseries so that the parents do not even recognise them as their own. For as history has so clearly shown, family affairs too frequently distort the attention and undermine the integrity of rulers, and it would seem that the only way of ensuring that love of family will not take precedence over love of the State is to abolish the family altogether. Thus deprived of property, of homes, and of family life, nothing can come between them and their service to the State. They will discharge their work as they should, and others, contemplating the extent of their sacrifice and preferring conjugal comfort and children to the stud-farm and the study, will not envy them nor, at that price, wish to discharge it for them.

The third of the precautions which Plato feels to be desirable in his good State is a biological one. He is a believer in eugenics, and since the duty of guardians and guards is to "beget children for the State," it follows that they cannot be allowed to mate when and with whom they like. They must beget children when the State directs and with partners whom it chooses. "The best of both sexes ought to be brought together as often as possible, and the worst as seldom as possible," Socrates says, "and the issue of the former unions ought to be reared, and that of the latter abandoned." 'An ingenious system of lots,' Plato believes, can be contrived to reconcile the worst to the infrequency of their marital relations—possibly one may reflect that it would have had to be very ingenious indeed to serve its purpose adequately. Brave men "will be allowed to enter into marriage-relations more frequently than others will, and to exercise more than the usual liberty of choice in such matters, so that as many children as possible may be obtained from a father of this character." A distinguished soldier on active service may claim special privileges. "No one whom he has a mind to kiss," says Plato, "should be permitted to refuse him that satisfaction." Preferences of others will not be considered. But brave eugenist as he is, Plato acknowledges that the children of the best may not be the best, though the chances are that they will, and that the children of producers may be natural guardians or guards, though the chances are that they won't. Where this happens, the children must be transferred to the classes for which they are best fitted. Plato's classes, therefore, are not the closed hereditary classes which they have been made out to be.

For good measure Plato adds a precaution of a religious kind to ensure the right working of his State. He introduces an allegory or myth which is to be incorporated in the traditions of the State, so that in time it will be accepted by all, including the guardians, and will reconcile all to their particular status in the State. The myth teaches that God mixed gold, silver, and iron in men, and that those mixed with gold are the rightful rulers, those with silver the true guards, and those with iron the proper producers. Hence each should accept the place which corresponds to the very nature that God has given him, and so promote the stability and justice of the State. Myths in the *Republic*, like parables in the Bible, show us truth in a graphic and intimate way. But this particular myth has done much to discredit Plato. For his description of it has been frequently mistranslated "noble lie," and used to suggest that he is instilling false opinions into minds unable to resist them. The translation of Vaughan and Davies, "a single spirited fiction," suggests more truly what Plato meant. He was not attempting to inculcate a belief which was false and known to be false, but which would, nevertheless, make it easier for the ruling class to suppress incipient discontent. He was trying to convey one of the most important of political truths—nothing less than the idea of Human Excellence, the truth that men are not born equal but with very different capacities, and that that will be the best State in which those different capacities are directed to the task for which they are best suited. Plato knew the importance of tradition and of the unseen. If, therefore, he was able to mould a religious tradition, that would, he felt, be one way of helping to preserve the good State. But that State was not founded on a lie. On the contrary, it was the vision of Truth itself that had given it birth.

This, then, was the Idea of the Polis that Plato believed to be laid up in heaven. Did he hope that it could be built on earth? Here his language seems contradictory. He tells us "the city is founded in words; for on earth I imagine it nowhere exists." Yet he also says: "It is not impossible; nor do we speak of things that are impossible, though even by ourselves they are admitted to be difficult." Actually the contradiction is more apparent than real. His republic is an archetype, and when Plato is thinking of it as such he knows that it can never exist in this world and says so. But an archetype is also a criterion whereby, in this case, existing States can be judged. Actual phenomena, as he says in the *Phædo*, "Aim at being," even though they fall short and are unable to be like their archetypes. There is no reason why they should not be strengthened in their aim, why they should not approach the archetype more nearly than they do at the moment, even though they can never reach it fully. Hence Plato can say that it is not impossible, though difficult, to make changes in existing States which will make them approximate more closely to the archetype. For in his republic we have at least a vision of the good. And some day somewhere that State may come into being which, imperfect as it must necessarily be, will still be a sufficiently close copy of the Idea to justify the title of the Good State.

The State and the Individual

Plato's theory of the State is an organic theory. He compares the State to the natural body of a man, saying that when a finger is hurt the whole body feels the pain, and that when a member of the State is hurt all will likewise suffer. That State, for him is the best in which the unity is that of the natural man. Moreover, he was not, of course, a liberal, as his attitude to truth shows. He emphatically did not believe "that the best test of truth is the power of thought to get itself accepted in the competition of the market." Rather he believed in a Gresham's law of ideas—that the bad would drive out the good, and he endeavoured in ways of which liberalism could never approve to make sure that they did not. He even expelled the poet from the republic, a proceeding which to Western democratic eyes is unpleasing—even though we should perhaps agree that this was only because to the Greeks the poet was far more than he is to us, since the cape of the Muse was also the mantle of the Prophet, and that all that Plato was seeking to do was to take the poet out of the pulpit. He was no democrat but the most formidable opponent that democracy has ever had. He attached little value to and took little interest in the majority of producers. And so it might well seem that he sacrificed the individual to the State.

Some of the views and practices to be found in the *Republic* would certainly suggest that he did. He says that the happiness of the whole is more important than that of the part, that the happiness of the State comes before that of any one of its three classes. He does not even allow to his two highest classes the right to their own bodies, which, as the regulations for marriage in the *Republic* show, are nothing more than the incidental means to the procreation of the State. He insists that his lowest class obey the rulers without question so that "the desires of the vulgar many may be controlled by the desires and wisdom of the cultivated few," and he makes the cultivated few give up all their private interests to those of the State. He says that the life of every individual has meaning only from the function he performs in the organism of the State. He maintains that the supreme good is the unity of the whole.

Nevertheless, it would be wrong to conclude that Plato sacrificed the individual to the State. It is worth remembering that the *Republic* is not primarily a discussion of Justice as applied to the social order. Its real interest is in Justice in the individual, and Justice is examined in the State only because the State is the individual writ large. For Plato is concerned not with civics but with souls—a concern not to be found in writers who can be legitimately accused of sacrificing the individual to the State. We cannot forget, either, that in the good State the individual is not denied but is fulfilled. The image of the teamster that Plato applied to Themistocles and Pericles he would have applied to himself. If individuals in his republic had been ungrateful, he would have seen in that a condemnation of it. And they would be ungrateful if they felt frustrated. But Plato is sure that they do not feel frustrated because they are fulfilling themselves as they can in no other way. And perhaps it can be agreed that in his republic is a better realisation of the principle "from each according to his ability, to each according to his needs" than has ever been achieved anywhere, certainly not excluding the U.S.S.R. The State, that is, exists for the perfection of the individuals within it, and the development of the individuals within it perfects the State. We look in vain in the *Republic* for any difference between the laws of public and private morality. The State conforms to the ideal of the individual man, and leaves to a later age the assertion that what is morally wrong can be politically right. Moreover, Plato's portrayal of the Unjust States hammers home the lesson that it is the falling away in personal conduct that leads to the lowering of tone in public life and to the passing of power into unfit hands for "constitutions are not born of oak and rock, but grow out of the characters in each city." It is, incidentally, one of these Unjust States, the Tyrant State, the caricature of his republic, that is to be compared with the Totalitarian States of the 20th century. It, like them, is driven by that fundamental vice that Plato calls "pleonexia," the hunger for more and more, which leads to the corruption of the soul. To compare his republic to them is to miss the whole point of Plato's teaching, which is that the purpose of the State is the production of noble characters, that the true greatness of States is to be measured by the personal worth of their citizens. And at last he leaves us with the idea that even though his republic cannot exist on earth man can by contemplating the eternal pattern build himself into the true State, can realise the State within himself. So the "celestial city," like the Kingdom of God, is really within us, and in our daily actions it is up to us to try to fulfil its laws, "so far as is possible to live like an immortal," as Plato says in the *Laws*. George Herbert's "Who sweeps a room, as for Thy laws, makes that and the action fine" is thoroughly Platonic. "It is unimportant whether the perfect state exists anywhere or will exist in the future," Plato says, "for the just man fulfils the law of that state and of no other." Anyone who can write that has not sacrificed the individual to the State. He has founded human personality not on man-made law but on eternal standards.

The Greeks and the Organic Theory of the State

It is unfortunate that limitations of space preclude a full analysis of Aristotle's contribution to political thought. For his mind was in no way inferior to Plato's. His conception of growth, his belief that everything moves to a perfect embodiment of itself and that the nature of anything is not what it is here and now but what it is capable of becoming under the best possible circumstances, has been one of the most fruitful ideas in political thought. He began that method of observation and of deducing general conclusions from actual practice which has, as it were, anchored political thought to earth. His interest in the "Politeia," his concern with the best good in existing circumstances, his conviction that we must take States as they are and do the best we can with them, his belief that political thought must combine a knowledge of political good and of political mechanics, his insistence on the value of the rule of law or "disembodied wisdom," his realisation that some constitutions would not grow in certain soils, all played a great part in the development of political thought.

But, after all, the stamp of the master is plainly to be seen in the pupil. For Aristotle man is a political animal, one who can only fulfil himself in the Polis. So Plato had believed. For Aristotle the State is a moral institution, existing not that man might live but that he might live the good life. From that view Plato never wavered. For Aristotle every true State must seek the welfare of all its members, not of a part only—and it was Plato who first taught this. In spite of Aristotle's criticisms, usually niggling though occasionally trenchant, of Plato, the difference between them is more formal than real.

Above all, Aristotle accepts the organic view of the State. The individual, he says, is to the State as the bodily organ is to the body, citizen and bodily organ being equally insufficient by themselves. "The State," he writes in a famous phrase, "is prior to the individual." We cannot, that is, conceive of the part until we have first conceived of the whole to which the part belongs. The part has meaning only in relation to the whole, as the hand has meaning only in relation to the body. And as a hand is not a hand unless it is attached to the body, so man is not man unless he is attached to the State. Again, when Aristotle speaks of the deformity of States it is to the analogy of the body that he turns. He reminds us that the exaggeration of any part of the State is like the exaggeration of any part of the body. And he criticises Plato because he says that Plato has not sufficiently realised that differentiation of parts is characteristic of the higher kind of organisms.

Moreover, as with Plato so with Aristotle, the charge that he sacrifices the individual to the State is misleading. For if to Aristotle the State is natural in the sense that without it men will not fulfil their nature, if it is natural in the sense that men cannot make it entirely as they would wish, cannot, for instance, determine its size according to the whim of the moment; if it is an organism, it is nevertheless one the growth of which they can help and the character of which they can change. The very intimacy of the Polis is such that in it the individual is not sacrificed but fulfilled. Hence for Aristotle it is true to say that the good of the State and the good of the individual are indistinguishable. He makes it plain that his State is a genuine whole, and that in any genuine whole there is no distinction between the general welfare and the welfare of the parts. He clears himself of the charge that Plato lays himself open to, namely that there is a difference between the happiness of the State, which is important, and the happiness of the citizens, which is not. "Happiness," he says, "is not a conception like that of evenness in number that may be predicated of the whole number without being predicated of its component parts. . . ." And it is worth remembering that the Greeks were in less danger than we are of seeking the good of citizens in power and in riches which in the nature of things cannot be shared by all. Like Plato, Aristotle uses the same word justice to denote the virtue of the individual and the virtue of the citizen. Like Plato he refuses to set the State above morality. "The same things are best for individuals and States," he writes. Clearly, for Aristotle as for Plato, the State and the individual are complementary not contradictory.

But if this is so, there is, nevertheless, an important point to be noticed in both Plato and Aristotle. The Organic Theory of the State, as a complete theory of the State expressed in terms of the fulfilment of men in and through it, must provide for the fulfilment of all men, not merely of some men. But it is manifestly impossible that all men should rule. Some must be ruled. Hence, as Aristotle saw quite clearly, the Organic Theory of the State implies a belief in the permanent inequality of men— "for wherever a single common whole is formed out of a number of elements, a ruler and a ruled is to be found." If all men's natures must be fulfilled and if some men must be ruled, it follows that some men must be natural leaders and some men must be by nature led. Plato's republic is based on the most thorough-going acceptance of this fact. Aristotle's exclusion from his state of mechanics and slaves, his distinction between parts that are integral and parts that are contributory, the one being citizens and the other not, similarly reflects it. This view that some must be naturally the ruled and some naturally the rulers is really an unavoidable result of organic teaching. It is true that Plato and Aristotle do not sacrifice the individual in the way that he might be said to be sacrificed, for instance, by Hegel. It is true that their State exercises a much more direct and more lively appeal than does Hegel's. But it is also true that Plato and Aristotle show what some will regard as an essential weakness of the Organic Theory of the State, though to others it will be no more than the truth, namely its deep conviction of the permanent inequality of men which so readily lends itself to the belief that some men are by nature no more than the instruments of others. My little toe is less important than my right hand, and my right hand less important than my head. If the analogy of body and State be taken too seriously, it can so easily follow that some classes of citizens are regarded as so much less important than others that concern for their welfare soon disappears. If one can accept the idea of Human Excellence, can believe that each acquires significance only in the making of his own highly specialised contribution to society, and can also believe that that contribution accords most miraculously with the structural needs of society, no doubt the Organic Theory of the State may seem sufficient. If one cannot, however, accept the idea of Human Excellence and all that it implies, the weakness of that theory will be clear.

Not the least importance of Plato and Aristotle is that in them we see the Organic Theory of the State in all its strength, and that at the same time we see its limitations clearly revealed. Yet nothing more inspiring in political thought has ever been written than these first and greatest works in the Rational-Natural tradition. As long as we are interested in the affairs of man in society, we will constantly find ourselves returning to the men who made political thought, to the masters whose voices can still reach over the years, from whose wisdom we can still draw strength for the tasks of today and inspiration for the days ahead.

CHAPTER II

THE STATE AS MACHINE

(THOMAS HOBBES; JOHN LOCKE; THE UTILITARIANS—JEREMY BENTHAM, JOHN STUART MILL)

The Failure of the Rational-Natural Tradition

THIS Rational-Natural view of the State which we have seen in the works of Plato and Aristotle inspired the Cosmopolis, or World State, of the Stoics and reappeared in the great work of the Jurists of the Roman Empire. Thence it passed over into Christianity, and was supreme in the Natural Law theory of the Middle Ages, even though admittedly then the State as we know it did not exist. At intervals in that long period another view of the State, the view of the State as Will and Artifice, strove for expression. It is to be seen in the so-called "Hard" Sophists, who taught that there are no ideal models to copy and that Justice is made by man himself. It is to be seen in the teaching of Epicurus who held that the State was not a divine inspiration guiding man's footsteps to Eternal Truth, but no more than a device of his own making to enable him to put up with one of life's major inconveniences—the existence of other people. It is the idea behind the Roman conception of Lex or Law which at first sight seems to correspond to the Greek idea of Nomos or Law, but which is in fact fundamentally different from it, Lex being thought of as creating something new while Nomos was thought of as discovering something that was already there, namely Eternal Truth. It appears again in the Hebrew and Christian conceptions of Divine Will and Creation, and it is reflected in St. Augustine's view of the peace of God. It strongly coloured the writings of the Nominalists of the 13th and 14th centuries, of William of Occam, Duns Scotus and Marsilius of Padua, for whom civil society is artificial, a mere contrivance of men to ensure peace and order, and what they themselves call Justice.

But it was only in the 17th century, when the individualism of the Nominalists reached full blossom, that the hold upon political thinking of the Natural-Rational view of the State began appreciably to relax. For by the 17th century the growth of scepticism had undermined men's belief in a Natural Law unchanging and absolute, since scientific discoveries had radically changed accepted views of Nature, Reason, and Artifice. To 17th-century philosophers the world was no longer composed, as it was to the Greeks, of living organisms. Nature was regarded as a machine, though a machine that was designed by God who could not himself be a machine. To some 17th-century thinkers men could not be regarded as machines either, for they have intelligence. Because of this, for instance, Galileo concludes that man as well as God must be conceived as being outside nature. But to others, as to Descartes and Hobbes, even men are machines and only God is outside the natural world and is not a machine.

It is understandable how widespread this view of nature as a machine should be, for the 17th-century was the beginning of the machine age. It is now that the windmill, the pump, the printing-press, the lock, the mechanism of the clock, captured the imagination of the Western World. More and more, men spoke of the energy of a substance, less and less of its soul or life. To the Greeks, Reason was not that which all men have in little and philosophers in large; it was the natural order itself, the very principle of the universe which "goeth through all things by reason of its pureness." For the 17th-century thinker, however, it had become a faculty by which men draw conclusions from their observations. It was no longer something which tells man what he ought to do, still less what he wants to do; rather it was that which taught him how to achieve what his passions desired. As Hume was later to say, "Reason is and ought to be the slave of the passions." To the Greeks, whatever was the work of man was but a copy of already existing Reality. To the 17th century, what man made was genuinely original and creative. As God created the world from nothing, so whatever man makes he also creates from nothing.

The Tradition of Will and Artifice

This new idea of Nature, of Reason, and of Artifice combined to create a new view of the State as being the result of Will and Artifice. Since Nature itself is a mechanism, society and the State must obviously be mechanisms. The artist who creates these machines is man, and who wishes therefore to understand the State must clearly begin by understanding its maker, man. His creation, the State, is a genuinely free creation, not a copying of something already existing. His act in creating the State is not an act of reason or science, it is not dependent on any knowledge of absolute standards, because these do not exist, and Right and Justice, for instance, come into being only with the State. It is an act of will and of artifice.

This view of the State as Will and Artifice begins with the individual being sovereign over himself, and is an attempt to answer the questions: How can men compose such a State? Why should they want to compose such a State? What sort of State can such individuals compose? The State, it concludes, must be the result of a genuine agreement on the part of individuals, a creative agreement which for the first time brings law and order into the world. It substitutes order for chaos and, as the price of the benefit, it extracts from man acknowledgment of obligations that he never knew before. But these obligations are no more than he has consented to, and indeed the only basis for their existence is his consent. Men want the State, this view maintains, because it provides something which Nature does not—that is, peace, order, and possibly prosperity. The lack of order, which it is for the State to remedy, arises not because men are bad but because they are men. The State's task is not to remove a defect of, but to impose a necessary check on, human nature. In civil society, therefore, man's slogan must be not "follow nature" but "reject nature." And the State that men make, since it must essentially be a limitation of their sovereignty over themselves, must establish a will over them that is superior to theirs. But there can be no question of its creating a superior reason—Will, not Reason, is the nature of the State. It will thus be an authoritarian State in the sense that its distinguishing characteristic will be the possession of supreme power—although of course its authoritarian nature will be more emphasised by some of the writers of this school than by others. But it will be authoritarian only because the people have consented in this way to limit their own sovereignty.

The State as Machine

This conception of the State as a machine continued to make an appeal to men long after the 17th century; its adherents today are numerous. Naturally many of the ideas of the 17th century are not acceptable to contemporary thinkers who regard the State as a machine. Nevertheless, they still retain the essentials of the 17th-century view. Indeed, all to whom the State is a machine have sufficient in common for it to be seen that they belong to this same Will and Artifice tradition of the State that we have been discussing.

Thus all see the State as something made by man to suit his particular purposes. Either implicitly, or more usually explicitly, they distinguish between State and Society as of course Organic theories of the State do not, regarding the State not as the whole of society but only as a special organisation of society. This distinction is extremely important to them, not least because it enables them—how satisfactorily is a matter of opinion —to meet the charge that men do not in fact construct States but are born into them, and that in consequence it is absurd to maintain that States which may have existed for centuries are merely machines, no more than governmental devices. Society, they admit, may be a natural growth, but at some stage of that growth, they say, it creates what it finds necessary for its continued survival, namely the State which is therefore to be regarded after all as a machine. Because in Mechanistic theories the State is something made by man, he must obviously be more real than his creation. A machine is not alive as an organism is —what significance and unity it possesses it derives purely from its creator. It is therefore something which exists for man, not, as Organic theories would have it, something for which man exists. It is something which establishes a superior will, not a superior reason, as Organic theories would have us believe. What characterises it is its possession and exercise of supreme regulating power. And this power it uses, not to create a common or general good, which does not exist, but to harmonise interests which do. The good of us all, Mechanistic theories of the State insist, may be inter-dependent, but it remains our good and is never that of a collective entity which we call the Community or the State.

It is the purpose of this chapter to examine these views in the writings of Thomas Hobbes, perhaps the greatest of English Political Theorists; of John Locke, who for a century was the acknowledged master of English and American, and even to some extent of European, political thought; and of the Utilitarians, whose intellectual dominance in the first half of the

19th century was as great as was Locke's in the 18th century, and who exercised an influence on the course of events as great even as his.

THOMAS HOBBES, 1588–1679

His Life and Writings

In the year of the Armada, Hobbes said, his mother gave birth to twins—himself and fear. He might perhaps have more truly said himself and pugnacity. He never thought it necessary to introduce much discrimination into the catholicity of his dislikes—brushes with Aristotle, the medieval schoolmen, Oxford mathematicians, the Pope and the Church of Rome in particular and all Churches in general, were not enough to satisfy his combative instinct, and at the age of eighty-five we find him translating the *Iliad* and the *Odyssey* into English verse with the charitable intention of providing his critics, who in their previous encounters with him had only been able to reveal their folly, some slight opportunity of displaying their wit. We may suspect that his parade of fear served its purpose in enabling him to say to his readers, "Human nature is as I say it is. Just look at me." And we may even reflect that not every philosopher would have the courage to draw attention in himself to what are normally considered defects of character in order to prove the validity of his theory.

He was the son of a vicar, which may explain his very thorough knowledge of Scripture and conceivably also his lack of enthusiasm for religion. He was educated at Malmesbury, which was near his home at Westport, and at Oxford, of which his main recollection seems to have been the "frequency of insignificant speech" he encountered there. On leaving the University he became tutor to the heir of William Cavendish, later Earl of Devonshire, thus establishing a connection that was to last for most of his life, and one which brought him into contact with leading figures of his day, such as Ben Jonson, Bacon and Clarendon at home, and Galileo abroad.

Though before he was fifty-two his only published work was a translation of Thucydides, he had long felt an interest in philosophy, an interest which was greatly stimulated by his discovery of the world of mathematics. His first philosophical work, *The Elements of Law,* was finished in 1640, but not published until 1650. With the outbreak of the Civil War, he removed to

Paris, writing *De Cive*, which was published in 1642. Here he became for a time tutor to Charles II, a post for which he might have been considered remarkably fitted since he believed on hygienic grounds in getting drunk once a month. But he held it for a short time only, for his suspected atheism seemed far too immoral even to that *émigré* court, which so enthusiastically practised the precept that profligacy is the prerogative of princes. However, his energies were not diverted by his brief excursion into royal pedagogics, and his masterpiece, the *Leviathan*, was published in 1651.

The following year he was back in Protectorate England, in which, to his surprise, he seems to have found a closer resemblance to his *Leviathan* than he had been able to discern in France. In England he rejoined the Devonshire household, where he remained for the rest of his life, publishing *De Corpore* in 1655 and *De Homine* in 1659. Charles II, in whom Hobbes's theory of human nature seems to be at least as well illustrated as in Hobbes himself, and who liked to be amused, received him at court after the Restoration. "Here comes the bear to be baited," Charles would say when Hobbes appeared, and since the bear could always be relied upon to give a handsome performance when baited, Charles thought him well deserving of the handsome pension that he gave him. Hobbes died at Chatsworth at the age of 91, full of years, full of works, and full, if not of honour, at least of notoriety.

In the dedication of the *Leviathan* to Francis Godolphin, Hobbes spoke of the possibility of his labour being "generally decried." In this he was not mistaken. Soon after the publication of *Leviathan,* his critics were in full cry after him, sounding the note of horror at his materialism and indignation at his despotism that has rung down the years. The role of major devil in modern political thought was not open to him, as Machiavelli had already been cast for the part, but if the wickedness of another had deprived him of pride of place, it was very generally recognised that he was Machiavelli's worthy if necessarily junior satanic colleague. Clarendon protested at his "lewd principles." Whitehall found *Leviathan* "as full of damnable opinions as a toad is of poison," "a rebel's catechism," "good doctrine for a Popish Cabal." Bramhill thought it "right dog's play," and believed that it would "put all to fire and flame." "Nilus after a great overflowing," he wrote, "doth not leave such a confusion after it as he doth; nor a Hog in a Garden of Herbs." Rosse was convinced that it would reduce all to "the condition of those who live under the Turk, the Muscovite, Prester John, and the Mogul." What else, Cowley asked, could be expected of "the Monster of Malmesbury"?

To those who, after the Plague and the Fire of London, were looking around for the cause of the wrath of God so plainly revealed, it appeared that any community which had not decisively spewed forth Hobbes and his damnable doctrines must expect to invite the attentions of the Avenging Angel, attentions which a committee of bishops sought to avoid in future by considering, albeit fruitlessly, ways and means of ensuring that a life that was so obviously poor, solitary, nasty, and brutish, would not be further prolonged. Yesterday his was "the meanest of all ethical theories" justifying "the most universal of absolutisms." And today Professor Willey can portray him as that devout if disputatious disciple of peace whose every statement was inspired by hatred of schoolmen and clerics or by love of that ordered living in a stable commonwealth of which the violence of Civil War in England and the selfish irresponsibility of revolution in France deprived him, and whose effortless skill in suiting his views to his circumstances must have been the admiration and the hopeless envy even of the Vicar of Bray.

But though his critics are legion and his confessed admirers few, Hobbes continues to be read and to make a powerful appeal. Though the exaggeration he allowed himself, the savage arrogance which is rarely far from his pages, may offend, the profound, incisive mind must attract, and his style, perhaps more elaborate, more sonorous, richer in imagery than we are accustomed to, but powerful and pungent enough to halt even our hurrying age, must delight. He possessed in full measure the "powerful eloquence" which he said "procureth attention and consent," and without which he believed "the effect of reason will be little." Indeed, he is one of the great stylists of English political philosophy, worthy to rank with such masters of English prose as Hooker and Milton and Burke.

In his pages the pertinent, the profound, and the pithy are waiting at every turn to reward the eager traveller. It is perhaps unlikely that he will ever be quoted extensively on those calendars which conceive it to be their duty not merely to indicate the date but to suggest a profound reflection for the day.

a fate to which he has, nevertheless, exposed himself, for the *Leviathan* alone is as full of quotations as Hamlet. "Words," we read, "are wise men's counters; they do but reckon with them, but they are the money of fools," or "Where men build on false grounds, the more they build the greater is the ruin," or "The understanding is by the flame of the passions, never enlightened, but dazzled." Here is homely, convincing common sense. "If Livy says the Gods made once a cow speak, and we believe it not, we distrust not God therein, but Livy." "Men give different names to one and the same thing, from the difference of their own passions: as they that approve a private opinion, call it opinion; but they that mislike it, heresy; and yet heresy signifies no more than private opinion; but has only a greater tincture of choler." Here is keen historical insight. Every schoolboy knows the passage: "If a man consider the original of this great Ecclesiastical Dominion, he will easily perceive that the Papacy is no other than the ghost of the deceased Roman Empire, sitting crowned on the grave thereof." And of how much of the world's history must we regard this as an illuminating text: "And from hence it comes to pass, that where an invader hath no more to fear than another man's single power; if one plant, sow, build, or possess a convenient seat, others may probably be expected to come prepared with forces united to dispossess, and deprive him, not only of the fruits of his labour, but also of his life, or liberty. And the invader again is in like danger of another"? Certainly a history of international relations could well be written under his inscription: "Men have no pleasure, but on the contrary a great deal of grief, in keeping company where there is no power able to overawe them all."

Again and again one finds the contemporary relevance of his words almost breath-taking. Those engaged today in building up the defences of the West would echo from the heart his words: "For all men are by nature provided of notable multiplying glasses, that is their passions and self-love, through which every little payment appeareth a great grievance; but are destitute of those prospective glasses, namely moral and civil science, to see afar off the miseries that hang over them, and cannot without such payments be avoided." Those who since the second world war have tried in vain to construct an international agreement on the control of atomic energy are bitterly aware of "this easy truth, that covenants being but words and breath, have no force to oblige, contain, constrain, or protect any man, but what it has from the public sword." Those who are wondering how best democratic institutions may be handed over to primarily primitive and possibly plural communities would have no difficulty in agreeing with him when he says: "To put an infant into the power of those that can promote themselves by his destruction, or damage, is not tuition but treachery."

One could multiply his aphorisms a hundredfold, as one could his comments on which we would do well to ponder today. But enough has been said to make it clear that he does not belong to those writers whose message is merely for their age. Of course he was influenced by the Civil War just as he was influenced by the schoolmen whom he so much disliked. Even profound and original thinkers cannot abstract themselves from their environment, as Plato and Aristotle make plain. But it is one thing for a thinker to be influenced by his age and another for him to be limited by it. Hobbes was no more limited by his age than Plato and Aristotle were by theirs. He was concerned with the particular problems of the 17th century, and the reflections of a great mind on contemporary problems can never lack interest. But he was more concerned with the general problems of mankind. Like every great artist, he was attracted by the universal in the particular—the local problem is of interest only because it reveals the general problem of human existence in a clear and familiar way. It is because this is so, because he is no more dated than Shakespeare or Plato or Aristotle, that he has confounded his critics and will do so as long as men feel, or are able to express, any interest in the questions: "What is man?", "What is the State?", and "Why should he obey it?"

His Political Theory—His View of Man

The Universe, for Hobbes, is a machine, a machine made up of particles moving according to a mechanical law which he believes that Galileo has shown can be determined. This movement, or motion as he calls it, is the very principle of the Universe. Man is a microcosm, an epitome of the great Universe. He also is a machine, more complicated than plants or beasts, but composed as they are, and as the Universe is, of moving particles. It is Hobbes's ambition to find the law according to which these particles move in man, and in man in relation with his fellows, as he believes that Galileo has found it for the Universe. Hence his insistence that any study of political society must begin with a consideration of the nature of man. Hence his reminder that "Read thyself" is advice which all men and particularly all statesmen should bear in mind, advice which they would find easier to follow when once they had read his works. Hence his claim, "I ground the civil rights of sovereigns, and both the duty and liberty of subjects, upon the known natural inclinations of mankind." Everything in man, including his thought, is, he believed, derived from his senses. Sense was itself but motion: "Original fancy, caused, as I have said, by the pressure, that is, by the motion, of external things upon our eyes, ears, and other organs thereunto ordained." From sense man acquires memory and imagination and prudence, all of which may be regarded as his receptive powers. These in their turn generate further movements in man's brain which may be called his active powers; these are his emotions or passions.

What man desires he calls Good, and Pleasure is the movement in his mind that accompanies it. What he dislikes he calls Evil, and the movement in his mind that accompanies it he calls Pain. Good and Evil, then, cannot be fixed and finite entities even for any individual because each individual's desires are not constant but changing. Still less can Good and Evil be the same for all men. Men call the succession of emotions in their minds prompting them to do or abstain from doing anything deliberation. And when a decision is reached men may be said to will whatever they decide upon.

Thus man is compelled by that very principle of motion which is operative in the Universe to will what he desires and only what he desires. It is impossible for him to will what another desires. He can be moved only by the desire to get what he wants and to preserve himself, and by the fear that he will be unable to get what he wants or to preserve himself. It is an illusion to think that he has any feelings which can be ascribed to other factors than these. Laughter and sympathy, for instance, may seem more generous emotions. But Hobbes would have agreed with the remark that W. S. Landor in his *Imaginary Conversations* ascribes to Lord Chesterfield that "Half the pleasure in the world arises from malignity, and little of the other half is free from its encroachments." Laughter, he says, is not a sign of good nature. It is caused "either by some sudden act of men's own that pleaseth them; or by the apprehension of some deformed thing in another, by comparison whereof they suddenly applaud themselves." "It is," he adds, "incident most to them that are conscious of the fewest abilities in themselves; who are forced to keep themselves in their own favour by observing the imperfections of other men." As for the pity that man sometimes feels, that "ariseth from the imagination that the like calamity may befall himself."

When man is successful in achieving what he wills, he is said to enjoy Felicity. This is not to be equated with Pleasure as the Utilitarians imagined that it was. It is "continued success in obtaining those things which a man from time to time desireth," and therefore it can give man no rest, for it is not a final end, but "a continued progress of the desire from one object to another; the attaining of the former being still but the way to the latter." It is a man's power that assures him success in the pursuit of Felicity, his lack of power that is the cause of his failure. Thus life is "a perpetual and restless desire of power after power that ceaseth only in death," since "man cannot assure the power and means to live well which he hath present, without the acquisition of more."

The individual whom Hobbes has thus described is completely self-centred. For Hobbes every single man is an absolutely solitary individual. Since knowledge comes from the senses and different senses cannot see the same world, a man and his world must be one and different from the world of other men. Different individuals have absolutely separate worlds, separate pleasures, truths, goods, and they belong to no order, moral or politic. Hobbes, so frequently portrayed as the great absolutist, is perhaps the greatest individualist in the history of political thought. His is an extreme doctrine of individualism embracing everything. He is a Nominalist of the school of Occam, and his individualism is quite unqualified—more so, indeed, than that of any other writer.

The individual whom he describes has, however, the possibility of breaking down his solitude because he has the power of speech. For in making a language men must agree that certain sounds mean certain things. Moreover, language is not only a means of communicating with others, it is the way in which we become conscious of our own thoughts. For "a name is a word taken at pleasure to serve as a mark that may raise in our minds a thought like some thought we had before." Moreover, in this way men are enabled to pass from names to definitions, to arguments and to reason, which is "nothing but reckoning, that is adding and subtracting, of the consequences of general names agreed upon for the marking and signifying of our thoughts." It is this faculty of reasoning which, together with religion, distinguishes man from the brute.

Reasoning, however, is artificial, while the passions are natural —man therefore is not primarily a creature of reason but of the passions. Moreover, man's reasoning is fallible—"as in arithmethic, unpractised men must, and professors themselves may often, err, and cast up false; so also in any other subject of reasoning, the ablest, most attentive, and most practised men may deceive themselves and infer false conclusions." And Hobbes is very well aware that if man has the ability to reason he has also "the privilege of absurdity; to which no living creature is subject but man." "And of men," Hobbes adds, "those are of all most subject to it that profess philosophy. For it is most true that Cicero saith of them somewhere: that there can be nothing so absurd but may be found in the books of philsophers." Nevertheless, Reason will help man in his pursuit of Felicity. But not even its assistance will enable him to overcome the difficulties that he will find in his way, which spring both from the circumstances in which he finds himself and from an inherent defect in his own character.

Circumstances place him among fellow-men whose very existence makes it difficult for him to satisfy his desires. For many will want what he wants, and will therefore be his deadly enemies. Moreover, men seek to outdo one another, for "man, whose joy consisteth in comparing himself with other men, can relish nothing but what is eminent." This urge to excel necessitates "a perpetual contention for Honour, Riches, and Authority." Contrasting men with bees and ants, Hobbes says, "Men are continually in competition for honour and dignity, which these creatures are not; consequently amongst men ariseth on that ground, envy and hatred and finally war." Roughly speaking, the powers of men are equal, the ingenuity of David always being sufficient to offset the strength of Goliath. Therefore men will always live in a condition of perpetual fear, of competition and war.

This will be the more certain because of an inherent defect

in man's intellect, vainglory or pride. This is "a vain conceit of one's own wisdom" and strength. For "such is the nature of men, that however they may acknowledge many others to be more witty, or more eloquent, or more learned; yet they will hardly believe there be many so wise as themselves; for they see their own wit at hand, and other men's at a distance." Men are thus apt to think themselves stronger than they are, to underestimate the necessity of fighting continually for what they want, to fear less than they ought to fear the frustration of their desires and even sudden death. Blinded by their brilliance, carried away by their conceit, Desire will outstrip Prudence in them and death will be their reward.

This, then, is the state of nature in which man lives. Neither right nor wrong, justice nor injustice, have place in it. Force and fraud are its cardinal virtues, and the only rule that men acknowledge is "the good old rule, the simple plan, that he should take who has the power, and he should keep who can."

"In such condition," says Hobbes, "there is no place for industry; because the fruit thereof is uncertain: and consequently no culture of the earth; no navigation, nor use of the commodities that may be imported by sea; no commodious building; no instruments of moving, and removing, such things as require much force; no knowledge of the face of the earth; no account of time; no arts; no letters; no society; and which is worst of all continual fear, and danger of violent death; and the life of man, solitary, poor, nasty, brutish, and short." Man's vainglory or pride unfits him for success in such a condition, but the condition itself is the result not of his defects but of his very nature. The state of nature, as Hobbes sees it, is "the ill condition which man by mere nature is actually placed in." And the problem for Hobbes is how to extricate him from a position which the very principle of the Universe, motion, has apparently designed for him.

His View of the State

Men would, Hobbes is sure, do anything to get out of this desperate position in which they find themselves.

They can, he believes, get out of it because they are creatures of passion and imagination, reason and will.

Passion and imagination teach them "the fear of death" and "desire of such things as are necessary to commodious living;

and a hope by their industry to obtain them."

Reason teaches them to obey Natural Laws, of which Hobbes enumerates nineteen that "concern the doctrine of civil society." The most important of these are that men should seek peace, without which they will not find Felicity, but that when they cannot obtain peace they should "use all helps and advantages of war," that they should surrender their equal right to possess all things, provided that all do likewise, that all men should keep the engagements that they make to do this, and that no man should be understood to have so acted as to make the further attainment of his Felicity impossible. All these Natural Laws or Articles of Peace can, Hobbes says, be "contracted into one easy sum, intelligible even to the meanest capacity; and that is 'Do not that to another which thou wouldst not have done to thyself.' "

Two things are to be noticed about these Natural Laws. First, they are not Natural Laws as commonly understood. For the great tradition of Natural Law that goes back to the Stoics is that of an Eternal Justice, a Perfect Morality, of which actual law is the imperfect reflection. Natural Law is thus a measuring-rod to apply to existing laws to find how far short they fall of the ideal. But Hobbes's Natural Laws are merely "counsels of prudence." They are what men who are able in calculating the changes and chances of this life would seek to do in pursuit of Felicity. They are, to those less able, Mr. Hobbes's ready reckoner, obviating mistakes in calculation. In writing of Natural Laws as he does, Hobbes is in fact saying that there are no such things as moral rights, no clash between a man's duty and a man's interest, but only an appeal from man drunk to man sober, only a difference between bad and good calculation. Secondly, Hobbes's Natural Laws do not imply that there is such a thing as a common good. They merely seek to bring into being those common conditions which are necessary to fulfil each individual good.

Will, finally, enables men to take the action that their reason dictates to compose a society. What is necessary is a "will not to will," not to insist on one's will on every occasion, to accept a limitation of the will. This can be arranged if men agree to transfer by means of a contract their absolute right to will whatever they like to some agreed-upon third party. Such a third party must have a particular characteristic. He must be the representative of each individual—that is, an artificial person distinct from the natural man. He can then will and act in place of each individual. But he must of course be the representative, having authority from him who is represented. His will cannot be the common will of all, for there is no such thing. But his representative will is a substitute for the conflicting individual wills, and this substitution is the only way in which many men can find unity. "A multitude of men are made one person when they are by one man, or one person, represented; so that it be done with the consent of every one of that multitude in particular. For it is the unity of the representer, not the unity of the represented, that makes the person one. And it is the representer that beareth the person, and but one person: and unity cannot otherwise be understood in multitude."

Such a contract must be perpetual and irrevocable, but it is not easy to make it so. Though begot by Reason on Fear, it is contrary to men's instincts. Moreover, men are notorious backsliders. Therefore "it is no wonder if there be somewhat else required, besides covenant, to make their agreement constant and lasting." That something is "a common power to keep them in awe, and to direct their actions to the common benefit." Clearly "covenants without the sword are but words." The representative of the people must also, then, be all-powerful over the people. Thus man, who is born free, solitary, and in intellectual and moral isolation, voluntarily accepts limitation of sovereignty to achieve something else. He composes a society by human agreement, an artifice. "This is the generation of that great Leviathan, or rather, to speak more reverently, of that mortal God, to which we owe under the immortal God our peace and defence. For by this authority, given him by every particular man in the Commonwealth, he hath the use of so much power and strength conferred on him that by terror thereof he is enabled to form the wills of them all to peace at home and mutual aid against their enemies abroad. And in him consisteth the essence of the commonwealth; which, to define it, is one person of whose acts a great multitude, by mutual covenants one with another, have made themselves every one the author, to the end he may use the strength and means of them all, as he shall think expedient, for their peace and common defence."

Hobbes believes that the third party, who is the beneficiary of the contract, the recipient of power, should be a king. As a man he will be selfish like all men, but the self-indulgence of one will be cheaper than the self-indulgence of many. There will be a limit to the number of mistresses of even the most amorous monarch, and an end even to the regality of their extravagance, but the goods of the State will be exhausted more readily than the ingenuity of a sovereign assembly in turning them to private ends. Moreover, "in a monarchy the private interest is the same with the public." A king cannot be rich, glorious, or secure, if his people are poor, contemptible, or weak. And as he has got to the top, all his ambition lies in strengthening the State; whereas members of a democratic or aristocratic sovereign assembly may be prompted by ambition to intrigue against the State in the hope of seizing power, to the great danger of the community. Indeed, Hobbes says "other governments were compacted by the artifice of men out of the ashes of monarchy after it had been ruined by seditions." Hobbes's personal prejudices are, however, unimportant. His is a doctrine of the absolute State, not of the absolute king. So long as it is admitted that Leviathan possesses absolute power, whether Leviathan be one, few, or many is a minor matter.

The characteristics of Leviathan are unmistakable. He is the sole source of laws, and he is of course the sole interpreter of laws. He is not subject to civil laws, although so long as he does not repeal them he is bound by them. Hobbes has no use for the traditional medieval idea that the king should be *sub lege*, subject to the condition that he should obey the law. Nor has he any use for the idea of fundamental law, of a law that cannot be changed. "I could never see in any author," he wrote, "what a fundamental law signifieth." Leviathan is the creator of Right and Justice. His edicts, or laws, therefore, can never be unjust or immoral—"for the law is all the right reason we have, and . . . is the infallible rule of moral goodness." Laws may, however, be inequitable or unnecessary. If they conflict with the Natural Laws, the articles of peace, they will be inequitable. If they forbid activity which is not dangerous to the peace, they will be unnecessary. But they will still be law, for law is always and only that which is the command of the sovereign. The Law of Nature can never be pleaded against Leviathan, for the purpose of the Law of Nature is the creation of Leviathan, who alone can interpret it. The Law of God can never be pleaded against Leviathan, for of that also Leviathan is the sole inter-preter. Conscience can never be pleaded against Leviathan, for "the Law is the public conscience by which man hath already undertaken to be guided. Otherwise in such diversity as there is of private consciences, which are but private opinions, the commonwealth must needs be distracted, and no man dare to obey the sovereign power, further than it shall seem good in his own eyes." There is, indeed, only one limitation on Leviathan's powers. He cannot command a man to kill himself. To do so would be the only act which would be a breach of the covenant on the sovereign's part—for it would imply that men can be said to seek Felicity in the extinction of all possibility of Felicity. And of course Leviathan must maintain himself—man owes no obligation to an authority that fails to protect him. If Leviathan fails to protect, men are then back in the state of nature and free to obey a *de facto* monarch. But while he exists, nothing can stand against him and nothing must be allowed to try. It is typical, for instance, that Hobbes greatly dislikes associations—"which are," he considers, "as it were many lesser common-wealths in the bowels of a greater, like worms in the entrails of a natural man."

Nevertheless, Leviathan is not such a one that he can tolerate no liberty. There is liberty under him. It is that which man enjoys in the silence of the laws. Leviathan has no passion for undue interference. "For the use of laws is not to bind the people from all voluntary actions; but to direct and keep them in such a motion, as not to hurt themselves by their own im-petuous desires, rashness or indiscretion; as hedges are set, not to stop travellers, but to keep them in their way." Men can expect the liberty "to buy and sell and otherwise contract with one another; to choose their own abode, their own diet, their own trade of life, and institute their children as they themselves think fit; and the like." Though it would be wrong to see in Hobbes an early exponent of *laisser-faire*. He believed that the distressed "ought not to be left to the charity of private persons" —they were Leviathan's responsibility. And he held that "there ought to be such laws as may encourage all manner of arts, such as navigation, agriculture, fishing, and all manner of manufac-ture which requires labour."

Hobbes believed, too, that intellect and conscience were be-yond the reach of Leviathan. Leviathan could certainly command men's behaviour and demand that they perform whatever ceremonies the public worship of the State dictates. But he should not inquire into private beliefs. Hobbes would have agreed with the letter that Lord Burghley wrote in 1584 to Archbishop Whitgift, protesting against "these your Grace's proceedings so vehement and so general against ministers and preachers, as the Papists are thereby generally encouraged, all ill-disposed subjects animated, and thereby the Queen's Majesty's safety endangered," criticising the Lambeth Articles, "which I have read, and find so curiously penned, so full of branches and circumstances, as I think the inquisitors of Spain use not so many questions to comprehend and to trap their preys." Leviathan, Hobbes wrote, "cannot oblige men to believe." "Thought," he said, "is free." We need only recall Hobbes's own vigorous stand against the authority of Aristotle to convince us that he is an opponent of all authority in philosophy, belief, opinion. Justification for the existence of the secret-thought police to be found in 20th-century totalitarian States is not to be sought in him.

This is Leviathan, the King of the Proud, with whom no power on earth can compare. It may be protested, Hobbes says, that such a power has never been acknowledged. But what, he asks, does that matter? "For though, in all places of the world, men should lay the foundation of their houses on the sand, it could not thence be inferred that so it ought to be. The skill of making, and maintaining commonwealths, consisteth in certain rules, as doth arithmetic and geometry; not, as tennis-play, on practice only: which rules, neither poor men have had the leisure, nor men that have had the leisure have hitherto had the curiosity, or the method to find out."

It may be said, Hobbes agrees, that men will not like Leviathan. Of course they will not, he says, when they give rein to the pride that is in them, "not considering that the state of man can never be without some incommodity or other; and that the greatest that in any form of government can possibly happen to the people in general, is scarce sensible in respect of the miseries and horrible calamities that accompany a civil war, or that dissolute condition of masterless men, without subjection to laws and a coercive power to tie their hands from rapine and revenge."

In any case, he says, what can they do about it? For "whosoever thinking sovereign power too great, will seek to make it less, must subject himself to that power that can limit it; that is to say, to a greater." If they reflect, they will see how great are its blessings. It will give them peace and the possibility of Felicity. More it cannot do. It cannot ensure Felicity, "for there is no such thing as perpetual tranquillity of mind while we live here; because life itself is but motion, and can never be without desire, nor without fear, no more than without sense." There is an old Chinese tale concerning the man in Hell about to be reincarnated who said to the King of Reincarnation: "If you want me to return to the earth as a human being, I will go only on my own conditions." "And what are they?" asked the King. The man replied, "I must be born the son of a cabinet minister and father of a future scholar of the First Class in the examinations, I must have 10,000 acres of land surrounding my home and fish-ponds and fruits of every kind and a beautiful wife and pretty concubines, all good and loving to me, and rooms stocked to the ceiling with gold and pearls and cellars stocked full of grain and trunks chockful of money, and I myself must be a Grand Councillor or a Duke of the First Rank, and enjoy honour and prosperity and live until I am a hundred years old." The King of Reincarnation replied, "If there was such a lot on earth, I would go and be reincarnated myself, and not give it to you!" Hobbes would have strongly approved of that story. But peace is worth having for itself. If the price, which is Leviathan, seems high, it is, after all, the price of life and is not too high to avoid death.

Hobbes's state of nature in which life is so wretched has frequently been criticised. But he would not have been impressed by the criticism that men have never lived without someone in authority over them. If that could be proved, it would still not affect his argument that this is how men would live if they had no authority over them. Nor would he have been very much impressed if proof were available that men had, in fact, so lived. If you want to pile Pelion on Ossa, he would have said, go ahead, but there really is no need. There is quite sufficient evidence, he would have maintained, that this is how men would behave in the absence of a sovereign. Hobbes, in fact, was not concerned with the history of the State, but with its validity. And he cannot be proved wrong by denying the existence of the state of nature.

It has frequently been pointed out, too, that the Social Contract is unhistoric and impossible, that the story of primitive societies has shown conclusively that men move from status to contract, which is possible only at a comparatively late stage of their evolution. Hobbes would have been as indifferent to these criticisms as to the criticisms of his state of nature. For the doctrine of the social contract, which was a self-evident axiom of 17th-century political thought, was not as a rule understood historically. It was understood in a logical not a chronological sense. It was concerned with the origin of the State, not in time but in reason. It was seeking not the beginning, but the principle of the State, its *raison d'être*. It was an attempt to answer the question, "Why do men obey the State?" not "What is the historical origin of it?" In employing it Hobbes was saying, "This is how I can best explain my idea of the State," and his device is legitimate since his is an analytical and not an historical problem. Denial of the reality of the contract can prove him wrong no more than can denial of the reality of the state of nature.

It has often been stated that what Hobbes has to say of Natural Laws is confusing and, anyhow, unnecessary. The charge is made that he deliberately switches the cards, that he calls powers rights, then treats them as if they were rights in the accepted moral sense; that his Law of Nature is both a brute instinct and a moral ideal, and that he takes advantage of either meaning to suit his case. It is true that he does not always define his terms with that force and clarity of which none can doubt him capable. It is true that he occasionally shifts his ground, thereby seeking an advantage that he would be the first to deny to others. But he is a remarkably consistent thinker, and his remarks on Natural Laws are neither as confusing nor as unnecessary as all that. In particular they serve as a forceful reminder of the fact that Leviathan's authority is legitimate only because of the consent of each individual. Men can be forced to obey a *de facto* sovereign power. But they have no moral obligation to do so in the sense that they have a moral obligation to obey the Leviathan that they have authorised to act for them. Hobbes's remarks on Natural Laws and Natural Rights may help us to remember that very important distinction.

From the time of Spinoza, who wrote that the monster of Hobbes's state of nature could never become the man of the compact, critics have commented that even if men were capable of making a social contract they would not make a contract such as this. Locke's words, "This is to think that men are so foolish that they take care to avoid what mischiefs may be done to them by polecats and foxes, but are content, nay, think it safety, to be devoured by lions," are well known. Yet, as George Bernard Shaw once pointed out, history is full of examples of men who embraced death in order to avoid destruction. Moreover, for Hobbes as for Burke, "politics ought to be adjusted, not to human reasonings, but to human nature; of which the reason is but a part, and by no means the greatest part." Given such an individual as the one with whom Hobbes starts, no other contract than this is conceivable. Admitting the fact that man's nature is constant, only such a contract as this can ensure that the natural result of man's nature, namely chaos, will not also be constant. The reflection of a lantern can be changed by the insertion of a lens through which its rays must pass without any alteration being made to the lantern itself, and the chaos which is the normal result of a man's quest for Felicity in a world in which he is not alone can be changed into peace without any alteration in man himself—but only by insertion between man and the screen of the world of the artificial lens, which is Leviathan.

Like all who have written at length, Hobbes is open to criticism in detail. It may be true that he fails to distinguish between State and Government, that he confounds the legal absolutism of the State with governmental absolutism, that he does not see that changes in the forms of Government do not imply the dissolution of the State. His tribute to virtue, "that which gives to human actions the relish of Justice is a certain Nobleness or Galantness of courage (rarely found) by which a man scorns to be beholding for the contentment of his life, to fraud or breach of promise," is unexpected, ungrudging—in spite of the "rarely found," and inconsistent with his view of man. So is the warmth of the words he uses in his conclusion : "I have known clearness of judgment, and largeness of fancy; strength of reason, and graceful elocution; a courage for the war, and a fear for the laws, and all eminently in one man; and that was my most noble and honoured friend Mr. Sidney Godolphin; who hating no man, nor hated of any, was unfortunately slain in the beginning of the late civil war, in the public quarrel, by an undiscerned and an undiscerning hand." But when all is said, his work is of the very greatest importance, and *Leviathan* is, in Professor Oakeshott's words, "the greatest, perhaps the sole, masterpiece of political philosophy written in the English language."

His Importance

Hobbes's significance can hardly be overrated. His work is the first statement of complete sovereignty in the history of political thought. The State in the ancient world seeks to model itself on standards to be found in Nature; it therefore reflects a moral order that already exists, but does not create something that is new. Political authority in the Middle Ages was regarded as the expression of Justice. It was limited by the august, divine law of which it was the imperfect reflection. It was limited, too, by the law of the community. The king, in the traditional medieval view, was under no man, but he was under the law. He was supreme in the affairs of State, in the sphere that the great medieval lawyer, Bracton, calls gubernaculum or government. But in the sphere that Bracton calls *jurisdictio* or law he was limited, limited by an unassailable law that set bounds to his discretion, bound by oath to proceed by law. Thus in the Middle Ages there was legal limitation of government, though there was not political control of government. To get the latter required a revolution—the English Civil Wars—and when the fighting had died down and the smoke cleared away, the beginnings of political control of government could be seen but the legal limitation of government had vanished. In its place was absolute sovereignty, recognising nothing superior to itself, bound by no moral law, wielding indeed, as Bishop Atterbury said at his trial in 1723, "a greater power than the sovereign legislature of the universe; for He can do nothing unjust." It was of this power as exercised by the king in Parliament in England that DeLolme said that it could do anything except turn a man into a woman or a woman into a man. And there is something in the view that it lost one empire, the American colonies; that it would have lost another if practice had not departed from theory in the nick of time; that it furnished the basis for much oppressive class legislation. If 19th-century evolution, on the whole, made it remarkably safe in England, it is difficult to feel that Professor McIlwain is being quite absurd in fearing that the future may yet find some new mischief for it to do. Certainly no one in the 20th century has the right to feel that the difficulty expressed by Alexander Hamilton in *The Federalist*—"In framing a government which is to be administered by men over men, the greatest difficulty lies in this : you must first enable the government to control the governed, and in the next place oblige it to control itself"—is a purely academic one.

Hobbes's is the first clear statement of this new view. Even Bodin, often regarded as the first to maintain explicitly the doctrine of State sovereignty, acknowledged that his absolute king should be subject to the common custom, the law of nature and the law of God. It was left for Hobbes to maintain that justice is created by law and that law is not the reflection of justice, and to preach the absolute and unrestricted sovereignty of the State. Philosophers are likely to have enough to answer for at the Last Judgment without being made to assume a responsibilty that is rightly to be borne by the course of events. Nevertheless, Hobbes must shoulder some of the blame, as he may claim some of the credit, for that marked deviation from medieval English political thought and medieval English political practice that was completed in the 17th century.

Secondly, even if Hobbes makes Leviathan all-powerful, he never forgets that it is something artificial. The State, he teaches, is a machine, an artefact, a contrivance of man. His very use of the contract is important here. The contract takes all mystery from the State, for there is nothing less mysterious than a contract. It presupposes the consent of all the parties to it, and the State becomes clear and understandable if political obligation can be explained in this way. Once men view the State as something made by themselves, they may think that they can build something other and better than Leviathan. The important thing is that they should see the State as a machine. There is no doubt that Hobbes helps them to do this.

Thirdly the Leviathan is not merely a forceful enunciation of the doctrine of Sovereignty and of the machine view of the State, it is also a powerful statement of Individualism. Hobbes does not let us forget that the State exists to serve man's need, and that its moral authority derives from the consent of the governed. Hobbes is no liberal or democrat, but he is an individualist, not because he believes in the sanctity of individual man, but because for him the world is and must always be made up of individuals. For him there is no such thing as the People, and no common will, no general will, no common good exists. Nor does Leviathan feed upon individuals. On the contrary, the sole justification for its existence is that it preserves them. The State is not the end of the individual, but the individual is most certainly the end of the State.

Fourthly, Hobbes is the first modern thinker to view the State as the conciliator of interests. In this he is the forerunner of the Utilitarians. It is no accident that Jeremy Bentham borrowed heavily from him here just as he did from Hobbes's ideas on Felicity. Succeeding ages have usually disagreed with him, but it is no exaggeration to say that they have found in him a mine well worth their while to work for the richness of the ore that it yields.

JOHN LOCKE, 1632-1704

His Life and Writings

Next to Hobbes, Locke is the greatest figure in the history of English political thought. Born in 1632, the son of a Puritan Somerset lawyer who served in the Parliamentary Army during the Civil War, Locke was educated at Westminster and Oxford —of which his recollections, like those of Hobbes, were not the most complimentary. The writings of Descartes awakened his interest in philosophy, and his friendship with Robert Boyle aroused his enthusiasm for the natural sciences. He became a student of medicine and then physician to Lord Ashley, later Earl of Shaftesbury. This association with the brilliant but erratic Shaftesbury was to influence Locke's life just as his connection with the Devonshires had influenced Hobbes's, and it gave him what Hobbes lacked, direct experience of practical, political affairs. For two years he held the important post of secretary to the Council of Trade and Plantations, of which Shaftesbury was president.

But if he had experience that was denied to Hobbes, Hobbes had rude health that was denied to him. Finding his political work more than he could cope with, Locke left England in 1675 and spent four years travelling in France. Back in England, he rejoined Shaftesbury for a short time, only to conclude that Oxford was better for his health than the energetic, and indeed dangerously unstable, presence of his patron. While he was at

Oxford Shaftesbury joined Monmouth in his rebellion, escaping the attentions of Judge Jeffreys by fleeing to Holland. Locke, though so guarded in his behaviour and cautious in his comments at Christ Church that Dr. Fell, the Master, wrote of him, "I believe there is not in the world such a master of taciturnity and passion," judged that his health would benefit from yet another continental trip, and retired to Holland. Not surprisingly deepening suspicion by his action and accused of complicity in Monmouth's rebellion, Locke showed himself as timorous as Hobbes was never tired of suggesting that he himself was, adopting an assumed name, and not returning to England, in spite of the pardon that was offered him, until the downfall of the Stuarts.

In Holland, Locke was again involved in Whig politics, helping with the plans for William of Orange's expedition to England. But invigorated by the sharp Dutch air and stimulated by the keen Dutch intellectual life, he found time to complete his studies. In 1689 his first *Letter Concerning Toleration* was published in Latin, an English version being published anonymously in the same year. That year also he returned to England. In 1690 his greatest work, the *Essay Concerning Human Understanding*, which had been nineteen years in gestation, appeared. This was followed in the same year by the two *Treatises on Civil Government,* the first being a refutation of Sir Robert Filmer's *Patriarcha*, and the second containing his own constructive ideas on the problem of political obedience. Both treatises appeared anonymously, but they were well known to be his work. In that year, too, his *Second Letter on Toleration,* and in the next year his *Third Letter on Toleration*, came out, and in 1693 his tract *Some Thoughts Concerning Education* was published. Theology and political economy occupied him largely in his declining years. Moreover, he retained his interest in and his connection with practical affairs. In 1695, when his paper against the Licensing Act helped to decide the issue, he played an important part in establishing the freedom of the press. In 1696, together with Newton, he helped to stabilise the currency, their joint advice resulting in the Recoinage Act of that year. In that year, too, he became a Commissioner to the Board of Trade and Plantations. His health once again failing he retired to Oates, in Essex, where he died in 1704, recognised, not as he thought that perhaps he might be, as an "under-labourer" occupied in "clearing the ground a little and removing some of the rubbish that lies in the way to knowledge," but as the great interpreter of the age, and indeed as possibly not the least of its builders.

The parallel between his life and that of Hobbes is striking. Each studied at Oxford, for which each had little use. Each on leaving the University formed connections which influenced his whole life. Each wrote against a background of hectic political life and finally of revolution. Each sought safety abroad; each peacefully ended his life in England, an acknowledged public figure. But there the resemblance ends. For though their views of human nature were not too dissimilar their conclusions were widely divergent; and in the reputations that were theirs they differed as much as men may. Hobbes, much the greater thinker, roused the wrath and resentment of Englishmen; Locke won their enthusiastic regard. His was the perfect justification for their perfect revolution—typically English alike in its lack of bloodshed, its respect for property, and its refusal to push matters to their logical conclusions. To the 18th-century Whig he was the Law and the Prophets. Bishop Warburton hailed him as "the honour of this age and the instructor of the future." Mr. Justice Best gave him the grave salutation of the English Bench, telling the jury of his "pure spirit" and "invaluable and immortal works." Nor was Locke's influence limited and his reputation confined to England. His voice spanned the Atlantic, rang in the ruins of empire, and spoke confidently to the future in the Virginia Bill of Rights and in the American Declaration of Independence. Echoing again in the French Declaration of the Rights of Man, it reached across the Channel and pealed over the babel of tongues. After its willing tribute to Locke, Europe was often to be moved by the thought of British power, but was rarely again to acknowledge the power of British thought.

No one would call Locke's *Essays on Civil Government* as exciting as the *Leviathan*. He lacks the colour and the sparkle and the power of Hobbes. His prose has none of the richness of texture that is Hobbes's, as his mind has none of Hobbes's penetration and profundity. Yet his appeal is a considerable one. He is neither boring nor banal. He is decently and decorously dignified, but he is never stilted. He has all the virtues of sobriety, and if those who appreciate its limitations occasionally long for a headier vintage, those virtues wear well and are important and very real. He is modest and unpretending. But together with something of the greyness of his Puritan father, he has all the Puritan's strong individuality and sturdy common sense, all the Puritan's deep instinct for setting bounds to the power of the State. And if it is not because of the charm of his pen that he ranks with the immortals, if indeed he was contemptuous of style, referring, for instance, to Montaigne's "peculiar sort of language" which seemed to him nothing but "pride and vanity," nevertheless his writing is vigorous and clear. And his touch can be light, as his comment on Barclay's advice that even tyrants must be resisted with respect reveals: "He that can reconcile blows and reverence may, for aught I know, deserve for his pains a civil, respectful cudgelling wherever he can meet with it." He is not, then, to be classed with those *bêtes noire* of Disraeli, "the nebulous professors who appear in their style to have revived chaos." On the contrary, his prose is an appropriate and serviceable instrument for one whose genius lay in consolidating ground rather than in winning new positions.

Above all, he is a mirror in which Englishmen may find themselves faithfully reflected. His individuals, with their virtues and vices, are as recognisably English as Hobbes's are not. The very insularity which makes his teaching inadequate as a universal answer to the problems of political obedience understandably increases his attraction for the English-speaking peoples. And in an age which is suffering, as is our own, from a surfeit of sovereignty, it is good to return to a thinker who is as convinced as he is of the bound's beyond which sovereignty must not trespass. In an age that is increasingly intolerant, a declining liberalism can renew itself by turning again to this apostle of toleration who insisted that the things that belong to Cæsar and the things that belong to God are easily distinguishable. So long as there are men who believe that few things have been more important and more damnable in our lifetime than the construing of the command, "Render unto Cæsar the things that are Cæsar's and unto God the things that are God's" into "Render unto Cæsar who is also God the things that are Cæsar's and God's," Locke can be assured of his appeal.

His View of Man

Locke's view of man is summed up in his *Essay on Human Understanding*. Desire, he says, is the spring of all human action.

Desire is a feeling of uneasiness identified with pain, a feeling of which men want to rid themselves. The object of all human action is to substitute pleasure for pain. This is the view of human nature which was copied by Bentham, which was later worked out more thoroughly and called "psychological egoistic hedonism." In Locke's words, "What has an aptness to produce pleasure in us is what we call good, and what is apt to produce pain in us we call evil."

So far his is a straightforward if not a very lofty view of man. But he adds to it a theory of morals which is not straightforward, is confused and confusing, and far from consistent with the view of man with which he begins. This is also to be found in his *Essay on Human Understanding*, in three chapters of which he demonstrates to his complete satisfaction that there are no universally binding moral laws. History shows clearly, he says, that the morality of one society is the immorality of another. "The saints who are canonized among the Turks," he points out, "lead lives which one cannot with modesty relate." This conclusion is in keeping with his view of man; it is, indeed, the only conclusion that is compatible with it. Yet in the last of those three chapters he commits himself to the view that morals, like mathematics, is a demonstrable science, subject to ascertainable, universal laws—a conclusion which, even though he did not think that mathematics were absolutely certain, one can only regard as very surprising and difficult to reconcile with the opinions he had begun by putting forward.

Moreover, as though to show that his conclusion is not merely an unconsidered afterthought which it would be charitable to forget in quickly passing by, Locke tells us what these universal laws are. They are the Divine Law and the Natural Law. The Divine Law is God's will for man's behaviour, which is made available to man both by divine revelation and by the use of his own reason, and which is, above all, to be looked for in the New Testament. The Natural Law is also an eternal law, the criterion of good and evil, discoverable by reasoning and commanding men to carry out the will of God.

It is typical, too, of the very contradictory nature of his theory of morals that, having said that men are incapable of desiring anything but pleasure, he maintains that they ought to act so as to produce the greatest amount of public or general happiness, and contends that the criterion of the goodness and the badness of their actions is their result expressed in terms of public happiness.

It must, then, be obvious that Locke's view of human nature is nothing like so profound, and certainly nothing like as consistent, as that of Hobbes. His problem, however, is very much the same as that of Hobbes. Why do such men as his wish to form civil society, and how can they do so? Locke's answer to that problem is very different from Hobbes's. It is essentially a justification, though written before the event, of the Glorious Revolution of 1688, a revolution which Hobbes would have regarded as anarchic and deplorable in the extreme.

In putting forward that answer, in advancing that justification, Locke makes use, as did Hobbes and so many thinkers of that 17th century to which the feudal contract was still a lively memory and the commercial contract comparatively new and very appealing, of the state of nature and of the Social Contract as devices which will help him to make clear his ideas. As with them, they are conscious abstractions rather than attempts to construct the actual origin of society, and it is therefore, even though he occasionally seems to believe in their actual historicity, no more valid a criticism of him than of them to point out that the state of Nature never existed and that the Social Contract never took place.

The State of Nature

The state of nature, says Locke, is a state in which men are equal and free to act "as they think fit, within the bounds of the law of nature." But it is not a state of licence, for though in it man is "free from any superior power on earth," nevertheless in it he has "the law of nature for his rule." From this Natural Law he derives certain natural rights, rights to life, liberty, and property. His right to liberty is his right to do whatever he wants so long as that is not incompatible with the Law of Nature. It is, therefore, conditional on "his having reason which is able to instruct him in that law." For "to turn him loose to an unrestrained liberty before he has reason to guide him is not allowing him the privilege of his nature to be free, but to thrust him out amongst brutes, and abandon him to a state as wretched and as much beneath that of a man as theirs." His right to property is his right to anything with which he has mixed his labour, provided he makes good use of it, since "nothing was made by God for man to spoil or destroy." But Natural Law not only accords man rights, it imposes duties upon him. It commands him "when his own preservation comes not in competition" to do what he can to preserve others. And it demands that he should keep his promises, for "Truth and keeping of Faith belong to men as men and not as Members of Society."

This state of nature, then, in which men have rights and acknowledge duties, is moral and social in character. Consequently it is wrong to conceive of it, as Hobbes did, as a state of war. It will not, that is, be a state in which life is normally solitary, poor, nasty, brutish, and short.

Nevertheless, it has its inconveniences. For if it is not a state of war, it is unfortunately a state in which peace is not secure. It is constantly upset by the "corruption and viciousness of degenerate men." It is, therefore, a "condition which, however free, is full of fears and continual dangers." It leaves unsatisfied three important wants—the want of an "established, settled, known law," the want of a "known and indifferent judge," the want of an executive power to enforce just decisions. Since production is so complicated that it cannot easily be said what was the contribution of different agents to the making of a joint product, an arbitrator, judging by an agreed upon law and able to enforce his decisions, is clearly necessary if men are to live amicably together. Without such an arbitrator men in the state of nature are, after all, "but in an ill condition," and "are quickly driven into society"—though the speed of the drive, unlike that of the Gadarene swine, is not of course such as to allow them to take no interest in their future condition and ultimate destination.

The Social Contract

To get out of the state of nature, Locke says, men make a contract to enter into civil society. This is a contract of all with all. This is a social, or more truly a political, contract, since it establishes political society; it is not a contract made with the government which is to be set up. And it is the only contract which is necessary.

It is a contract to which all must consent. But though itself unanimous, all parties to it agree henceforth "to submit to the determination of the majority"—since unless men agree to majority rule, decisions cannot be taken and the State cannot survive.

It is a contract which, once made, is irrevocable. He who has signed it "can never again be in the liberty of the state of nature," Locke writes, "unless, by any calamity, the government he was under comes to be dissolved, or else by some public acts cuts him off from being any longer a member of it."

It is a contract to which each generation must consent. For "a child is born a subject of no country or government." "Every man's children being by nature as free as himself, or any of his ancestors ever were, may, whilst they are in that freedom, choose what society they will join themselves to, what commonwealth they will put themselves under." But, Locke adds dryly, if they depart from the land of their birth they will not of course "enjoy the inheritance of their ancestors."

The contract they make is one in which men give up some, but not as Hobbes would have it all, of the rights they possessed in the state of nature. For it would be stupid to imagine that in "quitting the state of nature" men would agree "that all but one should be under the restraint of laws; but that he should still retain all the liberty of the state of nature, increased with force, and made licentious by impunity." All they agree to is to "give up every one his single power of punishing to be exercised by such alone as shall be appointed to it amongst them, and by such rules as the community, or those authorised by them to that purpose, shall agree on." Hence the contract is no more than a surrender of certain rights and powers whereby man's remaining rights will be protected and preserved. It is, then, not general as with Hobbes, but limited and specific.

This contract does not, as with Hobbes, put an end to the Law of Nature as it does to the state of Nature. Man in the State continues to be under that law, as he was before. As Locke expresses it—"the obligations of the law of nature cease not in society."

This contract, moreover, is the first step to the drawing up of a trust. People, having formed a society, must then institute a government. They do not do this by making a contract with the Government—that, as Rousseau was so clearly to point out, would be to invest government with too much dignity and authority. Men do this by drawing up a trust which creates Government as "only a fiduciary power to act for certain ends."

The community is thus both creator and beneficiary of the trust. Admittedly as creator of the trust the community might be said to make a covenant with the trustee or the Government. But as beneficiary of the trust, the community makes no contract with the trustee who accepts a unilateral obligation towards it. The acceptance of the trust by the Government is at the same time its undertaking not to exceed the limits laid down by the trust. Because Locke nowhere expressly denies that there is a contract between Government and People, and because his language is somtimes lacking in clarity, he has frequently been misunderstood. But there is no doubt that in his use of the word "trust" he is expressing precisely the idea which Milton had in mind when he wrote "the power of kings and magistrates is only derivative, transferred and counted to them in trust from the people to the common good of them all, to whom the power yet remains fundamentally and cannot be taken from them without a violation of their natural birthright."

Perhaps there is one final point to be noticed about Locke's idea of the Social Contract. It is closer to Rousseau's than to Hobbes's. Both Locke and Rousseau maintain that the institution of government is not a contract. Both believe that the contract does not remove the supreme power from the people. Locke writes of the "supreme power that [in spite of the institution of government] remains still in the people." Rousseau speaks of the "inalienable sovereignty of the people." The similarity must not, of course, be pressed too far—but it exists to a greater degree than has often been admitted.

The Nature of the State—Its Form

For the three great lacks of the state of nature—the lack of a known law, of a known judge, of a certain executive power—the three appropriate remedies would seem to be the establishment of a legislative, of a judicial, and of an executive authority. In civil society, or the State, Locke notes the existence of three powers, but they are not, as would naturally be expected, the above three. There is first of all the legislative, which he calls "the supreme power of the commonwealth." Secondly there is the executive, which includes the judicial power. The legislature need not always be in session, but the executive must be. Hence, he concludes, they "come often to be separated"; no bad thing, "because it may be too great a temptation to human frailty, apt to grasp at power, for the same persons who have the power of making laws to have also in their hands the power to execute them."

This is as far as Locke goes in enunciating the doctrine of the separation of powers which is enshrined in the American Constitution—and it is not very far. That doctrine, as in the American Constitution, is usually understood as implying that none of the powers is superior to any of the others, whereas for Locke the legislature is unquestionably the superior power. That doctrine, too, tends to make States in which it is applied hesitant and weak—a result which Locke would not necessarily have desired even though admittedly he was concerned to prevent the State becoming unduly strong. In any case, it is worth remembering that it is Montesquieu, not Locke, who is the author of the famous classification of powers into executive, legislative, and judicial.

The third power that Locke recognises is what he calls the federative—the power that makes *fœdera* or treaties, that which is concerned with the State's external relations. In theory there is a distinction between it and the executive power, a distinction which the danger of divided command will ensure that in practice is ignored.

It is, perhaps, to be regretted that Locke has not more to tell us about the federative power. He realises the great importance of foreign policy, and knows that its formulation, execution, and control presents a very special kind of problem to constitutional States, for, as he says, the federative power "is much less capable to be directed by antecedent, standing, positive laws than the executive; and so must necessarily be left to the prudence and wisdom of those whose hands it is in to be managed for the public good." But though he notices the existence of the problem, he has nothing constructive to say about it. Possibly, indeed, we might have to add that far from helping us to solve it, Locke's influence has been such as, in one most important case, to make it worse. It is commonly agreed that the Constitution of the United States of America emphasises the weaknesses inherent in the democratic conduct of foreign affairs. It does this even more by the vagueness of its clauses dealing with foreign policy, vagueness which is, as it were, a standing invitation for the executive and the legislature to struggle for the privilege of conducting American foreign policy, than by the unique constitutional devices it insists upon. The Founding Fathers were great disciples of Locke, and it may not, therefore, be too fanciful to see in the all-important vagueness of the American Constitution in this respect a reflection of the vagueness of his views on the federative power.

However, the form of the State is really for Locke a secondary matter. It may be a democracy, an oligarchy, an hereditary or an elective monarchy. Far more important than its form are its characteristics, for unless it can claim certain well-marked characteristics it is not a Political Society, it is no true State.

Its Characteristics

The first and most important characteristic of Locke's State is that it exists for the people who form it, they do not exist for it. Repeatedly he insists that "the end of government" is "the good of the community." "Political power," he says, "I take to be a right of making laws with penalties of death, and consequently all less penalties, for the regulating and preserving of property, and of employing the force of the community in the execution of such laws, and in the defence of the commonwealth from foreign injury, and all this only for the public good." The State, in fact, is a machine which we create for our good and run for our purposes, and it is both dangerous and unnecessary to speak of some supposed mystical good of State or country independent of the lives of individual citizens.

Locke goes further and insists that all true States must be founded on consent. It is true that he assumes that a minority will consent in all things to the rule of the majority, who have, he asserts, "a right to act and conclude the rest." It is true that he regards the consent of representatives as an adequate substitute for the consent of all. It is true that he is driven to admit that consent may be tacit rather than open and express, and that ultimately he is prepared to declare that a man gives tacit consent to a government by being simply within its territories. Nevertheless, it is both important and typical of him that he loses no opportunity of insisting on the importance of consent and displays considerable mental ingenuity in proving that men have consented to obey their rulers when it is in their interests to do so, and that when those rulers act harmfully they are doing so without the consent of their subjects.

The true State, too, Locke insists, must be a constitutional

State in which men acknowledge the rule of law. For there can be no political liberty if a man is "subject to the inconstant, uncertain, unknown, arbitrary will of another man." Government must therefore be by "established standing laws, promulgated and known to the people, and not by extemporary decrees." This must be the more insisted upon because in every State, Locke realises, the Government must possess discretionary or emergency power. So long as it is understood that this emergency power, which in England is called prerogative, is "nothing but the power of doing public good without a rule," its existence in States will be beneficial and not harmful. But it can only be supplementary to, and never a substitute for, the rule of law. The very necessity for the existence of prerogative is indeed one reason the more why men should never forget that "where the law ends tyranny begins."

Yet another most important characteristic of Locke's true State is that it is limited, not absolute. It is limited because it derives power from the people, and because it holds power in trust for the people. As "only a fiduciary power to act for certain ends," its authority is confined to securing those ends. It is limited, moreover, by Natural Law in general and by one most important Natural Law in particular. Civil Law, for Locke, is merely the restatement of Natural Law in detail and by authorised legislation. Civil Law, he says, adds nothing to our knowledge of right and wrong. All it adds is immediate punishment for wrong-doing and greater detail than Natural Law will give us. Thus Civil Law can never conflict with Natural Law, which remains as a standard of right and wrong superior to all powers within the State—"an eternal rule to all men, legislators as well as others." This applies to the external actions of States, since all men are united in one great natural community under Natural Law, and of course it applies to all their internal actions as well. Hence "the legislative, though it be the supreme power in every commonwealth, is not, nor can possibly be, absolutely arbitrary over the lives and fortunes of the people." The particular Natural Law which limits the power of the State is that which gives men a right to their property. The right to property, Locke insists, is a natural right which is in existence before political institutions. Indeed, he says, "the reason why men enter into society is the preservation of their property," and he is never in any doubt that "the legislative acts against the trust reposed in them when they endeavour to invade the property of the subject." Thus circumscribed by the existence behind positive law of moral principles which must override all positive law, the State can wield no absolute authority. As though to emphasise its limitations throughout the *Treatises on Civil Government* the word "sovereignty" never occurs.

The State, then, should exist for the good of the people, should depend on their consent, should be constitutional and limited in its authority. If it is not for the people's good, if it does not depend on their consent, if it is not constitutional or if it exceeds its authority, it can, Locke says, be legitimately overthrown. For, he says, anticipating Rousseau's idea of the permanent sovereignty of the community, "there remains still in the people a supreme power to remove or alter the legislative when they find the legislative act contrary to the trust reposed in them." This power the people exercise by "appealing to heaven," by resorting "to the common refuge which God hath provided for all men against force and violence"—namely by rising in revolution. "The true remedy of force without authority," he writes, "is to oppose force to it." He believes that a distinction must be made between "the dissolution of the society and the dissolution of government," and he is confident that the latter does not entail the former. Nor need it be feared, he says, that he is unduly encouraging rebellion. People will put up with many ills before they will embark on the dangerous course of revolution— they "are not so easily got out of their old forms as some are apt to suggest." "There is one thing only," he writes, "which gathers people into seditious commotions, and that is oppression." Persistently mistreat people and you must expect trouble— "cry up their governors as much as you will for sons of Jupiter, let them be sacred and divine, descended, or authorised from heaven, give them out for whom or what you please, the same will happen." Revolution, however, Locke is sure, ought never to be the act of a minority, for if it were it might indeed be thought that he was, as he strenuously denied, pleading for the "liberty for ambitious men to pull down well-framed constitutions, that out of their ruins they may build themselves fortunes."

Three further characteristics of the good State remain to be noticed. It is a tolerant State, which as far as can be will respect differences of opinion. It is a negative State, which does not seek to improve the character of its citizens nor to manage their lives, but which merely strives to secure their independence. Yet it is also a "transformer" State, transforming selfish interest into public good. Though it does not change man's character it, nevertheless, makes him behave as God would have him to, for it holds in check his self-interest and is the mechanism whereby men acting as they must are in the end brought to act as they ought to do—that is, for public happiness. Men will always seek to gain pleasure and to avoid pain. By regulating artificial pains, i.e. punishments, the State can see to it that the pleasure of doing things which do not contribute to the public happiness will be less than the attendant pain. The State thus brings pressure to bear on the individual in such a way that he acts for the public good, and the end—public happiness—is achieved even though the individual's motive—indeed, precisely because the individual's motive—is to do good to himself.

These are the characteristics without which the State is unworthy of the name. Locke knows how few States have possessed them. Conquest and violence, he is aware, have long stalked the world, and tyranny, which is "the exercise of power without right," whispers its enticements not merely to monarchies, but to all governments. But only where these characteristics can be observed can men be said to have entered Civil Society. And only where Civil Society exists will men understand that "the end of law is not to abolish or restrain, but to preserve and enlarge freedom." Only there will the age-old conflict of Authority and Freedom be perfectly resolved.

Locke's Importance

It is not difficult to criticise Locke, since he has not troubled to remove the contradictions and confusions from his writings. He was quite prepared to regard moral laws as finished and finite and their study as an exact science, and at the same time to see them merely as temporary and conditional, the relative products of different stages of society. He was ready to use words in different and not always defined senses. Property, for instance, as he speaks of it, may mean no more than we mean by it, or may imply nothing less than the life, liberty, and estate of the citizens. He is by no means averse to using terms so carelessly as to cloud his meaning. He attributes supreme power to no less than three sources—to the community, to the legislature, to a single person if the executive is vested in him and if he has also a share in the legislature.

Some of his ideas, too, are incompatible with others. His psychological egoistic hedonism is, for instance, incompatible with his utilitarianism, since if men can only desire their own happiness it is senseless to suggest that the general happiness is desirable. And if Locke is aware here, in speaking of the innate and unchangeable selfishness of man which is nevertheless supposed to be capable occasionally of altruism, of a contradiction that should be explained, there are occasions when he seems blind to the incompatibility of his various ideas. He is undoubtedly naïve in saying that his theory of consent is connected with his theory of Natural Law. His theory of consent means that justice and injustice are what men call justice and injustice—an action is right if it is considered right. This is of course a complete rejection of a Natural Law theory, according to which justice and injustice exist even though men deny them. Clearly where consent is part of the theory of institutions Natural Law must be absent.

Nor can it be denied that many of his ideas must today appear inadequate. His definition of property leaves much to be desired—"the grass my horse has bit, the turf my servant has cut, and the ore I have digged in any place where I have a right to them in common with others, become my property without the assignation of anybody." Ritchie's comment, "My horse and my servant are thus equally with my labour the means by which I acquire property; so that the capitalist employer of labour would, according to this clause, be fully entitled to the entire product created by his servants, if he can manage to get it," is justified.

When Locke says that "the very being of anyone within the territories of a Government" implies consent to that Government, it is obvious that he has so emptied the word "consent" of meaning that every Government that has ever existed could legitimately claim to have been based on consent. It is clear, too, that his social contract has become little better than a farce. Moreover, the 20th century has had greater opportunity than the 17th to know that there are many pitfalls in the path of those who are content with the definition of democracy as government by consent. In authoritarian countries the consent that the regime can normally count upon is all but unanimous—

thanks to the use of monopoly of mass propaganda and to the forcible suppression of dissentients. If consent, then, be the hall-mark of democracy, Fascist Italy, Nazi Germany, and Bolshevik Russia must be regarded as being much more democratic than those countries in which Governments have perforce to reconcile themselves to persistent, vigorous and often widespread opposition.

Locke, moreover, though a great fighter for freedom, was too disinterested in equality. His was the essential Whig faith, the belief in individual liberty combined with denial of social equality. To the 20th century he must therefore appear forgetful of the fact that while liberty may be very much more important than equality, and while too much insistence on equality may be most dangerous to liberty, nevertheless liberty itself is unlikely to survive long if equality is treated with too cavalier a contempt. Locke had forgotten what to Harrington was the greatest commonplace of political theory—the impossibility of freedom in a society where too great gulfs of class and wealth exist.

And Locke was, as all would agree, far too rationalistic. He was blind to the emotional forces that hold societies and states together. It is not merely the understandable desire to inherit his father's property that keeps an Englishman an Englishman and a Frenchman a Frenchman. In affirming that "all men are in the state of nature and remain so, till, by their own consent, they make themselves the members of some political society," Locke is expressing that extreme individualism of the Stoics which is so much less convincing than Aristotle's conception that men are by nature social and political beings.

Yet when all criticisms are made, Locke's worth and importance remain beyond dispute. His is the last great voice of one great tradition and the first great voice of another great tradition.

Though his theory of the state of Nature is not identical with that of his medieval predecessors, the Middle Ages believed, as he did, that all merely human authority is limited—by the Law of God and the Law of Nature. "In the court of conscience," Aquinas wrote, "there is no obligation to obey an unjust law." The Middle Ages held, as Locke held, that only the community was the legitimate source of political power. They maintained as he did, when they began to think of the law not as imme morial custom, but as something made, that it should be made by the community—as Bracton said that the English law was made, by the King "with the counsel and consent of the great men and the approval of the commonwealth." They were sure, as he was, that however august was the King's authority, it was limited not absolute. No distinction was commoner in medieval political thought and literature than that between the King, who ruled according to law, and the tyrant, who ruled against law. It is typical of medieval practice as well as theory that even strong Kings in time of war could never be sure of getting their way. Edward I told the Earl of Norfolk who was reluctant to join his expedition. "By God, sir Earl, you must either go or hang." And the reply, justified by the event, came, "By God, sir King, I will neither go nor hang." In insisting on the sacrosanctity of property also, Locke was carrying on that medieval tradition which regarded property and feudal institutions as something autonomous, not within the province of political power, a tradition which finds expression in the insistence of Magna Carta that the King cannot take action against the person or property of his subjects except by process of law, a tradition which survived in all its vigour so that when Sergeant Heyle told the Commons in 1593 that the Queen "hath as much right to all our Lands and Goods as to any Revenue of her Crown," we read "the House hawked and spat and kept a great coil to make him make an end." Locke's work is the very important continuation into the modern world of the great medieval tradition of political liberty.

But it is also the first striking formulation of the principles of the Liberal State, a very strong plea that the function of government is to remove oppression and increase liberty. He laid down the essential theses of liberalism—that the people is the source of all political power, that government cannot be justified unless it possesses their free consent, that all governmental measures are to be judged by an active citizen body, that men are reasonably moral and responsible and that the main object of government is to help them when they require it, but not to run their lives for them, and finally that the State must be resisted if it steps beyond its proper authority. The 20th century cannot share the confidence of the 19th that these theses are and ought to be of universal application. But Englishmen can believe that thanks to fortunate historical circumstances they can at least be applied to them. With their assistance Englishmen tamed Leviathan, and if in the 20th century Leviathan has cast off his chains to go devouring through the world, they may well feel that, after all, Locke has the root of the matter in him and that any sound and healthy political system will incorporate the greater part of the principles that he laid down.

THE UTILITARIANS

Perhaps it was neither Hobbes nor Locke, but a school which owed something to both of them, which made the greatest English contribution to political thought, though paradoxically it never produced a thinker as great as the one nor as typically English as the other. This was the Utilitarian school, which for over a hundred years, from the middle of the 18th to the middle of the 19th century, dominated English political thought.

The founder of Utilitarianism was David Hume; Priestley, Hutcheson, Paley professed it; it was fed from the foreign springs of Helvetius and Beccaria. But it was first around Jeremy Bentham, the most typical Utilitarian of them all, that a school began to form. His association with the energetic, able, and uncompromising James Mill, who converted him to Radicalism, and who, as the friend of Malthus and Ricardo, led Benthamism into ever closer relationship with the Classical Economists, brought into being that remarkable group of men whom today we generally refer to as the Utilitarians or as the Philosophic Radicals.

They were great individualists who made their own contribution to the development of Utilitarian theory. Nevertheless they have the characteristics of a school. Heine once deplored the habit of Englishmen of neglecting general principles in politics. He must, at least in this particular, have approved of the English Utilitarians, who were all firm believers in general principles. They were all sure that all men seek happiness, that pleasure alone is good, that the only right action is that which produces the greatest happiness, and that the sole justification of the State is that it makes possible this greatest happiness. They were all philosophic radicals, the theorists of representative democracy and of universal suffrage.

They had not merely their common faith and inexorable conclusions. They had also their active party representatives. In Grote, Roebuck, Buller, Molesworth, and for a short time in

John Stuart Mill, they had their spokesmen in Parliament. In Chadwick they had their greatest representative in the administrative machine. In Molesworth, in Buller, and to some extent in Gibbon Wakefield, they had their delegates in the Empire.

They were always in a minority and they were never popular. They were too coldly intellectual, too frigid and scholastic, and men were not flattered by their view of mankind. But for long they were without serious competitors. Their great contemporaries—Rousseau, Kant, St. Simon, Marx—were unhonoured in England; their critics at home were unconvincing. In consequence, their influence was out of all proportion to their numbers. Indeed, the English-speaking world today still bears witness to their teaching—in the words of G. M. Young, "it would be hard to find any corner of our public life where the spirit of Bentham is not working today." The nature of that teaching and the extent of that influence can best be seen in a study of the two greatest representatives of Utilitarianism—of Jeremy Bentham, the master, and John Stuart Mill, the greatest and the most errant of his followers.

JEREMY BENTHAM, 1748–1832
His Life and Writings

Bentham seems the caricaturist's dream of a philosopher. In infancy he was the prodigy who, escaping from his walk, made the footman light candles and draw up his chair to the table so that he might immerse himself in the joys of Rapin's *History of England*. In age he was the hermit of Queen's Square with his "sacred teapot" called Dick, who in the intervals of grinding away at reams and reams of barely decipherable studies written in the most peculiar of technical jargons "vibrated," as he put it, from one odd room to the next and exercised himself with his regular "ante-jentacular" and "post-prandial" "circumgyrations."

He came of a family of wealthy lawyers and he himself was intended for the law. His father was convinced from his early promise—he was learning Latin at three—that he was a future occupant of the Woolsack.

Not surprisingly, in view of his early education, he found his teachers lacking and his contemporaries stupid. It is not recorded what they thought of him. Doubtless his unfavourable impressions of Oxford were coloured by his involuntary association at

Queen's with prospective parsons whose ideas of preparing themselves for their vocations might have been thought even in that age and place peculiar. One drank till, as Bentham said, "his eyes turned purple." Another enlivened his theological studies by holding Bentham upside down at arm's length, thereby demonstrating the strength of muscular Christianity and the superiority of theology over philosophy. Perhaps by way of escape he sought the society of Methodists in the University, but his talents were still to be saved for the law. The University, whose tolerance was large enough to embrace drunkenness and horse-play, was appalled at the immorality of Methodist hymn-singing and prayer-meetings, and its action in expelling the Methodists saved Bentham from any temptations to which he may have been exposed of throwing in his lot with them.

Nevertheless, in Bentham's eyes, Oxford town more than made up for the deficiencies of Oxford University. For, returning to record his vote in the University parliamentary election, he found in a bookshop Priestley's *Essay on Government*, which contained the phrase which Priestley had taken from Hutcheson, "the greatest happiness of the greatest number." "It was," he says, "by that pamphlet and this phrase in it that my principles on the subject of morality, public and private, were determined. It was from that pamphlet and that page of it that I drew the phrase, the words and the importance of which have been so widely diffused over the civilised world. At the sight of it I cried out as it were in an inward ecstasy, like Archimedes in the discovery of the fundamental principles of hydrostatics, Eureka."

On leaving Oxford, Bentham took chambers in Lincoln's Inn, where on the £90 a year that his father allowed him he lived what he said was "truly a miserable life." His career as a barrister was short and inglorious. His father had a case or two waiting for him, which his son promptly "put to death," advising, for instance, that a suit upon which £50 depended should be dropped and the money saved. Instead of preparing for practice, he let chemistry and physics intrigue him, and even the fond father had to admit that visions of the Woolsack had faded so completely as to leave not a rack behind.

Yet Bentham's time was not being wasted. He was becoming more and more convinced that every man should, and that he in particular must, devote himself to the furtherance of human happiness. "Has a man talents? He owes them to his country in every way in which they can be serviceable," he wrote. And again, "I would have the dearest friend I have to know that his interests, if they come in competition with those of the public, are as nothing to me. Thus I will serve my friends—thus I would be served by them."

Moreover, he was being filled with the assurance that his particular job in life was to labour at the reform of the law, since he was rapidly becoming sure both that legislation was the most important of man's activities and that he, Jeremy Bentham, was possessed of a genius for it. "Have I a genius for legislation?" he asked. "And have I indeed a genius for legislation? I gave myself the answer, fearfully and tremblingly, 'Yes.'" He was right. In Dicey's words, he was "in very truth the first and greatest of legal philosophers."

He was, then, primarily a law reformer, intent on applying the scientific method to the field of law, on uniting law and science so that the whole human race might be rescued from superstition. He was only indirectly a political philosopher, though his work as law reformer led him to economics, logic, psychology, penology, theology, politics, and ethics.

He had almost a "Chinese box" mind, which led him continually from one project to the next and which rarely allowed him to finish anything. As Wilson wrote to him, "Your history since I have known you has been to be always running from a good scheme to a better. In the meantime, life passes away and nothing is completed." Much of what he was engaged upon appeared as "fragments" or "introductions." Such was his first published work, the *Fragment on Government*, which appeared in 1776. Such is perhaps his greatest book, the *Introduction to the Principles of Morals and Legislation,* which came out in 1789. He was most reluctant to publish, but fortunately his friends saw to it that he did. And, working steadily every day, he was amazingly prolific. His printed works in the standard Bowring edition fill eleven octavo volumes closely printed in two-columned pages, the best known of which being, besides the Fragment and the Introduction, the *Defence of Usury*, the *Discourse on Civil and Penal Legislation*, the *Essay on Political Tactics*, the *Theory of Punishments and Rewards*, the *Treatise on Judicial Evidence*, the *Papers upon Codification and Public Instruction*, the *Book of Fallacies*, the *Rationale of Evidence*, and the *Constitutional Code*. His unpublished MSS. are almost as voluminous.

That huge mass of material is still today a quarry well worth working. But it cannot be pretended that the study of Bentham, however rewarding, is the easiest and the most entertaining of studies. He could, when he so desired, write vigorously and well, as his demonstration of the impossibility of absolute equality, one of the best in the history of political thought, shows: "If equality ought to prevail today it ought to prevail always. Yet it cannot be preserved except by renewing the violence by which it was established. It will need an army of inquisitors and executioners as deaf to favour as to pity; insensible to the seductions of pleasure, inaccessible to personal interest; endowed with all the virtues, though in a service which destroys them all. The levelling apparatus ought to go incessantly backward and forward, cutting off all that rises above the line prescribed. A ceaseless vigilance would be necessary to give to those who had dissipated their portions, and to take from those who by labour had augmented theirs. In such an order—that of prodigality, there would be but one foolish course—that of industry. This pretended remedy, seemingly so pleasant, would be a mortal poison, a burning cautery, which would consume till it destroyed the last fibre of life. The hostile sword in its greatest furies is a thousand times less dreadful. It inflicts but partial evils, which time effaces and industry repairs."

But over-elaboration and too great a love of dissection and detail spoil his later works. Moreover, in the interests of scientific accuracy he thought it necessary to develop what he called a "new lingo," and what, understandably enough, his critics referred to as "this new peculiar branch of the great art of regeneration." Words and phrases such as annuality, trienniality, beneficialness, interest comprehension, pleasurably operating, potential impermanence, competition excluding, undangerousness, deceptitiously evidential, nonspuriousness, virtually universal suffrage plan, right and left hand complimentive distribution, pretty general civility proposition principle, break out like an ugly rash on most of his pages. When his critics said of him that he had adopted the language of Babel as the proper vehicle for the doctrines of political confusion at least as far as the language was concerned they were not far wrong.

Bentham, who had hoped that "torches from the highest

regions" would light themselves at his "farthing candle," was disappointed that his *Fragment on Government* did not win a still greater recognition. Yet it had one effect of the greatest importance. It won him the friendship of Lord Shelburne, and it was at Shelburne's home at Bowood that he met Etienne Dumont, who published a French translation in 1802 of his writings on legislation. The French National Assembly had already conferred the title of citizen upon Bentham for his "ardent love of humanity"—he had offered to set up his Panopticon, his prison or "mill for the grinding rogues honest and idle men industrious," in France and to become "gratuitously the gaoler thereof." Now the publication of the *Traités de Législation civile et pénale* gave him an international reputation long before he had established a national one. When he visited France in 1825, he was given a triumphal reception. As many copies of his books sold in St. Petersburg as in London, and the Emperor Alexander called for his co-operation in drafting a legal code. The Cortes of Spain and Portugal voted that his works should be printed at the national expense. Even distant South America felt his influence. 40,000 copies of Dumont's *Traités*, so Bentham said, were sold in Paris for the South American trade. General Mirando, whose hope of liberating Venezuela led him to death at the hands of the Inquisition, proposed to make Bentham the legislator of his new State. Santander was his professed disciple. Bolivar, as exile, addressed him in the most fulsome terms, and as dictator of Colombia paid him the compliment of banning his books. There is more truth than exaggeration in the words that Hazlitt wrote of him as late as 1825—"His name is little known in England, better in Europe, and best of all in the plains of Chili and the mines of Mexico. He has offered constitutions for the new world and legislated for future times. Mr. Hobhouse is a greater name at the hustings, Lord Rolle at Plymouth Dock, but Mr. Bentham would carry it hollow, on the score of popularity, at Paris or Pegu."

Yet if recognition was slower in coming to him at home than abroad, circumstances were conspiring to ensure that his influence in England would be greater and more lasting than anywhere else. In his youth he had been a Tory sympathiser. He "never suspected that the people in power were against reform." He "supposed they only wanted to know what was good in order to embrace it." But the rejection of his Panopticon scheme, which he had offered to the Government, made him see the Sinister Interest of Privilege in every path. Consequently when he became acquainted with James Mill in 1808 he was ready to make that alliance with Radicalism which was to be such an excellent means of perpetuating his influence and of carrying through the reforms he had advocated.

This Radical School thus established was, incidentally, not only the means of ensuring his influence, but of building up a legend which does not conform to fact. That legend claims that his genius suffered from the seclusion of his life. In J. S. Mill's words, he knew "neither internal experience nor external; the quiet, even tenor of his life, and his healthiness of mind, conspired to exclude him from both"—hence he was "not a great philosopher but a great reformer in philosophy."

None of his English school, however, knew him before he was sixty, an age at which it is not always easy to judge even from the conduct and conversation of philosophers what their experience has embraced. We know now that as a young man he proved the truth of the old Stoic saying that "the contest between a young girl and a beginner in philosophy is an uneven one"—he was very much in love with Mary Dunkly. And from his letters we must conclude that he had acted upon the advice which he gave to his brother, that a wise man will appreciate that address with ladies will be increased by considerable familiarity with those that are not. We can no longer picture him, as his school did, as a man of the most fugitive and cloistered virtue, who never knew the tug and tussle of the passions, whose only concession to the emotional in life was the gentle, dispassionate proposal of marriage which he made to a lady whom he had not met for sixteen years, and which clearly expected, as it received, the answer "no." In spite of the legend, we can no longer account for whatever defects there may be in Bentham's philosophy by speaking of the secluded character of his life.

Bentham lived to be eighty-two, working hard to the end, "codifying like any dragon," as he himself said. His ambition had been no small one. "J. B. the most ambitious of the ambitious," he wrote. "His Empire—the Empire he aspires to—extending to and comprehending the whole human race, in all places—in all habitable places of the earth, at all future time." He died happy in the thought that that ambition was well on the way to being realised. In the words of Leslie Stephen—"he is said to have expressed the wish that he could awaken once in a century to contemplate the prospect of a world gradually adopting his principles and so making steady progress in happiness and wisdom." And—typical gesture—he crowned a life of service by directing that his body be dissected in the interests of that science which was his god, that knowledge which he was convinced would supply the answer to all man's problems.

The Principle of Utility

Today we understand by "utility" that which is contrasted with the merely ornamental, agreeable, or pleasant. Bentham, however, meant by it not what is opposed to the pleasant or agreeable, but exactly what is pleasant or agreeable. He used it, in fact, as a synonym for our word "good," or our word "value."

But what does Bentham mean by goodness or utility? Everything that brings happiness is good, he tells us, and nothing that doesn't bring happiness is good. "An adherent to the Principle of Utility," he says "holds virtue to be a good thing by reason only of the pleasures which result from the practice of it: he esteems vice to be a bad thing by reason only of the pains which follow in its train."

The doctrine of Utility, therefore, is a hedonistic doctrine. When Bentham spoke of the good and bad consequences of an action he simply meant the happy or painful consequences of that action. He accepted the association principle of Hartley that all ideas are derived from the senses as the result of the operation of sensible objects on these, and he conceived of life as being made up of interesting perceptions. All experience, he believed, was either pleasurable or painful, or both. Pleasures were simply individual sensations. But happiness he thought of not as a simple individual sensation. Rather it was a state of mind, a bundle of sensations. Every pleasure was prima facie good and ought to be pursued. But happiness was not the piling up of all pleasures. It was the net result—that is, it sometimes entailed the rejection of some pleasures indulgence in which would have painful consequences.

The doctrine of Utility is a doctrine of a quantitatively conceived hedonism—it can recognise no distinction between pleasures except a quantitative one. If good equals happiness, then one action is better than another only if it produces more happiness. We can only speak of one pleasure being greater in quantity than another—otherwise we would be appealing to another standard of goodness. When we say that "poetry is better than push-halfpenny," we may either mean that it gives a different and better kind of pleasure or that it gives more pleasure. If we accept the principle of Utility, however, we can only mean the latter.

If the only difference between pleasures is a quantitative difference, how are we to measure pleasure and pain? No linear measurement can be applied to them, and it is obviously impossible to measure them by weight. Yet if we believe that the goodness and badness of actions is determined by the pleasures and pains that they produce, it is essential to be able to compare pleasures and pains. The doctrine of Utility must therefore also be a doctrine which teaches how pleasures can be measured. To enable us to do this, Bentham gives us his famous "felicific calculus." When we measure pleasures, he says, we must take account of their intensity and duration. We must take note of their certainty or uncertainty, since a pleasure that is more certain is greater than one which is less certain. Their propinquity or remoteness must also come into our calculations, a pleasure that is closer or more easily available being greater than one which is farther away and more inaccessible. We must consider their fecundity and their purity, since one pleasure is greater than another if its chances of being followed by sensations of the same kind are better and if its chances of being followed by sensations of the opposite kind are less.

This doctrine of Utility is a doctrine which is concerned with results not with motives. It maintains that the motive of an action is irrelevant to its goodness or badness—not, as Dr. Johnson held, that its goodness and morality depends upon the motive with which it is done. However, Utilitarians are prepared to compromise with the view that motive matters at least to this extent that they will admit that the motive of an action can be considered relative to its goodness or badness where it has an effect upon its results. If men act habitually from good-will they agree, their actions are likely to have better consequences than are the actions of men who act habitually from ill-will. Bentham, moreover, believes that consequences may be both "primary" and "secondary." The pain which the robbed man feels at the loss of his money is a "primary" evil. The alarm felt by all other holders of money, the suggestion that robbery is easy which may affect the conduct of others and thus weaken the "tutelary" motive of respect for property, are "secondary" evils. These secondary evils may be more important than the primary evil—as the example of a single man refusing to pay his taxes might be infinitely more harmful to the State than the loss to the Treasury of his personal contribution would suggest. A man's intentions or motives, Bentham says, are of the greatest importance in determining these secondary consequences of actions, and must therefore be taken into account by the legislator. In spite, however, of this compromise, it is clear that according to the doctrine of Utility we cannot say whether an action is good until its consequences are known.

It would seem to follow that Utilitarians cannot say that a whole class of actions is bad, but that only particular actions are bad. Circumstances must always be taken into account, and there are no uniform and certain consequences that can be said to follow actions of a certain class. If this be so, a difficulty arises of which the Utilitarians were well aware. If each action is to be judged separately, haven't we abolished a criterion of goodness, haven't we discounted morality in favour of expediency? Yet the doctrine of Utility aims also at being a doctrine of morals.

Different Utilitarians attempt to meet this difficulty in different ways. Paley and Mill argue that Utilitarian theory can, after all, give us a principle by which we can say that whole classes of actions are good or bad. An action, they say, is to be accounted good not because of its immediate happy consequences but because of its general or long-term happy consequences. If men ask themselves what would be the consequences if the same sort of action were generally permitted, they can determine what sort of actions are good and what bad. The accumulated experience of mankind will tell men what the probable consequences of certain kinds of action will be, will provide a rough, general rule whereby whole classes of actions can be judged. Bentham, however, asserted that since we can make an accurate estimate of the consequences of any particular action, generalisations about conduct are entirely unnecessary to a moral theory. He believed in "moral arithmetic," in the replacement of a general principle by an exact calculation.

The doctrine of Utility tells us, further, whose happiness or pleasure is to be sought—though there is more than a little vagueness about this, and there is remarkably little unanimity in the views of the Utilitarians on this point. Bentham gives four distinct answers to the question whose happiness is to be aimed at. Like Hobbes, he is a believer in psychological egoistic hedonism, holding that no man ever desired anything, because no man could ever desire anything, but personal happiness. He tells us first, therefore, that a man aims always and only at his own personal happiness. But secondly he tells us that man ought to aim at the happiness of everybody in general, since he says that an action is good whenever it results in a balance of happiness to somebody. Thirdly he says that man should strive to bring about the greatest happiness of the greatest number—a slogan which owes some of its success to its ambiguity, since if read in one way it could even justify the slavery of the Greek City State. Fourthly, in his later writings he says that man should seek the "greatest possible happiness." This last view, which was held by J. S. Mill, is on the whole that which is most characteristic of the Utilitarians.

This doctrine of Utility is one which tells us how to regulate our conduct—even though according to Bentham, somewhat paradoxically, no action can be disinterested and the conception of duty—that which you are punished for not doing—does not really exist. It tells us what is a right action as well as what is a good action. A good action is one which results in a maximum of pleasure—a definition which, incidentally, allows the infliction of pain if in the end a balance of pleasure is obtained, an idea which is the basis of the Utilitarian theory of punishment. A right action is one which would produce a larger balance of pleasure or a lower balance of pain than any other action possible in the circumstances. All actions whatsoever must be good or bad. All actions to which there is an alternative must be right or wrong. It is always bad to produce more pain than pleasure. It is always wrong to choose that of two actions which produces less pleasure than might have been the case in the circumstances. Whether a bad action is right and a good action wrong depends, then, on the circumstances. A bad action, which produces more pain than pleasure, is nevertheless right if the only alternative produces still more pain.

This doctrine of Utility, moreover, is supposed to be universal

—all other explanations of man's conduct are merely this doctrine in disguise. Bentham says, for instance, of the principle of ascetism, which finds any action good which has painful consequences and any action bad which has pleasurable consequences, that it is "merely the principle of utility misapplied." Ascetics, Bentham says, derive a perverted pleasure from their asceticism. Therefore asceticism is explicable in terms of hedonism, while hedonism is not explicable in terms of asceticism. Hence hedonism, or the principle of Utility, must be the true explanation of men's actions. If we say that conscience is the guide to the goodness and badness of actions, there are moments when conscience itself is uncertain and what we fall back upon then is, Bentham says, the principle of Utility. Whatever has been achieved of stability in the past, J. S. Mill agrees, has been achieved by the tacit acceptance of the principles of Utilitarianism. Behind every criterion of goodness has always been the principle of Utility.

Finally the doctrine of Utility is supposed to be objective, verifiable, unequivocal, and clear. The author of the *Federalist*, Bentham wrote, had said that justice was the end of government. "Why not happiness?" he asks. "What happiness is every man knows, because what pleasure is every man knows, and what pain is every man knows. But what justice is this is what on every occasion is the subject-matter of dispute." It was indeed because the principle of Utility seemed to present a criterion of goodness that was objective and not subjective, that was verifiable and not esoteric, that was, above all, easily recognised by everybody that Bentham chose it to combat the conscience or moral sense theory that held the field. According to that theory, moral judgments are self-evident judgments, they owe nothing whatever to experience, they cannot be questioned or doubted. Goodness cannot be translated into any other terms—it cannot, for instance, be happiness—and men know what is good by intuition. For all who believe in the moral sense theory, in the Law of Nature, Right Reason, or Natural Justice, Bentham has the utmost contempt. "The fairest and openest of them all," he regards as the man who says, "I am of the Elect! God tells the Elect what is right. Therefore if you want to know what is right, you have only to come to me." Wanting to make the conduct of human relations an exact science, it was in the principle of Utility, so immeasurably simpler and clearer as he thought than any other theory, that Bentham found his greatest guide.

Bentham's Idea of the State

The explanation of anything in terms of a limited end will be a limited and incomplete explanation. The Utilitarian explanation of the State is a complete explanation in terms of an unlimited end. It is an explanation which does not confine itself entirely to vague generalities, such as the assertion that the State exists to fulfil personality. The State, Utilitarians tell us, is a group of persons organised for the promotion and maintenance of Utility —that is, happiness or pleasure. This principle of Utility, not any inherently improbable Contract, is all that is needed to explain why men obey the State. What does it matter, Utilitarians ask, if our ancestors did or did not sign a bond? It is not their signatures but the principle of Utility that binds us. Utilitarians do not leave us with a phrase, but give us a complete, fully worked-out theory of the nature and purposes of the State.

The Utilitarian explanation of the State is not only an explanation in terms of an unlimited end, but also in terms of the particular character of the State which differentiates it from man's other activities. A theory which maintains that the end of the State is the promotion of Utility simply identifies the end of the State with the end of human life. Yet clearly the State has a particular part to play in human life, and such a theory does not tell us what. If the State is an institution for the furtherance of Utility, so is every other institution, and a theory which does not tell us how it differs from these will not help us very much. Bentham and the Utilitarians tell us in what way the State is peculiar—it is the sole source of law, which is the most certain of the four 'sanctions,' or overriding motives, which govern the lives of men. These are the physical sanction, which operates in the ordinary course of nature; the moral sanction, which arises from the general feeling of society; the religious sanction, which is applied by "the immediate hand of a superior invisible being, either in the present life or in a future"; and the political sanction, which operates through government and the necessity for which is the explanation of the State.

Thus for Bentham the State is primarily a law-making body, a group of persons organised for the promotion and maintenance of happiness, and acting through law to that end. Law is command and restraint, and as such is opposed to liberty. But it is necessary, and if it is simply explained people can be brought to realise that it is necessary, for the promotion of happiness—

which is, of course, its sufficient justification. Its great task is to reconcile interests—"so to regulate the motive of self-interest that it shall operate, even against its will, towards the production of the greatest happiness." This it does by attaching artificial pains, or punishments, to certain actions of a particular kind which would not be conducive to the general happiness. It cannot, and it ought not to try to, concern itself with all actions which would not be conducive to the general happiness. For law in its very nature is limited, and its nature shows the bounds which any true State must set to its actions. Law should take cognisance of and turn into offences only those bad, adult, other-regarding actions the punishment of which will increase the net balance of pleasure or decrease the net balance of pain. It should not, for instance, try to stamp out drunkenness, for this would lead to a complexity of laws of excessive rigour and would entail the use of an army of spies. Offences such as drunkenness, Bentham says, produce no general alarm, but such laws as would be directed against them undoubtedly would, and in addition new and more dangerous vices would appear. Morality, which like law aims at the production of happiness, must concern itself with such matters as with all self-regarding actions, but they are beyond the province of law. "Legislation and morals," as Bentham puts it, "have the same centre but not the same circumference."

Because law is command, it must be the command of a supreme authority. Indeed, it is only when such an authority is habitually obeyed that Bentham is prepared to admit the existence of civil society. His State, therefore, is a Sovereign State. It is the hallmark of a Sovereign State that nothing it does can be illegal. To speak of it as exceeding its authority is an abuse of language. This is true of the freest as well as of the most despotic of States, although a written constitution, he will admit, can limit governmental power.

His State, too, is the sole source of rights. The individual can never plead Natural Law against the State, for the Law of Nature is "nothing but a phrase." He can never take his stand on "Natural Rights," for they do not exist. Natural Rights, says Bentham, are "simple nonsense: natural and imprescriptible rights rhetorical nonsense—nonsense upon stilts." It is, however, perhaps worth noticing that Bentham contrives to give to the individual much of what he had enjoyed under Natural Law and

Natural Rights. In his regard for property he is so true to the teaching of Locke that not even his *bêtes noires*, sinecures, are to be abolished without compensations. He justifies this as being essential to the security of the individual, and it can fairly be argued that what he has taken away by his attack on natural rights he gives back by way of insisting on security. Moreover, he justifies opposition to the State if that opposition will produce less pain than continued obedience. In that case, he says, it is the individual's "duty and interest" to "enter into measures of resistance." But even then he will not say that the individual has the right to resist, for he is true to his theory that rights cannot be maintained against the State.

It will appear from this that Bentham's State is not one in which liberty is regarded as an end in itself. For liberty which is often thought of as one of the fundamentals of all government is not of such importance in the Utilitarian scheme of things. Happiness is the only ultimate criterion and liberty must submit itself to that criterion. The end of the State is the maximum happiness not the maximum liberty.

Like Paley, Bentham distinguishes between Natural Liberty, which is my liberty to do whatsoever I will and which clearly cannot be enjoyed in any sort of social or political life, and Civil Liberty, which is my liberty to do whatsoever I will so long as it is consistent with the interests of the community to which I belong. If laws are of the right kind—that is, of a Utilitarian sort—they will increase Civil Liberty; Natural Liberty they will of course decrease. Neither Paley nor Bentham are, however, quite consistent here. In both there is the presumption that everything that derogates from Natural Liberty is in some measure undesirable, a presumption which comes from the belief that the individual is the best judge of his own happiness and should therefore be left as free as possible to judge everything for himself. That presumption cannot be justified on their own principles. For the proposition that a man is the best judge of his own happiness cannot be proved by reference to the principle of Utility, and in any case it is not the individual's happiness which is the criterion of Utility. That criterion is the greatest amount of happiness altogether. Therefore, in spite of the personal predilections of the pioneers of Utilitarianism, it is wrong to suppose that the Utilitarian doctrine necessarily leads to *laisser-faire*. Utilitarianism can justify no restriction excep that which will produce a greater amount of happiness than its absence—but all restrictions, however great they may be, that do, it must of course demand. A good law is not one which increases liberty but one which increases happiness. And as Sidgwick saw, there may be a conflict between happiness and liberty. Paley and Bentham tend to think this unlikely. But their belief is not based on the principle of Utility, and because of their own attachment to *laisser-faire* it is the more important to remember that the State for them is not primarily concerned with liberty at all. Indeed, it is obvious how much more highly Bentham thought of security than of liberty. "Give me liberty or give me death" would have appeared to him the cry of a fool, for it was the price of heroism not its value that he understood. "Wars and storms are best to be read of," he said, "but peace and calms are better to endure."

Yet Bentham never forgets that his State is a contrivance whereby man seeks to ensure happiness. It is not therefore a State which, like Aristotle's, is prior to the individual. On the contrary, the individual is prior to it. He is endowed with reason, and is himself before ever he comes into the State, which thus in no sense can be regarded as more real than he is himself.

The State, moreover, is a trustee for the individual. And, more important, it is a democratic State. For Bentham, who was originally a Tory, slowly and somewhat reluctantly came to believe that "the sinister interest" of the few must be overcome by calling in the general interest as the only possible corrective. When at last he applied his "self-preference principle," which asserted that "in the general tenor of human life, in every heart, self-regarding interest is predominant over all other interests put together," he came to the following remarkable conclusion: "At no time have the constituent members of the governing body, at no time has the monarch, at no time has the hereditary aristocracy, at no time have the proprietors of seats in the House of Commons, at no time have the clergy, at no time have the judges, had any better endeavour or desire than to swell each of them his own power to its utmost possible pitch." At no time have they because at no time could they. But if everybody controlled everybody else, nobody would predominate; everyone's self-interest would be suppressed except when it coincided with the interests of all; and whatever was done would be that which all approved.

There is still, however, a difficulty that he has to face. Since men can only safely be counted upon to advance their own interests—Bentham even says "whatsoever evil it is possible for man to do for the advancement of his own private and personal interest at the expense of the public interest—that evil sooner or later he will do, unless by some means or other, intentional or otherwise, he be prevented from doing it"—and since direct democracy in large countries is impossible, how can it be assured that the representatives of the people will not legislate merely in their own selfish interest? Only by "minimising" confidence in them, by "maximising" control over them, by "making public functionaries uneasy," by enforcing every constitutional device—universal suffrage, annual Parliaments, vote by ballot, the election of the Prime Minister by Parliament, the appointment of civil servants by competitive examination—whereby the dependence of their representatives on the people would be increased. But if it be remembered that "if it be true, according to the homely proverb, that the eye of the master makes the ox fat, it is no less so that the eye of the public makes the statesman virtuous" all would be well.

Bentham's, furthermore, is a State in which all men have equal rights. All men have the right with all others to promote policy; all must be equal before the law; to ensure a greater equalisation of property is one of the State's most urgent tasks. Not that he believes that men are by nature equal. Indeed, this is another of those "anarchic fallacies" on which he pours such a torrent of abuse. But his perception that inequalities are inevitable did not blind him to the fact that too great inequality is an insuperable obstacle on the road to the greatest happiness. He recognised, and he was right in recognising, that a society which is without gross inequalities of fortune is happier than one which is not.

There is yet one more characteristic of Bentham's State which must be noticed. Though according to his principles the State can take far-reaching action so long as that will increase pleasure or decrease pain, though he himself, as has been said, passed "from an uncritical individualism to an uncritical collectivism," his State is nevertheless fundamentally a negative one. It has no integral relation with the moral life of the citizen. It seeks to change his behaviour: it cannot change him. It cannot help him to develop his character, to bring out the best that is in him.

For it is not the State that moulds the citizens, it is the citizens that mould the State.

His Importance

Coleridge once said that until we "understand a man's ignorance we are ignorant of his understanding." It is not too difficult to reveal Bentham's ignorance.

He was not an outstanding philosopher, though paradoxically he occupies an important place in the history of philosophy. He had, as it were, swallowed his first principles whole, but he had never digested them. He took his theory of knowledge from Locke and Hume, the pleasure and pain principle from Helvetius, the notion of sympathy and antipathy from Hume, the idea of Utility from any of half a score of writers. Lacking originality and full of prejudice in his speculations, he is as confused and contradictory in his own theoretical adventures as he is complacent. His *Introduction to the Principles of Morals and Legislation* opens with a famous passage: "Nature has placed mankind under the governance of two sovereign masters, pain and pleasure. It is for them alone to point out what we ought to do, as well as to determine what we shall do. They govern us in all we do. In words a man may pretend to abjure their empire: but in reality he will remain subject to it all the while. The principle of Utility recognises this subjection." This is indeed an arresting passage, but when analysed its words will be seen to have a far more definite ring than meaning. What does the sovereign mastery of pleasure and pain mean—that men should seek their own or anyone else's pleasure? In saying that pleasure and pain govern what we do as well as what we ought to do, is he saying that all men always do their duty? And what is meant by saying that the principle of Utility recognises this subjection? If men always seek their own pleasure, isn't it pointless to say that they ought to do something else? How can men have two different things as the absolute good—their own pleasure and the happiness of mankind?

Bentham goes on to reduce confusion to chaos, a fact not always appreciated as he himself is such a mint of precise ideas. But the questions he leaves unanswered are legion. How can the principle "every one is to count for one and nobody as more than one" be derived from hedonism or even made consistent with it? How can private interest be translated into public duty? How can it really be believed that even the closely watched legislator, if as selfish as Bentham portrays him, will forward his own interests only by forwarding the interests of all? How are pleasures commensurable at all? How much intensity, for instance, is to be counted against how much duration? Can any meaning be attached to a quantitative estimate of things which are by their nature not quantities but qualities, which differ in kind, not in amount? And if we admit, as Bentham does, that the intensity of a pleasure depends on the person experiencing it, are we not after all introducing a subjective element into what is presented to us as a purely objective felicific calculus?

Moreover, we do not need Carlyle's indignation at what he called the "pig philosophy," to remind us that hedonism of this kind is not very satisfactory, that happiness is much more than pleasure. Kant's two-fold end—that of meriting as well as receiving happiness—makes a greater appeal than hedonism, which is concerned only with receiving happiness. Is it really true to say that everybody knows what happiness is any more than it is to suggest that men eat, not because they are hungry but because they seek the pleasure that comes from satisfying hunger? And is it not significant that happiness deliberately sought is not obtained? If you want your own happiness, the worst way of going about it is to seek it expressly. The story of the old man who was fond of macaroons and who hid them between the books in his library because he said they tasted so much better when he came upon them unexpectedly is worth remembering. Aiming at other things, men may attain happiness and other things; aiming at happiness, men may achieve other things but they will not achieve happiness.

Besides, if in his portrayal of the hedonistic individual Bentham seems to have left life out of the picture, since men feel the conflict between duty and interest which he denies and the prompting of conscience which he ignores, in his study of the atomic individual he has left out both society and history. In refusing to consider man as moulded by history and society, he ignores the strongest forces that have made him what he is. It can indeed be argued that he sees only three separate entities, the Individual, Society, and Government, but that he never sees the totality which is the State. And in his over-insistence on the rational individual he has left out the emotions. So much is this the case that we can hardly recognise Bentham's man as a member of our species. We are not as rational as he is, nor can we attempt, as he must, to calculate quantities of pleasure.

We cannot regard Bentham as "the greatest critical thinker of his age and country." We have to see in him as much of the 18th century as of the 19th. He was the typical philosophe of 18th-century France, unaccountably carried too far north by a stork too stupid to appreciate national characteristics. His was the philosophe's unbounded confidence that knowledge, which would soon be complete—he wrote "the age we live in is a busy age; in which knowledge is rapidly advancing towards perfection"—was the answer to all the problems that have ever perplexed mankind. His was the philosophe's collection of assumptions, never admitted as such and never examined, which shows the extent of the gulf between the philosophe and the philosopher. His was the philosophe's rationalism and contempt for tradition. It is significant that for long he was so little thought of in his own country, and so highly regarded outside it wherever the philosophes had made their way. It is significant, too, that great as is his importance as a reformer of the law, not only were many of the reasons he gave for his proposed reforms fallacious but that English law has continued to resist his codifying and to reject his fundamental principles.

But, after all, it is better to be right for the wrong reasons than never to be right at all. Moreover, critical as one must be of Bentham's philosophy, it would be folly to ignore his achievement. This was great because, French philosophe as in so many ways he was, he nevertheless contrived to fit in so well to the structural needs of his English age. For his age, scared almost out of its wits by fear of revolution, had decided that nothing must change lest all be overthrown. Yet no age stood more in need of reform. The great captains of the Industrial Revolution, impatient of the history and tradition which seemed to them to be expressed solely in hampering archaic laws, were demanding that the efficiency, cheapness, and uniformity which they worshipped in their industrial undertakings should also be introduced into government and law. But if they were unwilling to accept Burke's Toryism and respect for landed nobility, they had of course no more liking for the anarchism of Godwin and Shelley, for Jacobinical principles and Natural Rights, for sentiment and rhetoric and revolutionary dogmatism which might

be asserted even against themselves, than had the governing aristocracy. They wanted reforms which would be sensible and
practical and far-reaching without being too far-reaching; reforms which would acknowledge the movement of power from
the aristocracy to themselves without doing anything to encourage its further movement from themselves to the masses.

In Bentham and his followers, who were also crying out for
efficiency, cheapness, comprehensibility and uniformity in the
law, they found the answer to their needs. Here were reformers
who were as bitterly critical of "The Rights of Man" and the
bloody effects of the victory of that watchword in France, as
Pitt, Burke, or even Eldon himself. Here were reformers who
lacked the sentimentality of Cartwright, the bluster of Burdett,
the egotism and fiery oratory of Hunt, the obvious inconsistences
and unreliability of Cobbett. Yet they were as trenchant and
vigorous and fearless in their attack on aristocratic privilege as
any new industrialist could desire. It was exactly what he
wanted to be able to read in the *Westminster Review*—"the rule
is good always to suspect the 'higher orders' and the higher the
more. They live only to pervert justice and right to the interests
of their own class; and if any good is gotten out of them, it
must be with a screw." His heart warmed to Bentham, who
complacently called himself "the most egregious and offensive
libeller men in power in this country ever saw," when in *The
Book of Fallacies* he found such a devastating exposure of the
forces opposing reform. The very chapter headings of that book
speak with an eloquence Bentham could not always sustain—
"the wisdom of our ancestors, or Chinese argument," "the Hob-
goblin argument, or no Innovation," "Official malefactors'
screen," "Attack me you attack Government," "the Quietist, or
'No complaint,'" "Snail's pace argument," "One thing at a
time," "Slow and Sure," and so on. And even if Bentham advocated universal suffrage, he and his school were as fully convinced as any captain of industry of the desirability and indeed
the inevitability of middle-class rule. James Mill had this to say
about it : "The opinions of that class of the people who are
below the middle rank are formed, and their minds are directed,
by that intelligent and virtuous rank, who come the most immediately in contact with them, who are in the constant habit
of intimate communication with them, to whom they fly for
advice and assistance in all their numerous difficulties. . . . There

can be no doubt whatever that the middle rank is that part of the community of which the opinion would ultimately decide. Of the people beneath them, a vast majority would be sure to be guided by their advice and example."

Though he failed to codify the English law, it is very largely because of him that Parliament has become the legislative instrument that it is today. Before him Parliament concerned itself very little with legislation. Indeed, in Blackstone's *Commentaries*, published in 1765, references to statutes are to a modern mind astonishingly few. It was Benthamism which brought to an end the era of legislative stagnation, and ushered in that period of increasing legislative activity which has not yet ended and under the cumulative effects of which we are living our lives today. Bentham had, furthermore, such an enormous influence on law reform that Maine says, "I do not know a single law reform effected since Bentham's day which cannot be traced to his influence." To that influence can also be attributed the creation of adequate legal machinery for the protection of the equal rights of all citizens. His influence on penology was almost as great—no one has ever done as much as he did to tell us how to prevent as many offences as possible as efficiently and as cheaply as possible.

His figure, too, can be seen behind all 19th-century measures for Parliamentary Reform. He inspired the logic of political democracy, as can be seen from that trenchant criticism of the Reform Bill of 1832 published in 1837 by the Birmingham Political Union, which begins: "The motive and end of all legislation is the happiness of the universal people." He supplied a new measurement for social reform—the "maximising" of individual happiness. Poor Law Reform owed much to him, as did the measures introduced to improve public health. Edwin Chadwick, whose work in scouring and scrubbing the nation was of such great importance, was his faithful disciple. And if Chadwick's lack of humour and sense of proportion—he was annoyed because in the middle of the Crimean War Napoleon III failed to send for him again to continue a fascinating discussion on sewage manure—repels us today, and if it is no longer so easy to regard an infinite capacity for making drains as the genius on which Englishmen pride themselves, since their ideal of a w.c. on every landing and a wash-basin in every room seems unimpressive compared with the American practice of two w.c.s on every landing and two wash-basins in every room, nevertheless, anyone who has smelled an Eastern city and resisted the conclusion that God gave Indians and Chinese noses for some purpose which escapes the West must give thanks for the Edwin Chadwicks of this world. Bentham's great interest in education, too, deserves for him an honourable place in the list of the educational reformers of this country. Via the Mechanics' Institutes, he can even be regarded as one of the pioneers of Adult Education. And if it was in Bentham's smithy that the tools of the law-reformer were tempered, it was here, too, that some of the weapons of Socialism were forged. For the principle of the greatest happiness and the practice of a legislating Sovereign Parliament ultimately lent themselves even more to the furtherance of collectivism than to the preservation of individualism.

Moreover, Bentham, it may be maintained, increased Englishmen's belief in the essential reasonableness of Englishmen and therefore their conviction that reform is infinitely preferable to revolution. Gladstone could say that no great end could be achieved in politics without passion, and the House of Commons was rarely as sedate and decorous as a Victorian finishing school for young ladies—one observer in the early 19th century reported that "the bestial bawlings of the Commons could be heard 50 yards away"—yet English political life was remarkably placid throughout the 19th century. And if beer and fights figured prominently in Eatanswill elections, nevertheless what breaking of heads Englishmen cared to indulge in at election time was not proof of their disbelief in, but was no more than incidental to, their faith in the proposition that it is better to count heads than to break them. The contribution of Benthamism to the steadiness of British politics is not to be ignored.

It should be added that Benthamism strengthened another not so desirable tendency of Englishmen, their habit, to which the Anglo-Saxon peoples seem particularly prone, of seeing all peoples as cast in their own mould and therefore as sharing their own ideas, opinions, prejudices. For Bentham taught that there were general principles, always and abidingly true and applicable to all men. He also taught that every political problem demands immediate empirical investigation. In teaching both lessons, Bentham anticipated Marx. He was, like Marx, an empirical universalist. In England his universal principle, the *à priori* abstract element in his teaching, could be minimised while immediate problems could be examined in all the detail that would have delighted him. But when Englishmen turned to foreign problems, lacking as they naturally did that detailed knowledge which they could so easily acquire at home, they were only too prone to believe that detailed investigation was not, after all, necessary as they could fall back upon the general principle that all men were fundamentally the same. Too apt to believe this and too ready to ignore foreign traditions, Englishmen have frequently made rods for their own backs. Believing that all must attach the importance that they do to things, they have frequently proved incapable of reading aright the international situation. They were, for instance, convinced that the Great Exhibition of 1851 was the ceremonial opening of an era of world-wide free trade, prosperity, and peace—a conviction which a little observation ought very quickly to have dispelled. Believing that all will behave as they do, they have often been blind to the facts of power. Because their Government does not flout their public opinion, they have attempted to base the League of Nations upon their belief that public opinion will be all that is required to restrain the abuses of power. And when they learn at last that all nations are not would-be Englishmen who express English thoughts in unaccountably perverted tongues, they are apt to cry out at the wickedness of the world and to regard with unalterable mistrust those who have taught them that lesson. It was said of Sir Edward Grey that he treated all foreign diplomats as though they were if not old Etonians at least old Wykhamists, and that when it was at last borne in upon him that not all representatives of Balkan countries had had the advantage of an English Public School education, he could hardly bring himself to continue negotiations with them.

It can also be argued that Benthamism, with its congenital distrust of the representatives of the people, whom it regards as plunderers of the public to be kept on the straight and narrow path only by the most rigid of controls, the most unremitting of supervision, has done public life the great disservice of hastening the day of delegative democracy. It has helped to turn the representative who, as Burke said, being a lover of freedom, is himself determined to be free to serve his constituents with his judgment, into the delegate whose judgment is in pawn to foregone conclusions, who is the slave of committees and caucuses

Bagehot warns us of the dangers of government by the constituencies : "The feeling of a constituency is the feeling of a dominant party, and that feeling is elicited, stimulated, sometimes even manufactured, by the local political agent. Such an opinion could not be moderate, could not be subject to effectual discussion, could not be in close contact with pressing facts, could not be framed under a chastening sense of near responsibility, could not be formed as those form their opinions who have to act upon them. Constituency government is the precise opposite of parliamentary government. It is the government of immoderate persons far from the scene of action, instead of the government of moderate persons close to the scene of action; it is the judgment of persons judging in the last resort, and without a penalty, in lieu of persons judging in fear of a dissolution, and ever conscious that they are subject to an appeal." If these dangers have in our own lifetime become acute, a good measure of the blame for this must be borne by Benthamism.

Benthamism has certainly the defects of its virtues. Even so we can look back to it with gratitude. For in addition to all the reforms that it encouraged, it liberated political theory from medieval political vocabulary, and, above all, it provided one of the most powerful of weapons against the coming of what William James used to call the "Bitch Goddess." It insists that the State exists for man, not man for the State. It proclaims that only where there are happy citizens can the State be considered good. "The interest of the community then is what?" Bentham asks. And he answers, "The sum of the interests of the several members who compose it." This is the greatest contribution of Benthamism to political theory, that it sees every question in terms of the men and women whose lives it will affect and never in terms of abstractions. And Benthamism denies the infallibility of the superior person who foists his own morality or type of happiness upon others. Winnowing the grain from the chaff need not be such a dusty process as to blind Englishmen to the debt they owe to Jeremy Bentham.

JOHN STUART MILL, 1806–1873

His Life and Writings

Nothing would have seemed more absurd to Jeremy Bentham and to James Mill than the proposition that it is better to travel hopefully than to arrive. Yet by the time of the death of the latter it is obvious not only that Utilitarianism is arriving, but also that in the process the force, the exhilaration, the bounding enthusiasm of its disciples is waning. Like many before and since, Utilitarians were finding the taste of victory insipid after the heady anticipations of the battle. Some gave up the cause, refusing to be further associated with a victory which now unaccountably seemed so little worth the winning. Others, who would not forsake the faith, sought to reinterpret it in the new conditions, while at the same time removing from it those things which were offensive both to its critics and to their own consciences. Of these the greatest was John Stuart Mill, the new leader of Utilitarianism. It can hardly be said that he succeeded in his task, for his removing, though he could never bring himself to admit it, was of such a wholesale kind that when he had finished reinterpreting and refurbishing Utilitarianism, Utilitarianism was singularly hard to find. If it can ever be said of any grave philosopher that he so far forgot himself as to pour the baby out with the bath-water, it can be said of him. Yet perhaps because he is the least logical, he is also incomparably the most satisfactory of the Utilitarians. For life is more real than philosophic systems, and a life and a truth that is not always present in more coherent and impressive philosophic systems is easily to be seen shining through all his inconsistencies.

He was born in 1806, destined for the purple—to be "a successor worthy of both of us" as his father James told Bentham—and educated for that high position as few have ever been. He was learning Greek by the age of three. By the time he was eight he had read all Plato and Herodotus and most of Xenophon and Lucian. With a little English, History, Arithmetic, and Latin added by way of light relief, he persevered with his Greek studies, reading Homer, Thucydides, Sophocles, Euripides, Aristophanes, Demosthenes, Æschines, and Lysias, Theocritus, Anacreon, and Aristotle's *Rhetoric*—his first "scientific treatise on any moral or psychological subject." It is pleasant to record that he was most attached to *Robinson Crusoe*. But such frivolities were not to be allowed to distract his attention, and he was soon grappling with the more exacting disciplines of logic, psychology, and political economy. His father was his teacher and constant companion, and by a combination of sarcastic tongue-lashing—he was "the most impatient of men"— and protracted Socratic cross-questioning, John's mental powers were soon astonishingly developed. And to complete the process he was himself set to teach his brothers and sisters—always under the reproving eye of his father.

He himself said, with characteristic modesty, that his education proved that it is possible to instil into a child a greater amount of knowledge than is usually acquired in childhood. It may well be doubted how many childish minds, as well as childish bodies, could stand the strain. Even John's health suffered and he became a prematurely old man. The cost of that education was high, but the achievement is not to be valued lightly. John had certainly been trained to use his mind, and in the enormous amount of work he produced, in which he used it to such good purpose, his training may, after all, find its justification.

After a year in France, in which he learned to appreciate things French and to deprecate many things English—in particular the English habit of "acting as if everybody else was either an enemy or a bore"—and in which incidentally he discovered the joys of travel and the beauties of nature, he took up his old studies, added Roman Law and began reading Bentham. This last, he said "was an epoch in my life; one of the turning-points in my mental history." At sixteen he founded the Utilitarian Society, an association of young men who met to discuss Bentham's ideas. He became a member of a small group which met at George Grote's house to discuss political economy, logic, and psychology. He joined "The Speculative Debating Society" and "The Political Economy Club." At seventeen he obtained a post in the office of the Examiner of India Correspondence in the East India Company, thus beginning a connection with the East India Company which lasted until its abolition in 1853. His duties here gave him experience of the actual conduct of affairs and brought him an adequate livelihood, but were not so onerous as to make it impossible for him to devote himself to what he considered more valuable matters.

He soon achieved distinction in the articles that he contributed to the *Westminster Review*. At the age of twenty he edited Bentham's *Rationale of Evidence*—a task which he says very simply "occupied nearly all my leisure for about a year." Then, really finding his feet in the morass of Bentham's manuscript notes, he undertook to see "five large volumes through the press." This, he says, greatly improved his style. It also proved too much even for his strong mind, and he fell into acute mental depression. He became convinced of "the paradox of hedonism"—seek happiness directly and it will not be found. Seek other things and it will be "inhaled in the air you breathe." He became convinced, too, that he had unduly starved the emotions and that in future he must make "the cultivation of the feelings one of the cardinal points in his ethical and philosophical creed." The poetry of Wordsworth and the philosophy of Coleridge helped him to find himself. It was a changed Mill—a man of deeper sympathies, of more generous feelings, of wider outlook—who emerged from this mental depression. He himself thought of it almost as a conversion—"And I am Peter, who denied his master," he said in later life when it was suggested that there should be a meeting of Bentham's followers.

That change in him was no doubt strengthened and confirmed by his association with Mrs. Taylor, who became his wife in 1851 on the death of her husband. Victorian susceptibilities were shocked by his open love for a married woman, and in his own person he had full opportunity to realise the truth of his contention that in England the yoke of law is light but that of public opinion heavy. He spoke of her as being a greater thinker than himself and a greater poet than Carlyle. Her judgment he thought "next to infallible." "If mankind continue to improve," he said, "their spiritual history for ages to come will be the progressive working out of her thoughts and realisation of her conceptions." That regard is a better testimony to the greatness of his heart than to the hardness of his head, but it is doubtless true that Mrs. Taylor helped to humanise his revised version of Utilitarianism.

After vainly trying, via the editorial chair of the *London Review* (afterwards the *London and Westminster Review*), to make an effective political force of men who had so little feeling for the realities of English politics as to refer to themselves as Philosophical Radicals, Mill began the publication of his greatest works. In 1843 his *System of Logic, Ratiocinative and Inductive* appeared and had an immense success. In 1848 the *Principles of Political Economy*, came out—with similar immediate and exceptional success. These and his *Essay on Liberty*, which was not, however, published until 1859 because of his wife's death, and which is beyond question the greatest and most compelling of his works, were completed before his retirement, and it is

obvious that in the fifteen years left to him after his retirement
his energy and output were alike considerably less than they
were before. However, he published two further essays, the
Considerations of Representative Government of 1860, and the
Utilitarianism of 1861. Four years later appeared the *Examination of Sir William Hamilton's Philosophy*; then in 1867 his
inaugural address on the value of culture, and in 1869 *The Subjection of Women*. Two posthumous works, the *Autobiography*,
published in 1873, and the *Three Essays on Religion*, published
in 1874, increased his already great reputation and mark a fitting close to a great career of scholarship and service.

If his retirement did not lead to any great outburst of literary
activity, it gave him the chance, hitherto denied him, of parliamentary experience. He was the Radical member for Westminster in the Parliament of 1866–8. He was not a great success. It
was not only that his somewhat singular programme—he announced that he would expend all his popularity as a writer in
upholding unpopular opinions—was not best suited to achieve
parliamentary eminence, nor that he occasionally lacked reality
as in his attack on the ballot, the secrecy of which he said would
make men vote for their selfish interests and not, as they should,
for the good of the State. He was, said Disraeli, who portrayed
him as cruelly and as faithfully as only Disraeli could, "the
finishing governess." Even Gladstone, who said, "When John
Mill was speaking, I always felt that I was listening to a saintly
man," also wrote to Granville about him—"Mill has failed as a
politician—not so much from advanced views, as from errors of
judgment and tact." No doubt when he lost his seat in 1868 he
was glad to retire once more to private life and his own pursuits.

He died at Avignon in 1873, being active to the end. Green
echoes Gladstone's remark that Mill was a saintly man. He considers Mill to have been an "extraordinarily good man." Perhaps
those comments are Mill's truest epitaph. In the whole history of
Political Philosophy there are few more appealing characters
than his.

His Alterations in Utilitarianism

In his desire to safeguard Utilitarianism from the reproaches
levelled against it, Mill goes far towards overthrowing the whole
Utilitarian position. The strong anti-hedonist movement of his
day, personified by Carlyle, determined him to show that the

Utilitarian theory, although hedonistic, is elevating and not degrading. Therefore he sought to establish the non-utilitarian proposition that some pleasures are of a higher quality than others. Bentham had denied this, maintaining "quantity of pleasure being equal, pushpin is as good as poetry." Mill offers a singular proof that Bentham is wrong. Men who have experienced both higher and lower pleasures agree, he says, in preferring the higher, and theirs is a decisive testimony. "It is better to be a human being dissatisfied than a pig satisfied; better to be Socrates dissatisfied than a fool satisfied. And if the fool or the pig is of a different opinion, it is because they only know their side of the question. The other party to the comparison knows both sides." Mill's assertion that pleasures differ in quality is no doubt a truer reflection of human experience than is Bentham's insistence to the contrary. It is, nevertheless, non-utilitarian. If pleasures differ qualitatively, then the higher pleasure is the end to be sought and not the principle of Utility. As Sidgwick, who was so ruthless and logical a thinker, saw, if we are to be hedonists we must say that pleasures vary only in quantity, never in quality. Utilitarianism, because it is hedonism, must recognise no distinction between pleasures except a quantitative one.

In the course of proving his thesis that the principle of Utility can admit a qualitative distinction of pleasures, Mill makes use of the non-Utilitarian argument that pleasures cannot, in any case, be objectively measured. The felicific calculus is, he says, absurd, and men have always relied upon the testimony of "those most competent to judge." "There is no other tribunal to be referred to even on the question of quantity. What means are there of determining which is the acutest of two pains or the intensest of two pleasurable sensations except the general suffrage of those who are familiar with both?" Mill was of course right in maintaining the absurdity of the felicific calculus —but if it is admitted that pleasures can no longer be measured objectively, a vital breach has been made in the stronghold of Utilitarianism.

Mill is concerned to establish the fact that pleasures differ in quality as well as in quantity, so that he can maintain the further non-Utilitarian position that not the principle of Utility but the dignity of man is the final end of life. In his *Liberty* he makes the non-Utilitarian complaint that "individual spontaneity is hardly recognised by the common modes of thinking as having any intrinsic worth, or deserving any regard on its own account." He approves of Humboldt's doctrine of "self realisation." "It really is of importance," he says, "not only what men do, but also what manner of men they are that do it." "What more or better can be said of any condition of human affairs," he asks, "than that it brings human beings themselves nearer to the best thing they can be?" To Bentham and to James Mill that would have sounded dangerously like that intuitionist gibberish which they were so constantly attacking. Not self-realisation but the achievement of pleasure and the avoidance of pain was the end that they set before men. Mill, on the contrary, is in effect saying that one pleasure is better than another if it promotes the sense of dignity in man. Thus our criterion of goodness is no longer the principle of Utility. We must now say that actions are good if they produce a higher sense of dignity in man. Mill is here introducing a conception of the good life as something more than a life devoted to pleasure. Speaking of "the paradox of pleasure," that happiness is to be found only indirectly, he says, "Aiming thus at something else, they find happiness by the way." This is to place moral ends above happiness, which becomes not indeed a state of pleasures but a state of mind which ensues when one pursues some moral end. Mill's introduction into Utilitarianism of this moral criterion implies a revolutionary change in the Benthamite position. Mill has once again made the State a moral institution with a moral end. Not utility but the promotion of virtue in the individual is what it must aim at. Thus Mill has defended Utilitarianism only by abandoning the whole Utilitarian position.

Mill's non-Utilitarian interest in the sense of dignity in man leads him to give a non-Utilitarian emphasis to the idea of moral obligation. Bentham had conceived of this as being merely the product of past associations of the selfish desires and anticipations of men. To Mill, to whom Bentham's view is far too simple and naïve, moral obligation is something very different. Fear, memory, self-esteem, he admits, play their part in its composition, but so do love, sympathy, religious emotion and occasionally even self-abasement. Thus Mill not only makes a real allowance for the emotional basis on which the State is founded, but goes far to admit T. H. Green's contention that public duties and responsibilities cannot logically be derived from private rights and interests. For Mill the sense of moral obligation cannot be explained in terms of the principle of Utility. Thus while his ethics are certainly more satisfying than Bentham's, Mill is responsible for yet another important alteration in Benthamism. This wish to encourage man's better self leads Mill to his non-Utilitarian interest in liberty, of which he gives two contradictory interpretations, each having this in common—that it is non-Utilitarian. To strict Utilitarians liberty is always subordinated to the principle of Utility. To Mill it is something fundamental, more of an end even than the principle of Utility itself. It is that passionate conviction, glowing through its pages that has made Mill's *Essay on Liberty* the great English classic that it is, with which only Milton's *Areopagitica* is fit to be compared. No finer defence of liberty of thought and discussion has ever been written. Believing that it is man's mind that changes society and that only free discussion can nourish fruitful ideas, he says that all mankind minus one lacks the right to coerce the single dissentient. For if it suppresses his opinion it injures the human race. The opinion suppressed may be true and "if not suppressed for ever, it may be thrown back for centuries." It may be partly true, in which case it is a necessary corrective to the accepted body of truth. It may be false, but controversy will strengthen true conviction. A creed accepted because of authority is a "mummery stuffed and dead." There is no slumber like that of a deep-seated opinion, and it can only be to the advantage of mankind to disturb it. Then they will acquire "the clearer perception and livelier impression of truth, produced by its collision with error." It will be seen that Mill is a firm believer in the survival of the fittest in the world of ideas, and that he is convinced that truth is fittest to survive. But even if men will not accept the inherently truthful, authority, Mill believes, cannot help. Call in Cæsar to save Christ and he at once destroys Him.

But important and powerful as is Mill's advocacy of freedom of discussion, this is not the main theme of his *Liberty*. Above all, Mill wants to promote the development of individual men and women, for he is convinced that all wise and noble things come, and must come, from individuals. To Mill there can be no self-development without liberty. It is this connection between liberty and self-development which interests him most, and even though he goes on to argue that liberty is also necessary for the happiness of society, it is clear that liberty is not to be expressed in terms of Utility, but is yet more fundamental than it.

Mill's first definition of liberty, and that to which he generally keeps, is that it is the sovereignty of the individual over himself. It is "being left to oneself." "All restraint *qua* restraint is an evil," he says. No interference with the individual's liberty of action is justified except to prevent him from harming others. Mill divides all actions into two categories. There are those actions which concern only the individual performing them, or self-regarding actions. There are those actions which affect others, or other-regarding actions. And he concludes that there should be no interference with self-regarding actions, but only with such other-regarding actions as produce positive, demonstrable harm to others. Mill will also admit, as a natural development of this position, that it is legitimate to oblige a man to bear his share in maintaining society—conscription is not to be regarded as an unwarranted infringement of his liberty. Mill's whole view is non-Utilitarian. It rests on the presumption that all restriction is evil—a presumption that cannot be justified by the principle of Utility. Nor, though he says that interference with the individual for his own sake is almost certain to be ill-judged, does he prove that there are sound Utilitarian reasons why society should not concern itself with self-regarding actions. Indeed, it is obvious that in insisting that self-regarding actions should not be interfered with, Mill is not being strictly Utilitarian. He is introducing a criterion other than that of Utility—the criterion, again, of self-development.

Mill's second definition of liberty is that "liberty consists in doing what one desires." This is obviously very different from the definition of liberty as being left to oneself. You would be justified, Mill says, in preventing a man crossing a bridge that you knew to be unsafe. "Liberty consists in doing what one desires, and he does not desire to fall into the river," he tells us. The man desired to cross the bridge, but it is legitimate to frustrate this desire so that the greater desire, which can be imputed to him, of not falling in the river can be achieved. This definition of liberty throws the door open to any amount of interference. If once it be admitted that somebody may know better than you know what you desire, and that liberty is to do what you desire, then even the activities of the Grand Inquisitor, torturing a man's body to prevent him being damned and thereby ensuring to him the salvation he desires, can be justified. Mill has gone far towards admitting the extremist idealist contention that one can be forced to be free. Bentham and James Mill would have been astounded and appalled at such apostasy as this on the part of one so carefully chosen and so tirelessly and so meticulously educated for the purple. In both his enthusiasm for and his definitions of liberty, Mill, then, makes the greatest of changes in Benthamism.

He makes yet another change of great importance in Bentham's teaching. Bentham, impatient of tradition, ignorant of history, and seeing the world as an extension of himself, had been convinced that his doctrines were of universal application. Mill, who recognises in his essay on Coleridge how wrong the philosophes were in tearing away the past, who admits that within any community there exists a feeling of allegiance, a strong and active principle of cohesion which can be explained only in terms of centuries long gone by and not in terms of Utility, who even agrees that the existence of a feeling of nationality is a necessary part of this cohesion, is not a universalist at all, but an historical relativist. He sees, for instance, as Bentham never does, that the people for whom a form of government is intended must be willing to accept it, able to keep it standing, and capable of the restraint and action necessary to achieve its end. The difference between their respective justifications of democracy is typical of the two men. Bentham justifies democracy because of the nature of man, regarding him as so inherently selfish that any other form of government will be government in the sinister interests of the governing class. Mill, while not denying that no other form of government than democracy can be trusted to keep the interests of the people always before it, is nevertheless very sure that not all peoples are fit for democracy. He explicitly says that democratic institutions cannot be recommended for a society whose citizens have not got the requisite quality of character. Thus whereas Bentham justifies democracy because of the nature of man, Mill justifies it because of the condition of man.

Mill's historical relativism enables him to emphasise something of the highest importance. He says, as does Bentham, that political institutions are the work of men. But he emphasises, far more than does Bentham, that Will is the basis of all institutions, including the State. And this Will, for him, is not only dependent on numbers, it has a qualitative foundation, and the Will which makes institutions takes on the form of a belief, almost of a religion. Hence Mill can say, as Bentham never could, "one person with a belief is a social power equal to ninety-nine who have only interests." Not the least important of Mill's alterations in Benthamism is that he comes to regard the State as a product of will rather than of interest, and that he recognises, as Bentham did not, that mechanistic theories of the State are fundamentally inadequate if they leave out the human will or if they neglect the personality of men.

In all these alterations that he makes in Benthamism, Mill may think that he is defending it, but in fact he is destroying it. Nevertheless, he introduces one change which is sounder Utilitarianism than Benthamism itself. In his writings the negative character of the State largely disappears. In his *Political Economy* Mill reveals a clear appreciation of the weakness of the assumption that the pursuit of individual happiness will result in social happiness. This assumption, he realises, ignores the fact that men differ in strength and ignores, too, the effect of historical conditions. If men's environment represents the accumulated inequality of the past, then they do not start equal in the race of competition. Land, industry, knowledge are the monopoly of a small minority. The whole legal system has been made for and by that small minority. This being so, Mill shows a good deal of sympathy for Socialism and wishes to use the State to remove obstacles in the way of the individual's development and to make life tolerable for the masses. Mill has none of Bentham's regard for property. There is for him no sacredness attaching to landed property. It is to be judged entirely by its utility, and by this test it must be concluded that private property in land is not expedient, it is unjust. Similarly Mill advocates compulsory education supported by the State out of taxation—and even though he does not wish to see the curriculum laid down by the State he insists that there must be general inspection by the State. He is ready to limit the right of inheritance, maintaining that no one must have more than a certain maximum. He supports factory legislation, at least in the case of children. He thinks that practical monopolies should be controlled by the State. He would limit working hours, and, in general, he goes far in asserting the right of the State to intervene in economic affairs. In all this he is being far more Utilitarian than Bentham, showing that on the grounds of general happiness, far more State activity is necessary than ever Bentham contemplated in his *laisser-faire* State. Though even here, when he is being more Utilitarian than Bentham, it should be noticed that Mill's non-Utilitarian principles make their appearance. In all disputed cases he regards the presumption as being against the State—a view which cannot be justified according to the principle of Utility. And he remains in favour of private enterprise since only through the struggle for personal independence can man develop the moral qualities essential to a man—an intelligible point of view, but one which depends on a scale of values which is non-Utilitarian.

The Reluctant Democrat

In his *Liberty* and *Representative Government*, Mill shows himself very distrustful of democracy, yet he is both a democrat and the greatest of English writers on democracy. No one has been less blind to the faults of democracy. No one has insisted more vigorously that it is not suitable for all peoples. But no one has been more convinced that where it is possible it is the best of all governments.

He is a democrat because he believes, as did Bentham, that such is the innate selfishness of men that each individual's rights and interests are best defended by himself. "The passion of the majority," he was sure, "is needed to conquer the self-interest of the few." However, he is not entirely consistent here. He admits that rulers are governed as much by the habitual sentiments of their class and by the traditions of their office, as by their selfish interests. And in his *System of Logic* he says that accountability is not necessarily the best way of obtaining identity of interest between ruler and ruled.

He is a democrat because he believes, as also did Bentham, that freedom is the means to prosperity and that without prosperity there can be no happiness. He would have heartily agreed with Bronterre O'Brien when he said, "Knaves will tell you that it is because you have no property you are unrepresented. I tell you, on the contrary, it is because you are unrepresented that you have no property."

But Mill is a democrat above all, not because he believes that democracy makes men happier, but because he is convinced that it makes them better. "One of the benefits of freedom," he says, "is that under it the ruler cannot pass by the people's minds, and mend their affairs for them without amending them." For he knows that the development of character depends on the exercise of character, and it is because of the beneficial effect of citizenship upon the citizen that it is so important. The only education in citizenship that is worth anything at all is actually being a citizen. Being responsible, serving on juries, casting one's vote, these are, Mill says, as necessary to the political animal as is the air that it breathes to the natural animal. In the whole history of Political Thought there is no loftier conception of voting than his—"In any political election, even by universal suffrage, the voter is under an absolute moral obligation to consider the interests of the public, not his private advantage, and give his vote to the best of his judgment, exactly as he would be bound to do if he were the sole voter, and the election depended upon him alone. His vote is not a thing in which he has an option; it has no more to do with his personal wishes than the verdict of a juryman. It is strictly a matter of duty; he is bound to give it according to his best and most conscientious opinion of the public good. Whoever has any other idea of it is unfit to have the suffrage. Instead of opening his heart to exalted patriotism and the obligation of public duty, it awakens and nourishes in him the disposition to use a public function for his own interest, pleasure, or caprice: the same feelings and purposes, on a humbler scale, which actuate a despot or oppressor."

But although Mill is sure that however poorly fitted men may seem for democracy they can only learn to swim in the water, he is sufficient of a Utilitarian, or perhaps one should say he has sufficient common sense, to say keep out of the water if you are certain of being drowned. His view that the only education in citizenship that is worth while is actually being a citizen is not incompatible with his other view that democracy is not possible for all peoples. But where society is ready for democracy, then he is certain that all its adult members, women as well as men, must participate in it. He was the advocate of women's suffrage. He was the first to speak for that in Parliament. He was intimately connected with the London Committee of the Society for Women's Suffrage. No one can be denied to be a democrat who sees as he does what an important part democracy has to play in that development of individual men and women which for him is the object of political association. "The worth of a state in the long run," he writes in a noble passage, "is the worth of the individuals composing it; a state which postpones the interests of their mental expansion and elevation to a little more of administrative skill, or of that semblance of it which practice gives in the details of business, a state which dwarfs its men, in order that they may be more docile instruments in its hands even for beneficial purposes, will find that with small men no great thing can really be accomplished; and that the perfection of machinery to which it has sacrificed everything will in the end avail it nothing, for want of the vital power which, in order that the machine might work more smoothly, it has preferred to banish."

By the mid 19th century, however, it was not as easy as for Bentham to concentrate exclusively on the theoretical virtues of democracy. For by then a democracy had existed for long enough for its practical drawbacks to be obvious. In 1835 De Tocqueville published the first part, and in 1840 the second, of his *Democracy in America*, the most brilliant and penetrating study of America ever written. Mill called it "the first analytical inquiry into the influence of Democracy." He was so impressed with its profundity that for many years he maintained a correspondence with De Tocqueville, a correspondence in which incidentally he makes his most violent comment on things political. "For my part," he writes, "I would walk twenty miles to see Palmerston hanged, especially if Thiers were to be strung up along with him."

The coming of democracy De Tocqueville regarded as inevitable, but he believed that it rested with man to make it a good or an evil thing. Democracy in America, he found, safeguarded the interests of the majority and greatly developed the faculties of the people; but it resulted in a general want of merit in legislative and public functionaries, and it produced a tyranny of the majority which, in Mill's words, did not "take the shape of tyrannical laws, but that of a dispensing power over all laws." "The people of Massachusetts," he added, "passed no law prohibiting Roman Catholic schools, or exempting Protestants from the penalties of incendiarism; they contented themselves with burning the Ursuline convent to the ground, aware that no jury would be found to redress the error. The laws of Maryland still prohibit murder and burglary; but in 1812, a Baltimore mob, after destroying the printing office of a newspaper which had opposed the war with England, broke into the prison to which the editors had been conveyed for safety, murdered one of them, left the others for dead, and the criminals were tried and acquitted." In no country, De Tocqueville considered, was there less independence of thought than in America. Once public opinion has settled a question, there can be no further discussion of it for, he says, "Faith in public opinion is a species of religion, and the majority its prophet." Mill comments, "The right of private judgment, by being extended to the incompetent, ceases to be exercised even by the competent; and speculation becomes possible only within the limits traced, not as of old by the infallibility of Aristotle, but by that of 'our free and enlightened citizens' or 'our free and enlightened age.' "

De Tocqueville's general conclusion, with which Mill agreed, was that as mankind advanced towards democracy there might be not too great liberty but too ready submission; not anarchy but servility; not too rapid change but "Chinese stationariness." The danger was that man would lose his moral courage and his pride of independence. He might not be able to resist the temptation to give the State too much power. He might "on condition of making itself the organ of the general mode of feeling and thinking, suffer it to relieve mankind from the care of their own interests, and keep them under a kind of tutelage; trampling meanwhile with considerable recklessness upon the rights of individuals, in the name of society and the public good." Democracy, in fact, might be but the prelude to a new era of slavery. As Nietzsche was later to say, "the democratisation of Europe will tend to produce a type prepared for slavery in the most subtle sense of the term."

Nor was De Tocqueville's the only voice critical of American democracy. Others were appalled at the materialism of a civilisation in which it had to be said that the whole of one sex was devoted to dollar hunting and the whole of the other to breeding dollar hunters. Dickens commented with all a novelist's freedom on the dollars, demagogues and bar-rooms which played such a part in American life. His listing in *Martin Chuzzlewit* of the New York papers—the New York Sewer, the New York Stabber, the Family Spy, the Private Listener, the

Peeper, the Plunderer, the Keyhole Reporter, the Rowdy Journal, is an extreme, but legitimate, caustic comment on the culture of democracy. Perhaps it is as well that he did not know that Seward, the American Secretary of State, was to come into a Cabinet meeting gleefully waving the latest Dime Novel, portraying the exploits of one Seth Jones, Indian fighter and scout. Dickens says of the democratic politician, "He was a great politician, and one article of his creed, in reference to all public obligations involving the good faith and integrity of his country, was 'run a moist pen slick through everything, and start fresh.' This made him a patriot." "Liberty," he concludes, "pulls down her cap upon her eyes, and owns oppression in its vilest aspect for her sister."

Mill was convinced that what was true of America was true of England also. Moreover, he believed that human nature "is so poor a thing." In his *Essay on the Subjection of Women* he asks us to consider how vast is the number of men in any great country who are little better than brutes. That whole essay, as Fitzjames Stephen says, "goes to prove that of the two sexes which between them constitute the human race, one has all the vices of a tyrant and the other all the vices of a slave." He is convinced of "the present low state of the human mind." He writes of "the extreme unfitness of mankind in general, and of the labouring classes in particular, for any order of things that would make any considerable demand upon their intellect and virtue." Men, he thinks, are so little given to reflection and so little capable of control that they are blind to the obvious effect of the "devastating torrent of children" on "the niggardliness of nature," which for him is so fundamental a fact. He says, in words which the 20th century will certainly one day have to recall, that "the niggardliness of nature, not the injustice of society, is the cause of the penalty attached to over-population." He is appalled at the "common, uncultivated herd," but he is no less dissatisfied with those who think themselves apart from it. He never lost that disillusion which at seventeen he expressed in a letter which bears all the arrogance of youth with none of its mitigating generosity—"at Yarmouth dined with a leading Radical; not much better than a mere Radical." The best he could find to say of the people of England who might, he thought, be sufficiently advanced to have a democratic government was that in England "the higher classes do not lie; and the lower, though mostly habitual liars, are ashamed of lying."

Holding such views of his fellows, it is not surprising that Mill is afraid of the stifling effect of public opinion, "whose ideal of character is to be without character." England, he says, is no longer producing great individuals—her greatness now is all collective. "Men of another stamp," he writes, "made England what it has been, and men of another stamp will be needed to prevent its decline." Pressure of society, he fears, is even dehumanising men. He laments, "by dint of not following their own nature they have no nature to follow; their human capacities are withered and starved; they become incapable of any strong wishes or native pleasures, and are generally without either opinions or feelings of home growth, or properly their own."

De Tocqueville's warnings could not but make more urgent these fears. Indeed, the example of America was the more challenging as the Founding Fathers themselves had been so suspicious of the people. To Hamilton the people was "a great beast." Adams said, "The People unchecked is as unjust, tyrannical, brutal, barbarous and cruel as any King or Senate possessed of uncontrolled power." If, now, in America, "the first minds of the country are as effectually shut out from the national representation, as if they were under a formal disqualification," it seemed as if Schiller was right in saying that the State where majority and ignorance rule must collapse ("Der Staat muss untergehn, früh oder spät, Wo Mehrheit siegt und Unverstand entscheidet"), and that the future was indeed grim.

The question Mill asks himself, then, is: How can I make democracy safe for the world, how can I ensure that this inevitable process will be for the good and not the evil of mankind? And his answer is well summed up in words which Lord Lothian once used with telling effect to an Indian audience, "Democracy is not a gift to be conferred, but a habit to be acquired. It cannot succeed unless it produces a race of aristocrats—and an aristocrat I would define as one who puts more into life than he takes out of it."

Mill was certain that democracy can produce aristocrats so defined. His basic assumption is that men are made what they are by their education. When he says in his autobiography that any child of normal intelligence, having the advantage of his training, would have developed as he did, he is not being falsely modest, but is speaking the simple truth as he sees it. Therefore he believes that right education can make men aristocrats. And by education he does not mean that which is exclusively concerned with books and academic studies. "The main branch of the education of human beings," he says, "is their habitual employment." He is an advocate of industrial as well as of political democracy. He believes, too, in education "in and through the exercise of social duties." Because if men realise democracy democracy will realise men, it should follow, he thinks, that democracy need never be short of those natural leaders without whose vision any people under any form of government will perish. And he believed that such aristocrats would be listened to if only men would make one all-important distinction—the distinction between False and True Democracy. "The democracy of numbers," which has been condemned, as he points out, by all the great masters of political thought "as the final form of the degeneracy of all governments," is False Democracy. The principle, "Every man to count for one; no man for more than one," is, he thinks, a principle of False Democracy. For it implies the belief that any man is as good as any other, a belief which not only ignores the obvious differences of intelligence and virtue between men but which Mill believes to be "almost as detrimental to moral and intellectual excellence as any effect which most forms of government can produce." "Exclusive Government by a class" is False Democracy. The principle of one man one vote, would mean such a government, a government of the least educated class, of the manual labourers.

True Democracy will give due weight and influence to all the different elements of society, and will thus obviate the undue preponderance of any. It will give men of worth plural votes—"but it is an absolute condition that the plurality of votes must on no account be carried so far that those who are privileged by it, or the class, if any, to which they mainly belong, shall outweigh by means of it all the rest of the community." It will insist on Proportional Representation. It will abolish the ballot since "people will give dishonest or mean votes from lucre, from malice, from pique, from personal rivalry, even from the interests or prejudices of class or sect, more readily in secret than in public." It will have a Second Chamber in which will be especially represented those factors in the national life which will never be adequately represented in an assembly popularly elected, so composed as to "incline it to oppose itself to the class interests of the majority, and qualify it to raise its voice with authority against their errors and weaknesses." True Democracy will never allow M.P.s to be paid, since thereby "the calling of a demagogue would be formally inaugurated." It will insist that representatives are true representatives and not mere delegates. It will not ignore the "radical distinction between controlling the business of government and actually doing it," but will realise that the true function of a Parliament is not to administer but to watch and supervise the administration. It will recognise the limits of the State's authority and will leave individuals to do things whenever they can do them better than the State, whenever, even if they cannot do them as well as the State, it is nevertheless desirable that they should do them as a means of self-education, and whenever there is a danger of adding unnecessarily to the Government's power. It will never be blind to the danger of a powerful bureaucracy, aware that "the governors are as much slaves of their organisation and discipline as the governed are of the governors." And it will be alive to the danger of majority tyranny, for it will know that "the silent sympathy of the majority may support on the scaffold the martyr of one man's tyranny; but if we would imagine the situation of a victim of the majority itself, we must look to the annals of religious persecution for a parallel."

Mirabeau once declared that "Representative Assemblies can be compared to maps which reproduce all the elements of a country in their due proportions so that the greater elements do not make the smaller elements disappear altogether." It was in the sense that he spoke of Representative Assemblies that the British Government in the 18th century could claim to be representative. The theory of representation held in England prior to the Reform Bill of 1832 was that representation should be of interests and not numbers, and it was precisely because the franchise was unequally and capriciously distributed that the House of Commons was said to be a real epitome of the nation. It was claimed that whereas under a system of universal suffrage every section of the people in a minority would have no representation, under the existing system there was no section of the community that had not the chance to return a member to Parliament.

Eighteenth-century Englishmen were extremely reluctant to exchange this representation of interests for a representation of numbers. "I see as little of policy or utility, as there is of right, in laying down a principle that a majority of men, told by the head, are to be considered as the people, and that as such their will is to be law," Burke declared. Coleridge denounced the authors of the Reform Bill as doing "the utmost in their power to raze out the sacred principle of a representation of interest, and to introduce the modern and barbarising scheme of a delegation of individuals." Canning was emphatic that, "For my part I value the system of parliamentary representation for that very want of uniformity which is complained of—for the variety of right of election." And Francis Horner, no Conservative, said, "I see a good deal of practical benefit result, even to the interest of liberty and popular rights, from the most rotten parts of the constituent body." There is indeed much to be said for Bagehot's claims that "the English Constitution of the last century, in its best time, gave an excellent expression to the public opinion of England," and that "the representation of the working classes then really existed."

The affinities between this old view of the Constitution and Mill's True Democracy are obvious. It is a paradoxical conclusion that this old view of representation which, in supporting the Reform Bills he himself was actively concerned to abolish, might yet have played an important part in reconciling Mill to democracy. Without it he might never have been a democrat. With it to shape his distinction between False and True Democracy there can be no doubt that he is entitled to be regarded as a democrat, albeit by 20th-century standards a reluctant democrat.

His Importance

The predicament of a man who was constrained by a process of indoctrination perhaps without parallel to profess loyalty to a system of thought against which in his inmost being he rebelled, who therefore persisted in believing that he was only refining whereas he was in fact undermining that system, has often been commented upon. Those for whom coherence and consistency are the major virtues will not look with admiration upon John Stuart Mill.

Moreover, it has to be admitted that Mill can be naïve and contradictory as well as confused. In his attempt to prove that happiness is desirable, he is responsible for one of the weakest arguments in the whole gamut of political philosophy. "The only proof capable of being given that an object is visible," he says, "is that people actually see it. In like manner, I apprehend, the sole evidence it is possible to produce that anything is desirable is that people actually do desire it. No reason can be given why the general happiness is desirable, except that each person, so far as he believes it to be attainable, desires his own happiness. This, however, being a fact, we have not only all the proof which the case admits of, but all which it is possible to require, that happiness is good: that each person's happiness is a good to that person, and that the general happiness, therefore, is a good to the aggregate of all persons." The difference which Mill ignores here between the words visible and desirable is of course fundamental. Visible can only mean what can be seen, but desirable means what ought to be desired as well as what is actually desired. Mill has only asserted that people do in fact desire happiness, not proved that they ought to desire happiness. And it is sophistry to suggest that because each man's happiness is a good to himself that it follows that the general happiness is a good to the aggregate of all men. Anything that adds to my happiness will add to the general happiness, but it does not follow that anything that increases the general happiness will add to mine. Mill's attempt to show that each should pursue the happiness of the whole as a means to his own pleasure completely fails to reduce altruism to egoism, and merely shows how logically impossible it is to believe as he did that happiness is the sole criterion of goodness and that men have only desired happiness. For if men can only desire happiness which alone is good, it must follow that whatever men desire is good. This is to abolish the notion of goodness altogether, for if an action cannot be bad it certainly cannot be good.

And if some of Mill's proofs are inadequate, some, which it is really much more important for him than for either Bentham or James Mill to provide, are entirely non-existent. He simply assumes, as they had done, that men should be treated as equals. But he makes pleasures differ in quality, as they did not, and it is easy in consequence to argue that the happiness of those whose higher faculties are well developed is worth more than the happiness of those who know only lower pleasures. Plato's republic would provide a greater development of the higher faculties than a democratic government in which the ignorant, selfish majority prevailed. Failure to defend the principle of basic equality of right among men is a real weakness in Mill's defence of democracy.

Few would deny that his view of liberty as the absence of restraint is inadequate. An age which has realised as Mill's was only beginning to that in an industrial civilisation rules are indispensable, and that if political power does not make them private power will, demands a more positive view of liberty than Mill was able to provide.

Similarly his individual will appear to the 20th century far too isolated and therefore unreal a figure. For Mill, who has far more idea than his father or Bentham of the emotional and historic forces that hold society together, has yet no appreciation of the formative role of associations in society. He remains on the whole hostile to corporate life within the State, although he is willing to recognise trade unions so long as they remain purely voluntary organisations.

Moreover, he himself goes far to admitting that he is hardly justified in basing his philosophy upon the autonomous individual when he attacks the ballot on the ground that publicity will check men making selfish use of their vote. For if men acting together are better in common than each would be individually, then it would seem that society is better than the individuals who compose it. And there would seem to be something wrong with a philosophy which makes so much of the autonomous individual when the autonomous individual can obtain goodness only when he ceases to be autonomous.

One may add, too, that Mill's acute sense of the weakness of his fellows is a remarkably insecure foundation for his belief in their liberty. It is, to say the least, difficult to reconcile his low view of human nature with what must seem to a later age, which has no longer the excuse that his had to believe in the inevitability of progress, the wild optimism that enabled him to write "all the grand sources, in short, of human suffering are in a great degree, many of them almost entirely, conquerable by human care and effort."

Besides, powerful and valuable as is his defence of freedom of opinion, it does not remove all doubts. He tells us nothing about the problem that so concerned Milton in the 17th century and that is of vital importance to us today. Should we tolerate the intolerant? What should our attitude be towards a small party working in the interests of a hostile foreign power who would use the freedom accorded to them to make freedom impossible for everyone else? Is there not a danger in attaching too much importance to discussion? There will, no doubt, always be believers in the eccentric theory that ignorance plus flatulence equals knowledge. And men can be forgiven if they sometimes respond to persistent probing as Doctor Johnson occasionally did to Boswell when he used to ask questions which the good Doctor declared were enough to make a man hang himself. Too much discussion may be a sign of weakness and instability; may, as Burke said, "turn our duties into doubts." Mill admitted as much in his essay on Coleridge—an admission that is very difficult to reconcile with the views he put forward in his *Essay on Liberty*. And we may well doubt if truth is as easy to discover as Mill thought, and if man's mind moves society to anything like the extent that he believed.

We will find it, in short, difficult to accept his view either of society or of politics. As individuals we both lack the power he ascribed to us and are not as amenable as he thought to the reason which he so constantly recommended to us. We cannot call into question all the traditions and customs into which we are born for we are the heirs of all the ages fashioned in the image of a thousand yesterdays and we will fly to all the moons that are before we learn to live each day as if it were our first— and that is what Mill is urging us to do. We should not forget, as he does, that the political process is one conducted under the permanent presidency of power and that if ideas contend men fight and use ideas as weapons in the fight. And we should doubt whether politics are as much concerned with perfection as he suggests when he says that "all the grand sources of human suffering are in a great degree, many of them almost entirely, conquerable by human care and effort," should wonder whether it is really the aim of politics to charter our course to the Garden of Eden and to give us the key when we get there.

Yet when all the criticisms that can be are brought against him, he remains far and away the most satisfactory of the Utilitarians. He touches depths that Bentham and his father never knew existed. He has his own unreality, but he is much closer to life than they are. Indeed, not the least of his importance is that, though unintentionally, he so completely demonstrates the inadequacy of Utilitarianism, its ethical aridity, its blindness to the emotions.

But if he does this, he shows also its real strength. He never loses sight of the individual men and women who make up the State. It exists for them, not them for it. Mill will have nothing to do with organic theories of State and Society. Moreover, like Locke, he is writing with Englishmen in mind, and his individual men and women, despite their exaggerated and artificial isolation, are recognisable Englishmen. And the problems which interested him then concern them no less nearly today. He wishes to determine the limits of collective control. Hence his much criticised division of actions into self- and other-regarding. Yet he never supposed that any other than a rough division was possible, and reliance on even so rough a rule seemed to him far safer than granting absolute moral rights to the majority. He was interested in the preservation of personality in the age of the large-scale—and so are we. To Ritchie writing in 1891 it might seem that Mill absurdly exaggerated the importance of eccentricity. We, who have felt the full weight of radio and cinema and newspaper, who have, as Nietzsche said, put the newspaper in place of the daily prayer, who know with Berdiæff how much "the machine wants man to adopt its image and its likeness," who have seen the terrible dehumanising work of that manufactory of souls, the Totalitarian State, can only feel thankful for Mill's fine protest against machine-made uninspiring dullness. He wanted to safeguard democracy against itself—a desire which contemporary uneasiness would suggest is certainly astir within us, even though we would naturally prefer to safeguard other peoples against their democracy than ourselves against ours. It would be to commit the sin of hybris and to invite the adverse attention of the gods to assert too confidently that he was necessarily wrong even in the means he suggested to this end. At least this is sure, that when in the storm and stresses of contemporary life Englishmen feel the need to refresh themselves in the faith of their fathers they will not think of Mill's works as they do of antimacassars and aspidistras—as dated and done with, displeasing to God, unprofitable to man and fit only to collect the dust.

CHAPTER III

THE STATE AS ORGANISM
(ROUSSEAU, HEGEL, GREEN)
The Inadequacy of the Tradition of Will and Artifice

TOWARDS the end of the 18th and increasingly throughout the 19th century men became dissatisfied with the theory which regarded the State as a machine. It was, they believed, unrealistic to look upon individuals as so many isolated atoms—as writers of the mechanistic school were only too apt to do. It was profitless to study men apart from society. It was wrong to set the desire for liberty which men feel against the necessity for authority under which they labour, defining the one solely in terms of the individual and the other in terms of the State. So misleading, in fact, was the antithesis "State" and "Individual," so dear to the hearts of those who regarded the State as a machine, as to make impossible any true analysis of man's relations with his fellows and with the State. Liberty is not mere absence of restraint. It is doing something worth doing, it is identifying ourselves with some law which we feel corresponds to our truest desires, our real self, whether we call that law the Law of Nature with the Stoics, the Divine Law with St. Paul, the Law of Reason with Kant, or the General Will with Rousseau. The State, they concluded, was not an enemy of liberty, but the only means of achieving it. It was unworthy of man to look upon him, as too often those who saw the State as a machine did, as a creature dedicated to the pursuit of pleasure and the avoidance of pain. That was to ignore that which in man makes him desire to be something more and better than he is, to forget that "Unless above himself he can exalt himself, how mean a thing is man." It was to overlook the truth that Lamartine so well expressed:

> "Borné dans sa nature, infini dans ses vœux
> L'homme est un dieu tombé qui se souvient des cieux."

Men thus felt a need for a more satisfactory answer to the question: "Why does the State exist and why should man obey it?" than any that could be supplied by the machine theory of the State. The 18th-century interest in history, the new tendency to give a general coherence to history in terms of growth and decay, strengthened that need. So did the development of nationalism, since it is easier for men to fall down and worship a State that is not presented to them as a mere machine of their own making. The State accordingly began to be portrayed as the embodiment of the nation. The basis of the State became a naturally homogeneous people, united by common descent and community of ideas, traditions, loves. The State-organism became the unconsciously evolved organisation which maintained the unity of the nation and gave expression to its will. State-personality was said to be attained when national self-consciousness had developed and had revealed itself in the constitution. The powerful attraction of new scientific discoveries made that need yet more acute. Throughout history men have shown themselves quick to believe that a new scientific advance could somehow be made of universal application. In the ancient world Pythagoras, recognising the great importance of mathematics, concluded that everything could be reduced to numbers. In the 17th century political and social theories were modelled on the type of mathematics then so highly thought of, in the 18th century on the physical sciences then developing, in the 19th century on the natural sciences then making so great an advance. To the "political algebra" of Rousseau, to the "social mathematics" of Condorcet, succeeds first the "social physics" of St. Simon, then the "social physiology" of Comte and finally his "Natural History of Societies." Though the modern theory of evolution at first seemed to strengthen the machine view of the State, it soon had the very opposite effect, and biology as well as the tradition of historical cohesion and the growth of nationalism fortified men's demand for some more adequate interpretation of the nature of the State. So did the economic and industrial development which drew men ever tighter into national societies as the 19th century wore on, and the breakdown of *laisser-faire* with men's consequent conversion to the advantages of collective responsibility and control. Reaction to the very materialism of a scientific age also played its part in making that demand still more insistent.

The Organic View of the State

A more satisfactory answer to man's speculation about the State was found in the organic view of the State, that view which regards the State no longer as a machine but as a living organism. The essentials of this view were already apparent under the Greeks, though later writers were to make far greater play than they had done with the parallel of the State and the human body. In modern theorists who refer to the State as an organism, no mere analogy or metaphor is intended. The State is regarded not as being like an organism, a person, an individual, but as actually being an organism, a person, an individual.

This view of the State was put forward by what may be called the biological school of political theorists that flourished in the 19th century. They pointed to the similarity of the growth of living beings towards a higher life and the development of political institutions. In both they found increasing differentiation of the parts and growth in the variety of needs felt. As higher forms of organic life are reached, they indicated, organisms become more definitely and delicately controlled, activities become increasingly self-directed until there emerges the self-conscious individual, and from the different development of individuals many classes, genera and species are evolved. So it was, they maintained, with political society. As the advance of civilisation produces increased social needs and activities, the organisation of the State becomes more complex and is endowed with greater power. The exercise of that power becomes more obviously self-directed, that is in the interests of the State itself rather than in the personal interests of those wielding the State's power, and finally States assume different forms in different environments until definite classes, genera, species can be seen. Sometimes, indeed, writers of this biological school displayed a wealth of ingenuity in finding close biological parallels between the State and the natural man. They spoke of the "tissues" of the State, of its systems of nutrition and circulation, of organs within it fulfilling specifically the functions of brain, nerve, fibres, heart, muscles, even stomach and nose. The Foreign Office of the State corresponded to this latter organ according to Bluntschli—a comparison which in the light of Soviet practice might have more to recommend it than could at one time have been thought. Bluntschli further maintained that the State was of the masculine sex, while the Church was feminine.

Others who were more moderate than the writers of the biological school, who were wise enough to appreciate the limitations of ingenuity, who were content to admit the differences between plants and animals on the one hand and States on the other, nevertheless maintained that the State was indeed an organism. Plants and animals, they said, were only two species of organisms, and together they did not exhaust the genus organism. The claim of the mollusc, they contended, to be an organism would not be rejected because it isn't a mammal, and the claim of the State to be an organism need likewise not be rejected because it isn't an animal. In any case, they maintained, in philosophical discussions the term "organic" must be allowed to have a broader application than to the phenomena of biology. There are, they said, three essential characteristics of an organism so understood. Firstly, there is an intrinsic relationship of the parts to the whole. The parts, though they may retain a certain relative independence, become what they are by virtue of their relationship to the whole. A part of a machine retains its essential character even when separated from the machine. A wheel is still a wheel though no longer working in a machine. But a hand is no longer a hand when separated from the body. In an organism when the parts cease to be parts they cease to be organic, and the relationship of part to whole is therefore intrinsic, while in a machine the relationship of part to whole is not. Secondly, in an organism development takes place from within. There can be no such inner development in a machine which may be altered by the substitution of new parts for old, but which cannot grow. An organism, on the other hand, cannot be altered by the substitution of new parts for old, but it can grow and thereby gradually transform itself. Thirdly, the end for which an organism exists lies within itself. It is the development of its own life and that of other lives in which it is reproduced. A machine, on the other hand, is a contrivance adapted to the realisation of an end outside itself. An organism, therefore, is a whole whose parts are intrinsically related to it, which grows and develops from within and which has reference to an end that is involved in its own nature.

The State, we are told, possesses these three characteristics, and must therefore be regarded as organic. Its members, it is true, do not "observe degree, priority and place" in quite the way that members of an animal organism must do if that organism is to survive. It must be admitted that as Wordsworth said in contrasting the sun and man:

> *"He cannot halt nor go astray,*
> *But our immortal spirits may."*

It must be further allowed that man's highest development sometimes seems in isolation from his social environment. Goethe declared that he had to tread the wine-press alone, and Hegel wrote: "In nothing is one so much alone as in philosophy."

> *"Two desires toss about*
> *The poet's feverish blood;*
> *One drives him to the world without,*
> *And one to solitude."*

That is true for all of us, for we must live within ourselves as well as among our fellows. And there is a truth that the Stoics would have recognised in the assertion with which Ibsen concludes *An Enemy of the People*—that "the strongest man on earth is he who stands most entirely alone." Yet we are all, even the strongest of us, very largely what inheritance and environment have made us. Indeed, it seems to be precisely in the strongest of men that the spirit of the times most personifies itself, so that Napoleon claiming to be the force of the French Revolution could say of himself: "I am not a person, I am a thing." So much are we part of society that, as Comte said, it is impossible even to give utterance to the "blasphemous" doctrine that we are independent of it, since the very expression of independence involves the use of language which is itself dependent on society. Thus the whole is essential to the parts, and however lonely a man's walk may seem, he can never completely dissociate himself from society. He can therefore be said to stand in an intrinsic relationship to it and to the State, which is society organised as a sovereign political body. In the State, too, we are told, we can see that inner development which is characteristic of an organism. Though the individual is moulded by society, it is nevertheless through the development of individual lives that society grows—that is, society, and with it the State, develops from within. Further we are asked to see in the State the third characteristic of an organism. It is an end in itself, and that end, whether we define it as the full life, the good life, the happy life, is included in its own nature. To regard it as an instrument of something else is therefore false and pernicious. Thus exhibiting all the characteristics of an organism, philosophically defined, the State, it is urged, is rightly to be regarded as an organism.

Some who wished to differentiate the State still further from the "natural" or "physical" organism, since this reveals no knowledge of the type towards which it tends and is powerless to accelerate or retard its own progress whereas the end of the State is one that makes an appeal to the rational nature of its members and one which their direct efforts must help to realise, preferred to call the State a "Super-organism," an "Organism of Organisms." Others spoke of it as a "Moral" Organism. Yet others referred to it as a "Real Person" or as a "Super Person," purifying or fulfilling the lesser persons of its citizens.

But however varied the nomenclature adopted by those who believe in the organic view of the State, they hold certain beliefs in common. They regard the State as an end in itself, something which subserves no other end. They see that end as the full development of all the latent capacities of the State and its members. They view the State as a whole which is greater than the sum of its parts. In Ritchie's words, "the body corporate is mysterious, like the personality of the individual." Therefore the interests of the whole are not necessarily the same as the sum of the interests of the parts. Thoroughgoing organic theorists, indeed, hold that the parts can have no real interests themselves, any more than hands or teeth or feet can have real interests. As only the interest of the individual to whom these belong matters, so only the interest of the State is essential. The parts must accordingly be subject to the authority of the whole. The parts may have some independent, if restricted, existence—they may have rights within the State, but they can never have rights against the State. The sovereignty of the State and the liberty of the Individual, so the organic theorists believe, are not really opposed. True freedom is to be found in obedience to the State's laws. Only when this is realised can the end of the whole be seen to be also the end of every part, for when it is realised and acted upon, the individual will be developing himself to the highest level of which he is capable and the State will be completely fulfilling itself. Further, organic theorists make no distinction between State and Society, and they do not regard all States as being equally good, since some are more completely integrated than others. The organic State is the ideal towards which civilisation is moving, not the point from which it starts, and not all States have advanced equally along that road.

This, then, is the organic view of the State, a State which is no mere contrivance of man, no mere device for getting things done, but which in Burke's glowing words is "to be looked on with other reverence; because it is not a partnership in things subservient only to the gross animal existence of a temporary and perishable nature. It is a partnership in all science; a partnership in all art, a partnership in every virtue; and in all perfection. As the end of such a partnership cannot be obtained in many generations, it becomes a partnership not only between those who are living, but between those who are living, those who are dead, and those who are to be born."

It is the aim of this chapter to analyse the ideas of three writers who in their very different ways illustrate the organic view of the State, of Rousseau who still made use of a good deal of mechanist terminology, who retained to the end a greater love of individualism than, strictly speaking, is compatible with organic doctrines, but whose contribution to the growth of the modern organic theory is nevertheless of the greatest importance; of Hegel who can be regarded as the representative *par excellence* of the organic State, and of T. H. Green who adapted it to English needs and who, reflecting as did Locke the English belief that logic is no necessary ingredient of political success, showed, as also did Locke, that common sense can frequently be more satisfactory in a political theorist than a ruthless determination to work out ideas to their logical conclusions.

JEAN JACQUES ROUSSEAU, 1712–1778

The Conflicting Interpretations

Few men have more affected the mind of the modern world than Jean Jacques Rousseau. His, so Bergson tells us, was the most powerful of the influences which the human mind has experienced since Descartes. He left the stamp of his strong and original genius on politics, education, religion, literature, and it is hardly an exaggeration to say with Lanson that he is to be found at the entrance to all the paths leading to the present. Yet there has been no writer about whom it has been more difficult to find agreement than about Rousseau. He has been greatly lauded and more maligned. He has been hailed as the philosopher who has seen most deeply into the nature of the State since Plato. Yet much of what the French, for whom the writing of recent history is an expression of political faith, have said of him had better remain untranslated. He was, for instance for Voltaire, who dispensed with irony in commenting on one whom the philosophes had wished to claim as their own and who contented himself with expressing philosophical disagreement in the measured language of cultured and considered condemnation, a "charlatan savage," a "hoot-owl," a "Swiss valet," a "bastard of the dog of Diogenes and the bitch of Herostratus." He has been regarded as the apostle of the Noble Savage, running wild in native woods, strong, magnificent, uncorrupted, and free. Rousseau made him itch to go on all fours, said Voltaire. Yet he has also been portrayed as passionately pleading for us to develop ourselves still further from the savage state, as a greater Statue of Liberty beckoning men with torch aloft lighting their way to a greater freedom and a higher culture than they have ever known. Even among those who share this latter view, however, there is deep disagreement. "Rousseau believed with passion in progress," Laski writes. "The idea of progress is one which we certainly cannot attribute to him," Cobban declares. No eminent writer, it is said, has ever been so full of contradictions. He tells us both that property is the root of all evil and that it is a sacred institution. He pleads for individual liberty and insists on absolute submission to the State. He wants toleration for all and banishes atheists from his republic. His work, comes the emphatic rejoinder, constitutes an essential unity. He is said to be a great thinker, one of the greatest. He never enjoyed "the distinction of knowing how to think," Morley replies. He is the extreme individualist, the latest and greatest of the individualist political theorists. Bonald declared that he wished "to make constant the inconstant, to order disorder," and Lamennais wrote that his work was "a sacrilegious declaration of war against society and against God." He is the extreme absolutist, the precursor of 19th-century German idealism. Constant said of him: "He is the most terrible ally of despotism in all its forms." Duguit wrote: "J. J. Rousseau is the father of Jacobin despotism, of Cæsarian dictatorship, and the inspirer of the absolutist doctrines of Kant and of Hegel." He is both extreme individualist and extreme absolutist. "A stern asserter of the State on the one hand," Vaughan wrote, "a fiery champion of the individual on the other, he could never bring himself wholly to sacrifice the one ideal to the other."

It is at least surprising to find that the man of whom so many different views are possible is a brilliant and lucid writer, a master of the finest prose. Indeed, there is none finer since Plato in the whole history of political thought. We dare not believe that he could not adequately express what he wanted to say. But he had the dangerous gifts of epigram and paradox, and the greatest of writers if he indulges them too frequently is open to misunderstanding. Such phrases as: "Let us lay aside all the facts, for they have no bearing on our problem," "The man who meditates is a degenerate animal," "Man is born free and is everywhere in chains," are more arresting, provocative, even inspiring, than clarifying. Moreover, Rousseau rarely troubles to define his terms very clearly, and indeed uses them—as, for instance, the term "nature"—in different senses at different times. And because he touched so many fields of thought that innumerable specialists have felt bound to take note of him, it is not surprising that they have interpreted him to suit themselves. The anthropologist takes his "natural" man to be the primitive man, the psychologist to be the unchanging man, the moralist to be the ideal man to whose development all the ages are leading. To the idealist philosopher the idealist in Rousseau is of supreme importance, to the individualist thinker the individualist in him alone matters. Knowing therefore the difficulty of classifying Rousseau in any school of political thought, it will be profitable to examine what he has to say, and then to sum up those reasons which have seemed strong enough to justify his inclusion among those who teach the organic theory of the State.

His Idea of Nature

Rousseau grew up in the rigorously Calvinist atmosphere of the small city state of Geneva, of which his father was a frugal if somewhat unstable master-craftsman citizen. Throughout his life, in spite of his conversion to Catholicism, in spite of Geneva shaking off her errant son, his affection for his home remained undimmed and strongly coloured his political thought. He himself was the most restless of men. Everything by turns and nothing long, he was never completely at home in any profession, in any science, in any religion. Now domestic servant, engraver, tax collector, private tutor, now music copyist, diplomatic secretary, musical performer and composer, he was more truly, as he said of himself, "the lonely wanderer." He could not tolerate external restraint. He was a man of great sincerity, hating sham, loathing the life of the salons and of Parisian society. He was a man of the deepest feeling, of great tenderness, of extreme susceptibility. Reverie he found easier than reflection. What touched his heart straightway unloosed his tongue.

When he came to Paris it seemed likely that he would ally himself with the Encyclopædists. Had he done so he would have been a made man. But he chose to unmake himself—he quarrelled with them and he refused to be presented at Court. Background and temperament made him protest against the artificiality around him. The philosophes, he said, "know very well what a citizen of London or Paris is, but not what a man is." And because their rationalism contented itself with what he could not, he became increasingly aware that their rational agnosticism was not for him. Voltaire, for instance, admired Catherine of Russia, and was unimpressed by the trifling circumstance that she had murdered her husband. Against the reason which could find excuses for that, Rousseau appealed to conscience, to the moral sentiment of man. In the *Discourse on the Origin and Foundation of Inequality*, he undertook to show what was the nature of man. In what seemed little short of deification of nature, he portrayed man as living in a past golden age, prompted by conscience, not yet led astray by the harlotries of reason, still uncorrupted by that perennial propagator of evil, that confidence trick of the ages whereby the rich induce the poor to accept them, that great deformer of man which calls itself society. Yet that was not really his view of man and his nature, that was not really his view of reason, that was not really his view of society. Because he was the enemy of one kind of reason, we must not conclude that he was the enemy of all reason; nor must we believe that black men with knobkerry and assegai in Africa, or red men with tomahawk and scalping knife in America, represented for him the end of all man's striving.

It is true that his belief that nature is always right was the foundation on which his whole thought rested. But he emphatically did not mean by this that animal desire should be man's only guide, that the nature of man was one with the nature of the brute, that to be natural man must be a savage—in spite of the passages in his writings in which he idealises the State of Nature, passages which are so vivid and colourful precisely because they reflect his own passionate rejection of restraint.

There are, he thought, two original instincts that make up man's nature. There is self-love or the instinct of self-preservation, and there is sympathy or the gregarious instinct. Since these instincts are more beneficial than harmful, it follows that man is by nature good. But self-love and sympathy will frequently clash, and when they do, how shall man know which to follow? He will wish to satisfy both, since that is his nature, and from this wish to do what will help others as well as what is necessary for himself is born a sentiment which is natural to man and older than reason, a sentiment which men call conscience. But conscience is only a blind sentiment, a desire which man feels to do right for himself and for others. It will not teach man what is in fact right, but will merely make him want to do what is right when he knows what that is. Conscience itself requires a guide—and that guide is reason, which develops in man as alternate courses of action present themselves before him. Reason teaches him what to do and conscience makes him do it. Thus it is obvious that for Rousseau, conscience and reason are in close attendance on man and together restrain the desire that is in him. Hence the "natural" man will be one in whom strong conscience and steadfast reason have successfully harmonised self-love and sympathy, the "unnatural" man one in whom these elemental instincts have been warped or suppressed while conscience sleeps and reason errs.

Reason, however, will seek not only to harmonise but also to develop man's instincts, to give them the fullest expression. For this, culture and society will be necessary. The freedom of action that man alone enjoys distinguishes him from the brute. At first sight it might seem that man living in a State of Nature must have much more freedom of action than man living in society. True, such a man will know independence, since he will be independent of the law of man and dependent only on those laws of things to which all earthly creatures are subject. Yet he will, in fact, be a slave to his appetites, in bondage to his pleasure.

Only society can give full meaning to the freedom of action which is man's, can turn independence into true liberty. In society, indeed, man will be dependent on the laws of man as well as on the laws of things. In society he will know duties as he never knew them before. But in society he will gain what independence could never give him, rights which are assured by a strength greater than his own, unmeasured freedom to do not what captivates his passing whim but what his inmost nature demands. In society his "natural" sympathy, for instance, will become rational benevolence. In society, if he can obey the law not because he has to but because he wants to, if he can give perfect obedience to his civil duty, he will attain moral liberty, he will be really himself. As a gardener who clears away the undergrowth from around the sapling and who by constant attention helps it to become a finer tree than it would have been without his loving care, so society will be to man. As the tree so cared for will be more truly a tree than if it had been left unaided, so man will be more truly "natural" than if left to live out his life in a primitive state.

Perfection of man's nature by his reason and through society is man's destiny. Why, then, has he never fulfilled it? Compound of self-love and sympathy, with conscience added unto them and reason to help, man has only to be true to himself to make his way to the stars. But it is not easy for man to be true to his nature. It is, in fact, so hard that Rousseau doubts if there ever has been or ever will be a natural man. For man's self-love, which satisfies his real needs, is only too apt to become pride, which creates imaginary and utterly insatiable needs, and which is incompatible with man's instinct of sympathy. From pride all evil has grown and gone ranging round the world devouring men. Pride seduces reason herself until, forgetting man's true nature, she proves the most reckless and irresponsible of guides. She builds an imposing culture around nature, but she is like the gardener whose art is to warp and twist the tree until he imposes upon it a form not naturally its own. The society which she develops, therefore, moulds man not according to but against nature. And as the malformed tree is less truly a tree than it would have been if left severely alone, so man in such a society is less truly "natural" than if left in his state of nature.

We can now see what Rousseau means in exhorting man to

return to nature. If he wishes to be saved, he must renounce pride and content himself with that self-love which is natural to him. He must rescue reason from pride, so that, leaving conscience uncorrupted to follow the right and leave the wrong, she will lead him to virtue, fulfilling, not distorting, his nature, until it becomes plain to all that the most "natural" of men will also be the most virtuous and the most cultured. It can be said, then, of Rousseau that "nature" for him was ahead of, not behind, political development. His protest, in his book *Rousseau Judge of Jean Jacques*, that he had never intended to put the clock back is valid. Far from seeing man's nature as at its best in the Noble Savage, it is clear that he viewed nature as did Aristotle, for whom the nature of a thing was what it was capable of becoming under the best possible circumstances. This idea runs all through Rousseau's work, giving it an underlying unity. In the *Discourse on the Sciences and Arts,* he attacks the false art which deforms nature and corrupts man. In the *Discourse on the Origin and Foundation of Inequality* he portrays the natural man and shows how a society which denies his nature warps him. In *Emile* he deals with the education that can be expected to produce the natural man. In the *Social Contract* he writes of the ideal state in which alone the natural man can reach his full stature. In the *Savoyard Vicar's Profession of Faith* he speaks of the religion of the natural man. And if this essential unity is rather the unity of poetry that one feels than the unity of philosophy that one sees, that is no matter for surprise when dealing with a man like Jean Jacques Rousseau, and it is none the less unity for that.

His Idea of the State

It is in the *Social Contract* that Rousseau's idea of the State is most clearly seen. This work was originally planned as part of a bigger whole which was never completed. It is, however, a unity in itself. It is unlike his other works in that it was meditated upon for years before it was written. It is much more rational, much less emotional, than the rest of his writing. And it is unquestionably much the most important of his works. In it is to be found most boldly set out his recognition that "everything is at bottom dependent on political arrangements, and that no matter what position one takes, a people will never be otherwise than what its form of government makes it." In it is to be found most clearly his answer to the question, "What is the State and why should I obey it?"

He starts with the belief that the family is the only "natural" society. All other society, he thinks, is of man's making and artificial. But he rejects the view that society other than the family must rest on force. It rests, he concludes, on agreement. Men register their agreement to come together in society in the Social Contract. The idea of some such contract was, of course, a commonplace of political philosophy of his day. The Social Contract was not, however, in his view a contract whereby the first society was established—although at times he is tempted to regard it as such. It is a contract whereby the right society will be set up—in the future, not in the past; the society which will substitute "justice for mere instinct," which will give to "man's actions that moral character which they lacked before," which will change man from "a stupid and limited animal" into an "intelligent being and a man."

The Social Contract is not a contract which men make with their future ruler. The Government is merely their agent. To make a contract with it would not only give it a dignity to which it ought not to pretend, it would place men under the rule of some individuals or groups, which would be nothing but slavery. Such a contract would defeat the ends for which men come together, those ends being the fulfilment of their nature, which slavery would make impossible. For men not only need society in which to develop; without freedom they cannot develop. Therefore their problem is to create a society "in such a way that each, when united to his fellows, renders obedience to his own will, and remains as free as he was before."

This is possible, Rousseau says, where the law leads and men do not obey other men but obey only the law. "How can it happen," he asks, "that men obey without having anyone above them to issue commands, that they serve without having a master, that they are all the freer when each of them, acting under an apparent compulsion, loses only that part of his freedom with which he can injure others?" "These wonders are the work of the Law," he replies. "It is to Law alone that men owe justice and liberty; it is this salutary organ of the will of all that makes obligatory the natural equality between men; it is this heavenly voice that dictates to each citizen the precepts of public reason, and teaches him to act in accordance with the maxims of his own judgment, and not to be in contradiction to himself." But what is the Law? Rousseau calls it the "universal voice." It is the voice of the General Will. And what is the General Will? Unfortunately it is not easy to answer precisely. Though it is the most important and most fertile idea in all his political writings, Rousseau is very vague in what he has to tell us about it.

If I join an association, I may continue to think only of my own selfish interests. If I and all my fellow members do this, there will not be much life in it. On the other hand, I may begin to think not of my own selfish interests but of its interests. Only if I and all my fellow members learn to think in this way will the association grow strong and live. If we do think in this way we will be generating a public spirit or, as Rousseau would say, a General Will for the association. What is true of lesser associations is true of the State, and the General Will is thus the will of all the citizens when they are willing not their own private interest but the general good; it is the voice of all for the good of all.

Rousseau goes further and says that my will which wills the best interests of the State is my best will, is, indeed, more real than my will which wills my private interests. "The most general will"—that is, the will for the good of the State—says Rousseau, "is always the most just also." All actions are the result of will, but my will for the good of the State is morally superior to any other will, private or associational, which may from time to time determine my conduct.

Rousseau has still something more of the greatest importance to add. So far the General Will as he has defined it has been the attribute of individual citizens—of all citizens willing their best wills for the general good. But he also believes it to be an attribute of the State itself. Every association, he thinks, which calls forth the public spirit of its members, also calls into being a "group mind" which is something other than and bigger than the sum of the minds of the individuals composing it. Many who have known the intimate life of associations have agreed with him. Maitland, for instance, said that any who had experience of committees came to recognise the emergence therein of an "It that is not us," of something that was not the same as the sum total of the individual outlooks of the members of the committees. Rousseau called such a Group Mind developed by the State

"Un Moi commun"—a common Me. "The body politic," he says, "is also a moral being possessed of a will." The General Will it appears therefore is a "Group Mind," as well as being the compound of the best wills of all citizens willing the best interests of the State.

It follows from all this that the General Will must be Sovereign. Since it is my best will, my own real will, I ought always to want to follow it. If in fact I don't, if the affections of the flesh so war within me that what I should I do not and what I should not that I do, then the General Will can legitimately compel me to obey it. Indeed, it is the only authority that can legitimately coerce me, for it is my own will coming back to me even though I do not always recognise it as such, and in following it I am fulfilling myself and am thus finding true freedom. "Whoever refuses to obey the General Will shall be compelled to do so by the whole body," Rousseau writes. "This means nothing less than that he will be forced to be free; for this is the condition which, by giving each citizen to his country, secures him against all personal dependence." Since also the General Will is a Group Mind which is bigger than mine though mine is a part of it, I must obey it on that score too. "If the State is a moral person whose life is in the union of its members, and if the most important of its cares is the care for its own preservation, it must have a universal and compelling force in order to move and dispose each part as may be most advantageous to the whole." The State, in fact, must have absolute power "as nature gives each man absolute power over all his members also."

The General Will, therefore, though by definition it can only deal with matters of public, not private, interest, can alone be the judge of what constitutes public or private interest. The General Will, moreover, cannot allow anything to stand between it and the complete loyalty of its citizens. It would, Rousseau believes, be better that lesser associations than the State should not exist, but if they do they must always be subordinate, and if any conflict of loyalties should ever occur, citizens must always obey the State. So jealous a God is the General Will that Rousseau thinks it should even substitute for the old religions of the world a new civic religion which all who would remain members of the State must accept, deviation from which, once accepted, should be an offence punishable with death.

The General Will must also, he says, be inalienable and indivisible. Hence it cannot be represented in parliamentary institutions. "As soon as a nation appoints representatives," he says, "it is no longer free, it no longer exists." England, he declared, was only free during elections, after which it is "enslaved and counts for nothing." "The use which it makes of the brief moment of freedom renders the loss of liberty well deserved," he adds. Nor can the General Will be delegated in any way whatever. Any attempt to delegate it will mean its end. As he said: "The moment there is a master, there is no longer a sovereign." Nothing less than all the people together can be trusted to will the General Will. As Rousseau expressed it, it is only "the voice of the people" that is "the voice of God."

The General Will must be a will which is general in every sense and which is particular in none. It must take account of the voice of every citizen, since it was agreed in the Contract that each is received as an "integral part of our group." It must bind all equally, since that also is implied in the Contract in which each surrenders his all on equal terms, so that it is "in the interests of none to make them onerous to his fellows." It must deal only with the generalities of legislation, with the common cause and not with private interests—though it alone will decide what is the common cause and what are private interests. It is, in fact, only the fundamental laws that shape the constitution of the State that Rousseau regards as law, and therefore as the product of the General Will. All that we know as civil and criminal law would not be law to him, but only decrees of the Government and not to be invested with the sanctity of the General Will.

It must follow from this that the General Will, as Rousseau insists, cannot be an executive will. The people ought not to be responsible for the details of Government. Those who make the law should not carry it out, for it is the characteristic of the Sovereign General Will that it must be impersonal, and the decrees of Government may frequently be particular and personal. Hence Rousseau makes a clear distinction between the Government and the Sovereign People. The People entrusts its executive power to its agent, the Government, though it may retain a limited right of supervision over it. As it is thus subordinate to the Sovereign, the actual form of the Government is a matter of secondary importance, varying according to the particular circumstances and needs of men. S long as the General Will is Sovereign, it does not matter if the Government is a democracy, an aristocracy or a monarchy—whichever in the existing circumstances is most suitable will be the best. Rousseau's preference is clear. It follows from the reasons he advances for separating the Sovereign and the Executive that he can hardly regard democracy as the best form of Government. Democracy, he believes, is too perfect for men—as they are "it is contrary to the natural order that the majority should govern and the minority should be governed." Since men are too imperfect for kingship, kings have a habit of becoming tyrants. Hereditary aristocracy is, in general, the worst of all forms of Government and elective aristocracy the best. But all men are not alike, and what suits one will not suit another. Variety in the forms of Government is therefore natural and of little moment so long as one thing is constant—the Sovereignty of the General Will.

The General Will, Rousseau adds, is infallible. In what he says here, he is not at his happiest or most lucid. He means little more than that the General Will must always seek the general good. "The General Will is always right and tends to the public advantage," he says. He does not mean by this that whatever the State does must always be right. If the General Will is always right, it is not always known. It does not follow, he adds, "that the deliberations of the people are always equally correct. Our will is always for our own good, but we do not always see what that is; the people is never corrupted; but it is often deceived, and on such occasions only does it seem to will what is bad." For the *raison d'état* that has been put forward to excuse every crime in the decalogue, Rousseau has no manner of use. "If it be said," he writes, "that a Government can sacrifice an innocent man for the welfare of the whole, I hold this maxim for one of the most execrable that ever tyranny has invented." So that in saying that the General Will is always right, Rousseau means only that men must never forget that they come together for the sake of the good life and should do nothing to make that good life impossible. He is not saying "Because the State is moral, it cannot deny itself and act immorally," but "If the State acts immorally it is denying itself and is no true State." That is an intelligible, even desirable, position to assume, though unfortunately it is lacking in any clear indication of what constitutes an immoral action and who is to determine its immorality.

We now know a good deal about the General Will. It is the result of all men willing their best wills for the good of the State. It is the "Group Will" of the State. It is Sovereign. It has certain marked characteristics. But still we do not know how it is to be found, though we can appreciate from what Rousseau had to tell us about its infallibility that finding it is unlikely to be a simple matter. Unfortunately Rousseau cannot help us here. He can never tell us how we can be sure of finding the General Will. At times he seems to suggest that the General Will is to be sought only when all unanimously agree—though he has already told us that the Will of All is something very different from the General Will. At times he implies that the General Will is the will of the majority—though he tells us elsewhere that this can only be so if "all the characteristics of the General Will are still in the majority." At times it appears that the residue left when differences of opinion expressed by all the citizens have cancelled one another out is to be regarded as the General Will. Yet again the General Will may be embodied in one man —a Legislator who will show people what is good for them. This, however, is only likely at the beginning of the State's life, and if it occurs the Legislator must not be regarded either as Sovereign or as Magistrate. He is to be seen merely as the proposer of laws, not compelling but persuading the people to accept them, with God up his sleeve as the ace which will win him the game. "This," Rousseau says, "is what has in all ages compelled the fathers of nations to have recourse to divine intervention and credit the gods with their own wisdom, in order that the peoples, submitting to the laws of the State as to those of Nature, and recognising the same power in the formation of the city as in that of man, might freely obey, and bear with docility the yoke of the public happiness." So much vagueness about something as important as the finding of the General Will is to be regretted. Rousseau, who has told us so much about the General Will, has still not told us enough; indeed, he has left us in such a position that nobody can be sure what the General Will is on any particular question.

Rousseau's inability to tell us exactly how we may find the General Will perhaps reflects his belief that it would never be easy for men to will it. The illustration of the General Will that he gives in *Émile* is sufficient proof of that. There he recounts the story of the Spartan mother who, on rushing to the runner to ask news of the battle and being told of the death of her five sons, answered: "Vile slave, was it this I asked thee?" Demanding how the battle had gone and learning of the victory, she ran to the temple to give thanks to the gods. Such a triumph of public over private interest could not, Rousseau knew, have been easy. Yet without that triumph there could be no General Will. So difficult, indeed, did he think it would be for men to will the General Will that he believed that the majority would not be capable of it. His republic was not for them. Not sufficiently intelligent, nor sufficiently public-spirited to know liberty, they would know instead the yoke of a master.

But Rousseau was sure that some men were capable of possessing liberty. They would find it, he was convinced, only in States of a particular kind. Such States must be small, so that when necessary all citizens could gather together. They must be conservative, so that little legislation would be required. The State in which alone freedom appeared to him to be possible could be no other than the small, non-industrialised city-state of the type that he knew at home in Geneva. Bentham was right in saying that except for the laws of the Republic of San Marino, the laws of no European State would be recognised as valid by Rousseau. What he thought of larger communities can be seen from his pregnant remark: "The greatness of nations, the extent of states; the first and principal source of the misfortunes of the human race." Rousseau was sure, too, that his Contract had no meaning for those who failed to find the General Will. Failure to arrive at it meant for him that the State was unable to accomplish the purposes of the Contract, the fulfilment of each individual. When this proved to be so, the individual was free to return to the State of Nature. But, above all, Rousseau was sure that only where the General Will reigned could man's nature be developed, only there can his great challenge "Man is born free but is everywhere in chains" be seen for what it is, not a deplorable but a legitimate fact because man, who is not fully human except as a citizen, can reach his full stature only in the great community of the State. There, in greater freedom than he had ever known, more truly man because of the blossoming and fulfilment of his nature, perfected man would at last enter upon that rich inheritance which had been locked away in the bosom of the ages awaiting his coming.

Rousseau's Place in Political Thought

We can now try to answer the question: Where does Rousseau stand in the history of Political Thought? His great debt to the Greeks is obvious enough. His work is the long-delayed re-assertion of the Aristotelian view that man is a political animal whose nature can be fulfilled only in the State, which is therefore no longer the result of his vice but the condition of his virtue, the chief agent of morality. Plato's voice rings strongly through his words, telling us again that subjection to the State is a matter of ethics rather than of law. Nor can it be doubted that his attachment to the city-state is as much the result of Greek inspiration as of Genevan example.

Rousseau believes, then, as did the Greeks, that the full life of man is possible only in society. He also believes that ultimately only the individual matters. His *Émile* makes it clear that the pupil is to be educated for his own sake, not for that of others. His sense of independence is to be stimulated, he is to be taught to regard himself always as an end and never as a means. Similarly Rousseau has Mme de Wolmar declare in the *New Héloise*: "Man is too noble a being to serve simply as the instrument for others, and he must not be used for what suits them without consulting also what suits himself. It is never right to harm a human soul for the benefit of others." In this spirit he repudiates, as we have seen, the doctrine of *raison d'état*. In the margin opposite Helvétius's view that "all becomes legitimate and even virtuous on behalf of the public safety," Rousseau writes: "The public safety is nothing unless individuals enjoy security." His Protestant background, his powerful, eager, if somewhat peculiar conscience, his hatred of "the hideous head of despotism" which would never allow him to associate himself with the Benevolent Despots, his love of liberty which found such passionate expression as his assertion: "When a man renounces his liberty he renounces his essential manhood, his rights and even his duty as a human being," which led him to comment on Aristotle's view that some men are slaves by nature, that men can only be slaves by nature if they have first been made slaves against nature, and which led him to prefer the abuse of liberty to the abuse of power—these are real in Rousseau and must not be forgotten in the insistence that only in society did he believe that the good life can be lived.

From his writings, in short, two answers to the question,

"What is the nature of the State and why do I obey it?" emerge. The first is that the State is a collective person, and that I obey it because only in so doing am I really myself, am I truly free. The second is that the State is an association entered into by man, or even a mechanism built by man for his own purposes, and that I obey it to achieve those purposes and only in so far as I persuade myself that I am achieving them. The first answer, corresponding to his doctrine of the General Will, reflects an organic view of the State; the second, corresponding to his use of the Social Contract, reflects a mechanistic view. Rousseau tries to hold both, which is why so many conflicting interpretations of his work are possible.

But we must ask if the two views to which Rousseau is attracted can really be held simultaneously, and, if not, which of the two we must regard as claiming his major allegiance. Can the State be both organism and association or machine? Can the General Will be made in any worth-while sense compatible with the Social Contract? The answer must surely be that the two views are not compatible and that not all of Rousseau's strict qualifications can make them so. For if the General Will is supreme, the Social Contract is unnecessary and meaningless, and if the Social Contract is necessary and significant, the General Will cannot be supreme. In insisting on both the General Will and the Social Contract, Rousseau is not so much demonstrating his skill as synthesiser as illustrating the danger of falling between two stools, in that he retains a sufficiently lively sense of the importance of the individual conscience to make him accept only with hedging and with reluctance the implications of the organic State, but a sense far too weak to give any encouragement to the individual to resist the collective majesty of the State.

Actually there can be little doubt that ultimately it is the organic view of the State that Rousseau embraces. That is to be seen in his description of the State as "a moral and collective body," "a common me." It can be seen clearly in his doctrine that my best will is not necessarily my actual will and that since there can be no infringement of my liberty in my being compelled to obey my own will even though I do not recognise or acknowledge it as such, I can be forced to be free. It is reflected in his determination that no association or Church be allowed to come between the individual and the State. It is apparent in what he says of Christianity, every word of which breathes the recognition that the most uncompromising enemy of the organic State is a religion with other-worldly values. It is particularly clear in his insistence that all within the State shall conform to the Civil Religion on pain of expulsion or death, and in his view that the State may teach compulsorily those doctrines which are held by the majority. And if further proof be required, it is plain to be seen in Rousseau's ideal of Patriotism, in those declarations, which are alive with the organic thinker's passionate love for the whole of which he is a part, that "the patriotic spirit is an exclusive spirit which makes us regard as a stranger and almost as an enemy any who is not a fellow citizen," or that "a child, when first opening its eyes, should see its motherland, and should be able to see nothing else until its death."

The frontispiece of the first edition of the Social Contract was a picture of Leviathan with his head cut off. Yet we must conclude that against Leviathan Rousseau was unable to provide adequate safeguards for the individual. He failed to reconcile the two views he held that the good life was possible only in society and that ultimately only the individual mattered. On the contrary, he succeeded only in dwarfing the individual. If he had succeeded in reconciling those two views, then one of the most common and compelling criticisms—namely that they are utterly unable to make provision for the individual conscience and for individual longings for liberty—could no longer be brought against the organic theorists. As such a man as he was failed to reconcile them, at least that criticism of the organic school still stands, and perhaps one must even conclude that it cannot be answered. In any case, we do not need the undoubted fact that organic theorists who followed him drew much of their inspiration from him to make us hail him as an upholder of the organic State. His own work bears the hall-mark of the true organic writer, and accordingly it is with the organic theorists of the State that he must be classed.

GEORGE WILLIAM FREDERICK HEGEL, 1770–1831

His Life and Writings

The most outstanding advocate of the organic theory of the State and one of the most important and influential thinkers of modern history was Hegel. Born in 1770 in Würtemberg, he passed his youth in the intoxicating days of the French Revolution, with which for some time he felt a warm sympathy, as did so many young men of his generation, but against which he ultimately strongly reacted. Private tutor, lecturer at Jena University, headmaster in Nuremberg, he became on the publication of his three-volume work on the Science of Logic the most loudly acclaimed of German philosophers. Appointed to a professorship in Heidelberg, he wrote his *Encyclopædia of the Philosophical Sciences*, the fullest treatment of his general philosophical system that he ever produced. From there he accepted the chair of philosophy at Berlin University, of which he later became president. Here he acted as the official philosopher of Prussia, exercising an influence such as few professors have ever done, becoming as it were the academic voice of Prussianism, just as von Roon and von Moltke were to be its military and Bismarck its political voice. Here he wrote his *Philosophy of Right*, and gave the lectures which after his death were published as the *Philosophy of History*, working out that theory of the State which has gone marching down the years, siring new and strange political philosophies, and giving ever louder expression to his own convenient conviction that the heir of all the ages was the Prussian monarchy and that the latest files of time were those daily thumbed over by the busy bureaucrats of Berlin.

By so many for so much of the 19th century he was hailed not merely as the official philosopher of Prussia, but as *the* philosopher of the age, just as Aristotle and St. Thomas Aquinas had for so long been regarded as *the* philosophers of their times. Critics called him "a flat-headed, insipid, nauseating, illiterate charlatan, who reached the pinnacle of audacity in scribbling together and dishing up the craziest mystifying nonsense." They applied to his writing Shakespeare's words "such stuff as madmen tongue and brain not." They said of his theory of the State that it grew "not in the gardens of science but on the dunghill of servility." German philosophers have always been as notorious for the acrimony of their philosophical discussions as for the weightiness of their philosophical writing. But most believed that he had synthesised all knowledge as Aristotle and Aquinas had done in their day, that he had found the fundamental laws which govern all reality. He said of himself: "Although I could not possibly think that the method which I have followed might not be capable of much perfecting, of much thorough revising in its details, I know that it is the only true method. It is clear that no method can be accepted as scientific that is not modelled on mine." He was sure that he had solved all the riddles of the universe. His modest opinion of himself was accepted as no more than the truth, so much so that after his death his devoted pupils wondered what was left for philosophy, mourning like Alexander the restricted state of the world. Even English philosophy, which traditionally was of that empirical kind which he so disliked and which he regarded as a trashy over-the-counter commodity fit only for a nation of shop-keepers, felt his influence, and in Green, Bradley, and Bosanquet tackled the difficult problem of how to express his philosophy in English without making it appear gibberish.

Although there is some truth in Lord Acton's words that "Ideas . . . are not the effect, but the cause of public events," political philosophers have not usually exercised a very important immediate effect on the world of practical politics. They have, as a rule, done more to interpret an existing world than to shape a new one. Hegel himself believed that it was the function of philosophy to explain but not to create. "When philosophy paints its grey in grey," he wrote, "one form of life has become old, and by means of its grey it cannot be rejuvenated but only known. The owl of Minerva takes its flight only when the shadows of evening are fallen."

Yet few philosophers have had a greater effect on the everyday world than he had. For he displayed a remarkable insight into the political realities of his time. He foresaw, for instance, the industrial, constitutional State then painfully struggling into life. He once said: "Political genius consists in identifying yourself with a principle," and with a sure instinct he identified himself with the principle of nationalism. His teaching that each people had its particular genius, its own "spirit of the people," that each people had its own peculiar political institution which had grown as it grew, and that the institutions of one people could not be imposed on another, even his contradictory message that some nations less virile than others had forfeited their right to political independence which thereby safeguarded that liberty which a people seeking national liberty has always highly prized —the liberty to deny liberty to others, all was bound to make a tremendous appeal to that nationalism which was to prove itself the strongest of 19th-century forces.

Later German statesmen were proud to acknowledge their

debt to him. Bismarck's work, with its insistence on the organic nation State, maintained by force, directed by an all-powerful monarchy and bureaucracy, admitting in international relations no principle higher than its own welfare, bears the clear reflection of Hegelian inspiration. So, too, does Nazism and Fascism. Their extreme nationalism, with their attendant, unprincipled conduct of international relations and their glorification of war as the purger and purifier of society, their acceptance of the constantly exercised, all-pervading power of the State, their authoritarianism, their acclamation of the Leader or Hero, their stress on the importance of guilds and corporations in the Corporate State, their insistence, seen clearly in Hitler's constant reference to his intuition and in Mussolini's frequent assertion that theory follows not precedes action, that instinct plays a greater part than reason in political life, are directly derived from Hegel. And if through Bismarck and the triumph of an armed and organic nationalism, Hegel's influence can be seen leading to Nazism and Fascism, through Marx and Engels it can also be shown operating strongly on Lenin, Stalin, and Communist Russia. Marx, whose powers of vituperation were as highly developed as his instinct to make use of them, was very gentle in his criticism of Hegel, seeing in his philosophy of the State "the most logical and the richest" ever produced. Even today Communists regret the little attention shown to Hegel in this country, contrasting British neglect unfavourably with official Soviet Russian recognition of his merit. Indeed, it can very plausibly be argued that Russia today is, after the collapse of Germany, Italy, and Japan, the most outstanding example of the Hegelian organic State.

Hegel's great influence on philosophy, on political philosophy, on politics, is not, then, to be denied. Unfortunately he is as difficult to understand as he is important. Language has frequently been accorded pride of place among the major arts of deception. Chinese scholars of old were not above indulging in the genial joy of writing so obscurely as to tax the erudition of their correspondents. But it has been left for German philosophers, appealing to a people conditioned by language and leaning to the view that obscurity and profundity are synonymous terms, to make occasional Chinese academic naughtiness their habitual practice, and there is no more trenchant commentary than Hegel's works on that most inappropriate of Nazi slogans :

"Deutsch sein heiszt klar sein"—"to be German is to be clear."
A technical terminology more shapeless, ugly, and impenetrable
than any other jargon, a truly awful style made still more un-
seemly by a love of ponderous paradox, yet adequately matched
by that wonderfully involved construction that makes the
Philosophy of Right such a difficult book to follow, these are
the hall-marks of Hegelian writing.

Moreover, the clearest, most subtly exact and delicate of writing would have been none too clear to convey Hegel's message.
His idea of the State is naturally enough merely part of his
general philosophy, and at the very least anyone who would
understand it must take into account a view of world history and
its patterns that is usually learned, sometimes convincing (as, for
instance, his presentation, in the *Constitution of Germany*, of
German history since the Treaty of Westphalia), at times ter-
ribly thin and inaccurate (as, for instance, his whole treatment
of Oriental history), but always involved and confusing. And to
the very considerable difficulties presented by the language and
by the construction of his books and by his highly peculiar his-
toricism, there is yet one further difficulty in understanding him,
that involved in grasping what he claimed to be a new kind of
logic, the dialectic which seemed to promise all things to all
men, but which, it is not surprising to learn since its appeal was
so universal, was not capable of precise definition. Realising,
then, his importance and the difficulty of explaining him clearly,
we must look more closely at his view of world history and at
the new method of interpreting it which he introduced.

Spirit and Dialectic

Hegel starts with the assumption that the universe is a coherent whole. In this organic unity what he variously calls the Idea,
or Spirit, or Reason, or the Divine Mind, is the only reality.
Everything, including matter and the external world, is the creation of this Idea or Spirit or Reason. Hence it is true to say that
"Reason is the sovereign of the world." It is the nature of this
Spirit or Reason, Hegel tells us, to know all things. As befits
one who borrowed so much from Aristotle, Hegel is using nature
here in the Aristotelian sense of that which anything becomes
when fully developed. At the beginning of the world-process the
Spirit or Reason does not, in fact, know anything; its nature is
as little achieved as is the nature of Aristotle's man before he

enters the Polis. Gradually, however, as it develops throughout the history of the world, it learns to know more and more, until it is led, finally and inevitably, to its goal which is perfect knowledge of everything, another way of saying, since it itself is everything, perfect knowledge of itself. As Hegel puts it: "The truth is the whole. The whole, however, is merely the essential nature reaching its completeness through the process of its own development. Of the Absolute it must be said that it is essentially a result, that only at the end is it what it is in very truth."

History is the process by which the Spirit passes from knowing nothing to full knowledge of itself, is the increasing revelation of the purposes of the Rational Mind. "The history of the world therefore," says Hegel, "presents us with a rational process." The Spirit on the way to its goal makes many experiments. Everything is, as it were, a mask which it tries on, which proves useful to it for the time being, and which it ultimately discards. "The universal mind at work in the world," he writes, "has had the patience to go through these forms in the long stretch of time's extent, and to take upon itself the prodigious labour of the world's history, where it bodied forth in each form the entire content of itself which each is capable of grasping, and by nothing less could that all-pervading mind ever manage to become conscious of what itself is." Or as he expresses it more briefly in his famous aphorism: "The rational is the real and the real is the rational."

It is to be noted that he is using "real" here in the sense of the important, or the fundamental. "In common life," he says, "any freak of fancy, any error, evil and everything of the nature of evil, as well as every degenerate and transitory existence whatever, gets in a casual way the name of reality." But it is not right to speak of that as "reality"; it is only "idle, worthless existence." Nevertheless, though he understands by "reality" that which is underlying and significant, not that which is merely empirical, he does not hesitate to conclude that "the insight to which philosophy is to lead us is that the real world is as it ought to be." Hence in his theory of the State he rejects Fichte's teaching that only the ideal State is rational whereas existing States are irrational, and he maintains on the contrary that actual, existing States are rational and are accordingly to be treated with all reverence. Hegel's strong tendency to idealise the actual is thus a logical consequence of his conviction that whatever happens happens because the Spirit needs it and that whatever the Spirit needs is right.

A doctrine which teaches that everything is as it ought to be and which idealises the actual has strongly marked conservative tendencies. But obvious and important as Hegel's conservatism is, we cannot conclude that his teaching is exclusively or even mainly conservative. For he believes that everything is experimental and destined to be transcended. Each form adopted by the Spirit helps it along the road to complete self-fulfilment, but each form represents only one step along that road and there are many, many more ahead. Throughout history the Spirit is incessantly giving birth to itself, suffering, dying, and rising to new glory. Thus Hegel's is a doctrine of change, and of change constantly for the better, a promise of assured progress. Change is thus as strongly marked a characteristic of his teaching as conservation. Indeed, if we had to find a heraldic device suitable for him, there would be a strong case for making it the phœnix constantly reborn, rising anew from the flames, rather than the changeless, timeless owl settling at Minerva's ear.

But Hegel not only tells us that history is the record of the march of the Spirit through the world, he explains in detail the process by which the Spirit changes from one being to another. In doing so, he introduces his famous principle of dialectic. The word "dialectic" is from the Greek "dialego"—to discuss or debate. As demonstrated by the constant questioning of Socrates, it was the process of exposing contradictions by discussion so as ultimately to arrive at truth.

It was not, however, thus that Hegel viewed dialectic, though another classical example might help us to understand what he meant by it. The Greeks had observed that anything if pushed too far will tend to produce its opposite. Absolute monarchy they noted, if pushed to the extreme of despotism, leads to violent reaction and to the establishment of democracy. Democracy if taken to the extreme of mob rule results in the climbing to power of a dictator. Later it was suggested that the rhythm of change was rather more complicated than the early Greeks had believed, that it was a triple instead of a dual rhythm. Monarchy changed first into aristocracy and only then into democracy. Democracy changed into dictatorship and only then into monarchy.

It was these ideas of the later Greek thinkers rather than the Socratic notion of dialectic which inspired Hegel. He believed that every being, except, that is, Reason or the Spirit when it has reached its goal, contains not only itself but in some sense its opposite. He believed also that the rhythm of change was triple not dual. But he breaks away from the everlasting classical treadmill. His conception of the triple rhythm of change is one that not only permits, but insists on the idea of growth. Every being, as Hegel expressed it, is to be understood, not only by what it is but by what it is not. The opposite of Being is Non-being, and Being and Non-being are alike summed up and carried further towards reality in Becoming. Each stage, or thesis, reached by the Ideal, until it has arrived at its goal, must fall short of perfection. Its imperfections will call into being a movement to remove them, or antithesis. There will be a struggle between thesis and antithesis until such time as a synthesis is found which will preserve what is true in both thesis and antithesis, the synthesis, in its turn, becoming a new thesis, and so on until the Idea is at last enthroned in perfection. The thesis "Despotism," for instance, will call into being "Democracy," the antithesis, and from the clash between them the synthesis "Constitutional Monarchy," which contains the best of both, results. Or the thesis, the family, produces its antithesis, bourgeois society, and from the resultant clash the synthesis, the State, emerges in which thesis and antithesis are raised to a higher power and reconciled.

The synthesis will not, Hegel insists, be in any sense a compromise between thesis and antithesis. Still less will it be an outright victory of one over the other. Both thesis and antithesis are fully present in the synthesis, but in a more perfect form in which their temporary opposition has been perfectly reconciled. Thus the dialectic can never admit that anything that is true can ever be lost. It goes on being expressed, but in ever new and more perfect ways. Nor, since everything is rational, can the dialectic ever admit that there can exist contradictions which can never be solved. Reality, in Hegel's words, may be like a "Bacchic dance in which there is not one of the constituents that is not drunk"; but the drunkards are divinely guided and reel always in the direction of home, and the end of all dialectical debauches is the attaining of the absolute which can be eternally contemplated without any imperfection or contradiction appearing in it.

It might be thought that this view of dialectic is not so very unlike that of Socrates, according to which contradictions are obstacles in the way of truth which we endeavour to remove when we become aware of them. Hegel would deny the similarity emphatically. For him contradictions are not obstacles preventing us reaching truth, but are essential to our very understanding of truth. Without them there would be no progress. He feels so strongly about this that in his dialectic he claims to have invented a new logic, a synthetic logic which is very different from the old analytic logic. This new synthetic logic, he maintains, eliminates the law of contradiction, according to which two contradictory propositions cannot be true at the same time. According to the new logic, then, something may at one and the same time be both true and false. "In itself it is not, so to speak, a blemish, deficiency or fault in a thing if a contradiction can be shown in it," he writes. "On the contrary, every determination, every concrete, every concept is a union of moments which pass over into contradictory moments. Finite things are contradictory in themselves." Moreover, it is not men who remove these contradictions, but Reason herself. It is not us, but the very force within the thesis and antithesis, which is Reason, which promotes development. Contradiction, or the dialectic, is therefore a self-generating process—it is "the very moving principle of the world."

Because it is this, dialectic is a theory which explains how it is that history is the story of the continuous development of the Spirit. Since all the former steps of the Spirit are preserved in the new ones taken, it emphasises the essential continuity of that story of the increasing revelation of the Spirit. But, typically, it also stresses the very opposite of the continuity of the historical process. It explains also that history is the story, not only of the quiet unfolding but of the bounding forward of the Spirit. Ideas, institutions, things change slowly and almost imperceptibly until a point is reached beyond which their very nature is suddenly transformed—as water after a gradual process of heating will suddenly become steam. This moment of sudden change, when seen in human history, might seem to involve in the catastrophic collapse of the old order such anarchy as would refute the view that change is always for the better. Certainly in such moments of change men may be extremely unhappy. But collapse, however apparently catastrophic, will not prevent what was true in the old order persisting, nor should it blind us to the fact that its attendant anarchy is but the path to a good greater than any known before. As for man's happiness, that, says Hegel, in what seems an odd echoing of the view "Happy the people which has no history," is no criterion. "The history of the world," he writes in the *Philosophy of History*, "is not the theatre of happiness. Periods of happiness are blank pages in it, for they are periods of harmony—periods when the antithesis is in abeyance." Dialectic thus claims to be a new system of synthetic logic, replacing the old system of analytic logic, a principle of self-movement through contradiction towards the final goal of perfect realisation of Spirit, a conception of ordered, rational progress which explains away periods of apparent anarchy accompanying the collapse of old orders as being themselves the misunderstood signs of progress to higher goods, a theory which is both essentially conservative and fundamentally revolutionary.

His Idea of the State

Against this background of Hegel's doctrine of Spirit and Dialectic, we can now turn to his view of the State and find his answer to the question: "What is the State and why do I obey it?" From what he has already said, his answer to that question must clearly be an answer in terms of the Spirit seeking its goal. But it is, after all, men with their interests and passions who compose the State. Hegel does not deny the existence of these interests and passions. On the contrary, he speaks of them very frankly. In words of which Gladstone was later to make considerable use, he wrote: "We assert, then, that nothing has been accomplished without interest on the part of the actors, and if interest be called passion, we may affirm absolutely that nothing in the world great has been accomplished without passion." Therefore Hegel's answer to the question: "What is the State and why do men obey it?" is an answer in terms, not only of the Spirit seeking its goal, but of men seeking to satisfy themselves in activity. "Two elements," he writes, "therefore enter into the object of our investigation, the first, the Idea, the second, the complex of human passion; the one the warp, the other the woof of the vast arras-web of Universal History." All things, according to Hegel, are forms assumed by the Spirit on its way to self-knowledge. Through its multiple embodiments it progresses from the inorganic world to the organic world of plants and animals, until it eventually comes to an imperfect consciousness in Man. Man is the highest physical or animal embodiment it has ever attained, or ever will attain, Hegel adds. Beyond Man there will be no further physical evolution.

But man is never a lone individual. He lives with others, and is dependent on them, as they are on him. Hence it is meaningless to consider him apart from the congeries of institutions which serve his needs and which are themselves the embodiment of the Spirit as it makes its way through the world. The earliest of these institutions which history reveals is the family, serving man's sensual needs, affording him and his a primitive protection, providing a precarious provision for simple needs. It is a unity which, as in China even in our own lifetime, is regarded by its members as being more real than themselves. The family, a unity incorporating the rational idea of mutual love, is thus the thesis from which Hegel begins his analysis of the State.

But the family is too small for the adequate satisfaction of man's wants, and as children grow up they leave it for a wider world. That world is what Hegel calls the world of bourgeois society, and it is the antithesis which is called into being by the original thesis, the family. Unlike the family, which is a unity regarded by its very members as being more real than themselves, bourgeois society is a host of independent men and women held together only by ties of contract and self-interest. Whereas the characteristic of the family is mutual love, the characteristic of bourgeois society is universal competition. But however cold and unattractive in comparison with the family bourgeois society might seem, there is a rational meaning to be discerned in it as well as in the family. The whole process of trade and industry in bourgeois society becomes a new organisation for the supply of human needs, so that man in that society is producing for his family, satisfying his own wants and at the same time serving his fellows, which makes bourgeois society take on a rational and universal significance. Moreover, bourgeois society evolves laws, even though not necessarily just laws; it creates a police force; and becomes more and more State-like in form. As it develops it produces guilds and corporations, which teach their members to think not of their own interests but of the interests of the whole to which they belong, and which, because they do this, reveal, not the social instinct, which is competitive, but the State instinct, which is co-operative. The thesis, the family, a unity held together by love, knowing no differences, is thus confronted by the antithesis, bourgeois society, an aggregate of individuals held apart by competition, knowing no unity, even though it is manifestly struggling towards a greater unity which it has nevertheless not yet attained.

The synthesis, which preserves what is best in thesis and antithesis, which swallows up neither family nor bourgeois society, but which gives unity and harmony to them, is the State. It does this because it is a super-organism, which is both family and society raised to a still higher power, and in which each, by consciously identifying himself with the whole, wills the interests of the whole, which he recognises as his own. Hence in Hegel's peculiar language it can be said: "The essence of the modern State is that the Universal is bound up with the full freedom of particularity and the welfare of individuals, that the interest of the family and of bourgeois society must connect itself with the State, but also that the Universality of the State's purpose cannot advance without the specific knowledge and will of the particular, which must maintain its rights. The Universal must be actively furthered, but on the other side subjectivity must be wholly and vitally developed. Only when both elements are there in all their strength can the State be regarded as articulated and truly organised."

There are several characteristics of this State that we must notice. To begin with it is no exaggeration to say that it is divine. It is the highest embodiment that the Spirit has reached in its progress through the ages. It is "the Divine Idea as it exists on earth." In all sobriety it can be called "the march of God on earth." It follows that Hegel makes no attempt, as does Rousseau, to square the circle and admit the possibility of a social contract. The notion that the State, which is the product of a long, unconscious but nevertheless divinely guided growth, can be explained in terms of a contract Hegel rejects with the utmost contempt.

The State also is an end in itself. It is not only the highest expression to which the Spirit has yet attained, it is "the final embodiment of Spirit on earth." There can thus be no spiritual evolution beyond the State, any more than there can be any physical evolution beyond man.

The State, too, is a whole which is far greater than the parts which compose it and which have significance only in it. "All the worth which the human being possesses," Hegel writes in the *Philosophy of History,* "all spiritual reality, he possesses only through the State." Individuals, therefore, must obviously be completely subordinated to the State. It "has the highest right over the individual, whose highest duty is to be a member of the State."

The State, moreover, is unchecked by any moral law, for it itself is the creator of morality. This can be seen clearly in its internal affairs and in its external relations. Firstly it lays down what shall be the standard of morality for its individual citizens. It goes without saying that they can never plead conscience or the moral law against it. Kant had believed that they could, that the individual conscience or the "practical reason" of the individual was the guide of guides to cling to. Hegel, going beyond Kant to Jean Jacques Rousseau, maintained that conscience can only tell us to do what is right. It cannot tell us what is right. Conscience itself must be informed by the traditions of the community. "The wisest men of antiquity," he says, "have laid it down that wisdom and virtue consist in living conformably to the customs of one's people," which are indeed "the collective reason of the past." And the State is the truest interpreter of the tradition of the community. Only it can tell us what is good, and conformity with its decrees, or Social Ethics, is thus the highest morality. "What the absolute aim of Spirit requires and accomplishes, what Providence does," Hegel writes, "transcends the imputation of good and bad motives. Consequently it is only formal rectitude, deserted by the living Spirit and by God, which those who take their stand upon ancient right and order maintain." More simply, whatever the State does is right, however high the apparent cost. And if the innocent are sometimes hurt, what else is to be expected? We can only say of the State: "So mighty a form must trample down many an innocent flower; it must crush to pieces many an object in its path."

Secondly, the State can recognise no obligation other than its own safety in its relations with other States. Its own welfare is its "highest law." "It is a generally acknowledged and well-known principle that the particular interest of the State is the most important consideration," he declares in the *Philosophy of Right.* Against this no plea based on hypothetic morality can be allowed. In the *Ethics* he writes categorically: "The State is the self-certain, absolute mind which acknowledges no abstract rules of good and bad, shameful and mean, craft and deception." International Relations, therefore, are relations between Sovereign States who believe that what is in their own interests is right and that the only sin is to act knowingly against those interests. "The fundamental proposition of international law [that treaties should be kept inviolate] remains a good intention," he writes. "States look upon the stipulations which they make with one another as provisional." Hence "when the particular wills of States can come to no agreement, the controversy can be settled only by war."

Moreover, war "is not to be regarded as an absolute evil." "The universal love of mankind" is an "insipid invention." War is itself virtuous activity. If one may misquote Acton, it can be said that for Hegel peace corrupts and everlasting peace would corrupt everlastingly. "War is the state of affairs which deals in earnest with the vanity of temporal goods and concerns —a vanity at other times a common theme for edifying sermonising. War has the higher significance that by its agency the ethical health of peoples is preserved in their indifference to the stabilisation of finite institutions; just as the blowing of the wind preserves the sea from the foulness which would be the result of a prolonged calm, so also corruption in nations would be the product of prolonged, let alone 'perpetual' peace." Moreover, "successful wars have prevented civil broils and strengthened the internal power of the State." Indeed, the very weapons with which wars are fought are, Hegel maintains, thoughtfully breathed into being by the Spirit in its royal progress. The gun, for instance, he tells us, "is not a chance invention." It can be said of it as of gunpowder: "Humanity needed it, and it made its appearance forthwith." In the most real of senses, then, guns and gunpowder do indeed bear the stamp of civilisation. It can be no surprise after this to read that the rights of uncivilised peoples are a mere formality—"the civilised nation is conscious that the rights of barbarians are unequal to its own and treats their autonomy as only a formality."

We cannot dismiss these views as an unpleasing but unimportant Prussian prejudice, nor even explain them away by suggesting that in periods of mounting communal emotionalism, such as was the German War of Liberation, safe scholars frequently react in a way more savage than serene. For Hegel's teaching is not merely based on his observation of the practices of his day, although as one who had aspired to be regarded as the German Machiavelli, he was not of course blind to them. It is a statement of inescapable necessity logically deduced from his general philosophy. On the one hand he held that the State was the final abode on earth of the Spirit. "Each State stands for and embodies an idea," he said, "or to be more exact, each State embodies a particular phase of the Universal Idea." Yet on the other he believed that the World Spirit or Reason making its way through history required the existence of a multiplicity of States. No single State, he taught, could ever embody the whole Universal Idea. But at different times different dominant States helped to carry the Spirit forward. "In history," he wrote, "the Idea unfolds its various phases in time and the dominant phase at any epoch is embodied in a dominant people." Only through the conflict of States could such dominant peoples emerge and the Spirit reach more perfect fulfilment.

War, then, plays an important part in world history. Hegel makes Schiller's expression "Die Weltgeschichte ist das Weltgericht" ("World history is the world court of justice") his own. In war it is the World Spirit which itself decides which of the contesting States is its true embodiment and which gives the victory. Success in war justifies war and is conclusive proof that the victorious State is the truer personification of the World Spirit than its defeated opponent or opponents. There is, however, a qualification to be made here. The State chosen for victory by the World Spirit is never conscious of its destiny. Hence no State can urge in justification of a war it has begun that it is acting merely at the behest of the World Spirit, though it can always make that claim in justification of a war it has won. Hitler could not claim in 1939 that he was the mouthpiece of the World Spirit hurling its gage of battle at the feet of lesser embodiments of itself. Had he won in 1945 he could, however, have excused his aggression in 1939 by triumphantly claiming that Germany was acting then as the World Spirit dictated. Unpleasant as is his doctrine, Hegel could not conceivably have held any other view than this. A genuine pacific settlement of disputes between States would presuppose the possibility of State interests being reconciled in the light of some higher interest. But as no such higher interest is possible, genuine, peaceful settlements are out of the question. However, whether or not we can share Hegel's optimism that in the long run the State which is the fullest embodiment of the Spirit and which is chosen to carry on its development will prevail, we can undoubtedly agree that Hegel is whole-hearted in his view that the State and only the State is the creator of morality.

Yet this State, which is divine, which is an end in itself, which is a whole greater than its constituent parts, and which determines morality but is itself unchecked by it, is, Hegel insists, a means of enlarging not restricting freedom. He goes further and says that only in the State can man find freedom, while without it he is completely in subjection. Freedom, he adds, is the outstanding characteristic of the modern State. He criticises the Greeks because they did not recognise that the State must rest on respect for personality. Their acceptance of slavery he saw as a proof of their failure here. He claims that it has been left for the youngest of historic peoples, the Germans, "to attain to the consciousness that man, as man, is free." Indeed, so highly does he think of Freedom that he writes: "The history of the world is none other than the progress of the consciousness of Freedom." What, then, does he mean by Freedom?

The Spirit, he says, is free, for it has its centre in itself and self-containedness is the very essence of Freedom. Matter, on the other hand, is not free, for it is subject to the law of gravity and always tends to a point outside itself. Therefore the development of the Spirit is the development of Freedom, and human history is thus the history of Freedom. Human history culminates in the State in which the Spirit finds its final embodiment. Therefore the perfect State is the truly free State, and the citizen who gives perfect willing obedience to the perfect laws of the perfect State has perfect Freedom.

Yet even the perfect laws of the perfect State may seem something external to the individual and imposed on him, and if they are imposed on him, how can he be free? Hegel answers they are not external to the individual, not imposed on him by any outside force, but are what he himself wills. The individual is also an embodiment of the Spirit, though not of course as perfect an embodiment as the State. He has sufficient of the Spirit in him to wish to identify himself completely with it, but not sufficient to make that identification automatic, easy, or even possible without help. He is capable of acting selfishly, with no thought for others, following the instincts of the brute. When he acts in such a manner he is out of relation with the scheme of things. The Spirit is sleeping within him, and he is not free but a slave to error and desire. Only when he seeks to identify himself with the Spirit is he doing what he would really wish to do, is he acting not according to momentary desire but according to his real will. Only in so far as he succeeds in acting according to his real will, in grasping the purposes of the Spirit and willing those purposes as his own, is he free. Freedom for the individual can thus never be the abstract and uneducated power of choice, but only the willing of what is rational, of what the Spirit would desire, and the power to perform it.

But how shall man know what his real will is? How can he identify himself with the Spirit if he can be led astray by brute desire and selfish interest? The State is there to tell him. It is the schoolmaster which brings him knowledge of the Spirit, of Absolute Reason. His real will impels him to identify himself with the Spirit. The Spirit is embodied in the State. Therefore it is his real will to obey the dictates of the State. Indeed, the dictates of the State are his real will. Thus the commands of the State give man his only opportunity to find Freedom. It does not necessarily follow, however, that he will avail himself of that opportunity. He may obey the State because he is afraid of the consequences of disobedience. If he obeys because of fear, he is not free, he is still subject to alien force. But if he obeys because he wishes to, because he has consciously identified himself with the will of the State, because he has convinced himself that what the State demands he would also desire if he knew all the facts, then he is subject only to his own will and he is truly free. The State, says Hegel, is "that form of reality in which the individual has and enjoys his freedom provided he recognises, believes in and wills what is common to the whole."

To do justice to Hegel, which is not always easy, it must be admitted that this proviso is of the very greatest importance. He certainly believes that the State will help men to fulfil themselves, but he also believes that only when men fulfil themselves will the State itself develop. The State is necessary to make men free, but free men are necessary to make the State perfect. We must, however, still remember that freedom for Hegel is obedience, even though voluntary obedience, to the State.

Freedom so defined is, to say the least of it, an authoritarian kind of freedom, which is not made less authoritarian by the fact that Hegel's State is, unlike Rousseau's republic, a State rich in associations, guilds, corporations, and a State which is constitutional and not arbitrary. None of the associations, not even the Church, has the smallest right against it, and the Constitution, though important because it enshrines the rule of law, in fact detracts very little from its omnipotence. After this, Hegel can hardly surprise us when he adds that Freedom has nothing whatever to do with the right of people to elect their own officials or make their own laws, or with such degenerate matters as freedom of speech or of the Press.

It is clear that Hegel, in writing thus of the State, is referring to no particular State. We must not be misled by his personal feelings: infatuation for Italy is as legitimate, or, to write more accurately, no more illegitimate than predilection for Prussia. Hegel is speaking of the ideal State—the State in idea as it exists nowhere in time and place. In such a State the Spirit can contemplate itself with continual complacence, unable to discover in itself contradiction or flaw, all-knowing, all-powerful, eternal, God at last entered into His heaven.

But what is entirely true of the ideal State is always to some extent, Hegel maintains, true of the actual State. For however much it may be declared to violate right principle, it "possesses always, if it belongs to the developed States of our times, the essential elements of its true existence." Actual States, he insists, will always be more rational, will always be truer embodiments of the Spirit, than the individuals who compose them. Therefore those individuals can never have the right to resist what they consider to be unjust, and the State here and now possesses all those characteristics which we have seen to be those of the State in idea.

"The State," Hegel said, "must be comprehended as an organism." In all essentials his is the most complete organic view of the State. It is a natural growth. It is a whole greater than the parts which are intrinsically related to it and which have meaning only in so far as the whole gives them meaning. It is an end in itself. It develops from within, shaped by the rationalising of the Spirit and helped on by that very development of its citizens which it alone makes possible. And this is true of existing States as well of the State in idea. Since this is the

State's nature, the question, "Why should I obey it?" is as intelligent as the question, "Why should my hand obey me?" It would be no true hand if it did not, and I would be no true man if I did not. My hand is fulfilled in me, and I am fulfilled in the State, and there is nothing more to be said about the matter.

An Appraisal of Hegelianism

Except for a few such as Bosanquet and Bradley, Hegel's view of the State has never made a strong appeal to Englishmen. It is of course such a contradiction of their traditional political thinking and such a condemnation of their most popular political practices that they have tended to regard it as something that is useless, that is dangerous, and that ought to be abolished. They have seen it—as did Hobhouse, who wrote his attack on it, *The Metaphysical Theory of the State,* to what seemed to him the most appropriate of accompaniments, the thudding of German bombs dropped by Zeppelins in raids on London—as something sired in war and giving issue to bigger and better wars. Yet it is difficult to deny it all virtue.

To begin with, it is not a static theory of the State. It portrays the State as a relative organisation expressing at each stage of its development the degree of rationality at which mankind has arrived. One hardly knows whether to call his theory of the State a conservative theory which nevertheless admits the necessity of growth, or an evolutionary theory which nevertheless stresses the importance of conservation. In any case, his view of the developing State is one which must command respect.

Hegel's teaching is valuable, too, because it insists on man's dependence on society. Individualism, treating the State as an aggregate of isolated units, largely ignores man's social character. Too often the State, in the theories of Individualism, is hostile to those lesser liberties of associations which, like cells, go to make up the State. Hegel redresses the balance. He is right in showing how much man is influenced by society. He made the idea of liberty richer by showing that man's conception of it largely depends upon the institutions which have trained him and given him his education. In this his idealism is thoroughly realistic, and has been confirmed by recent psychology, which has proved how the early impressions made on our minds always remain.

It can also be said of him that he made politics something

more than a mere compromise of interests, and that he made law something more than mere command. It is not an ignoble doctrine that the police State is inadequate and that the State must be viewed as part of man's moral end.

Finally his whole work is a valuable reminder that we would do well not to minimise the importance of the natural growth of a community. He said, for instance, of Constitutions: "What is called making a constitution is a thing that has never happened in history; a constitution only develops from the national spirit identically with that spirit's own development." Both Germany and Japan have taught the world how dangerous the organic State can be, and it has been frequently wished that they had drunk a good deal less deeply of Hegelian springs. But perhaps it is to be regretted that the makers and the admirers of the Weimar Constitution had not pondered longer over what Hegel had to say about Constitutions. And perhaps a closer knowledge of the *Philosophy of Mind* might have suggested to General MacArthur the unwisdom of his loudly announced conviction that he had successfully "processed" Japan into Western democratic modes of thought and Western democratic practices.

But if something may be said in favour of Hegel, much must also be said against him. His claim to have revised the law of contradiction and to have substituted for it, in the Dialectic, a new and more fruitful logic, is singularly unconvincing. His Dialectic is not a new method of logic. Whatever in any vague sense seems contrary to anything else, as punishment is to crime or centrifugal to centripetal force, he claimed as illustrations of dialectical contradictions. Yet it is obvious that such oppositions have nothing to do with logical contradictions—they can be explained by non-contradictory statements in complete conformity with the principles of the old logic at which Hegel affected to sneer. Moreover, the Dialectic is a method of reasoning which is capable of much too easy and general interpretation to claim scientific accuracy. Any historical situation may be interpreted to represent thesis or antithesis or synthesis, according to its political evaluation by the interpreter. The Dialectic, therefore, provides a wonderful instrument for always being right. It enables all defeats to be regarded as the beginnings of victory. For instance, for two years after 1933 German Communists refused to recognise that Hitler's victory had been a defeat for the German

Communist Party. We may very well doubt the value of a method of analysis which enables Hegel to worship the State as God and Marx to damn it as the Devil. We may even conclude that just as the doctrine of Natural Law was popular in the 18th century because it allowed all men to deduce from Nature those principles of justice which appealed to them, so the Dialectic became popular in the 19th and 20th centuries because it enabled men to deduce from history those theories of man in relation to the State which they wished to see generally accepted.

If the Dialectic is unconvincing, the uses to which Hegel puts it are frequently unpleasant. With a wave of his wizard's wand he turns things into their opposites with the practised ease of the most polished necromancy. "The aim of science," he says, "is knowledge of objective truth"; and adds: "The State must protect objective truth." This seems a promising enunciation of a famous liberal doctrine. But before we know where we are, we have arrived at the position "the State has, in general, to make up its own mind concerning what is to be considered as objective truth," and all that is left of the liberal creed is a skeleton disappearing disconsolately over the horizon.

Hegel turns the edge of the principle of freedom by identifying freedom with obedience. He turns the edge of the principle of equality by identifying equality with discipline. He turns the edge of individual personality by treating human beings as merely conduit pipes of the divine energy and merging them in the State. Freedom, equality, personality—the magic wand has turned them all into their opposites, and the aridity of the achievement must dull our appreciation of the wizardry of the artist.

Few of us, moreover, could agree that the State is the chosen representative of God, even though we recognise the great importance of the part it has played in bringing about the order which is necessary for all intellectual development. For the State has not been the sole factor in furthering this growth of rationality. It would be completely unhistorical to ignore the part played, for instance, by the Church in this. It is plain that actual States frequently imperil all that has been won in this respect in the past, and every day it is becoming more obvious that the claim that each Sovereign State is sufficient for its members is the greatest danger to modern civilisation. The Juggernaut, passing in triumph over the crushed bodies of its devotees, has become an offence to civilised consciences, and the Deity incarnate in Sovereign States which are all strongly attached to the practice of mutual throat-cutting, and who can therefore only advance through the suicide as it were of different forms of itself, is not a Deity which can command our respect. For such a devouring Spirit, William James's appellation of "Bitch Goddess" would not indeed be too strong. Men may find it wiser to limit rather than to insist on the sovereignty of each State. For if the world can progress only through the continued suicide of different forms of God, its progress is likely to be most reminiscent of that of the Gadarene swine, and in this atomic age, to misquote T. S. Elliot, mankind to end not with a whimper but with a bang.

One great value of Hegel's evolutionary view of the State is that from it naturally follows the belief that everything should be open to criticism. Yet by assuming the operation of the Divine Mind even in imperfect States, Hegel builds up a strong presumption against any criticism of existing States. He is too strongly inclined to the view that whatever is is right because it represents the historic process at any given moment of its evolution. When such a view is accepted too passively, that process itself is in danger of coming to an end.

But all criticism of him can be summed up in the charge that while he sought to give a more satisfactory definition of Liberty than that provided by those who regard the State as a machine, he in the end sacrifices the individual to the Great Leviathan. Far from curbing Leviathan, he has merely dressed it in the garments and given it the airs of Mr. Pecksniff, and made it oppress us for our own good. Preaching the fulfilment of humanity, he has opened the floodgates wide to those surging tides of inhumanity that have threatened since he wrote to engulf the world. Ardent apostle of Reason, he has done more than most to prepare the way for that age of Unreason in which we live. The evil that he has done has lived after him and is writ large in the world today.

THOMAS HILL GREEN, 1836–1882

His Task

About the 1870s, as Dicey has taught us, a great change took place in the nature of English legislation. From the 1830s it bore the stamp of the individualism that saw in "the systematic extension of individual freedom" the cure for "the evils which bring ruin on a commonwealth." From the 1870s it carried the mark of the collectivism "which favours the intervention of the State, even at the sacrifice of some individual freedom, for the purpose of conferring benefit upon the mass of the people." This trend towards collectivism did not necessarily imply the undermining of Utilitarianism, the prevailing political philosophy of the mid-century; for the individualism that was expressed in the doctrine of *laisser-faire* was not an essential part of that political philosophy which, as Herbert Spencer pointed out, could lend itself perhaps even more readily to justify collectivism than individualism. Indeed, Socialism in England has not hesitated to acknowledge its indebtedness to the Utilitarianism which, in Dicey's words, provided it with a legislative dogma—the principle of Utility, a legislative instrument—the active use of parliamentary sovereignty, and a legislative tendency—the extension and improvement of the mechanism of government.

Yet in the period of transition from individualist to collectivist legislation, Utilitarianism tended to be discredited. It had been too closely associated with prejudice against State action, and men who were now more ready than formerly to listen to Southey maintaining that the State could if it would prevent the greater part of social evils, to Arnold protesting against "one of the falsest maxims which ever pandered to human selfishness under the name of political wisdom—I mean the maxim that civil society ought to leave its members alone, each to look after their several interests, provided they do not employ direct fraud or force against their neighbour," to Carlyle fulminating against *laisser-faire* as "false, heretical and damnable if ever aught was," could not remain entirely unaffected by their contempt for Hedonism and by their exhortations that men should follow higher paths than Utilitarians could tread. Arnold's plea that men should follow not their ordinary but their best self, Carlyle's insistence that true liberty consisted in man's "finding out or being forced to find out the right path, and to walk thereon," while not widely popular, no longer seemed such ungodly heresies in the 1870s. Even those curious racial theories—theories of the Folk which became so familiar in the 20th century, which are to be found in *Past and Present*, wherein Carlyle preaches the doctrine of the strong, silent man and in which he proves himself surely the noisiest advocate of Silence, the most eloquent Apostle of the Inarticulate that the world has ever seen—are not entirely unacceptable in the 1870s. For by now the mental climate of the century is clearly changing, and is foreshadowing that odd mixture of hysterical emotionalism, of racialist mumbo-jumbo, and of sound community feeling which we know as late-Victorian Imperialism.

Possessed of too much common sense to soar to these high altitudes, in which giddiness is no uncommon affliction, and discredited by its close association with *laisser-faire* individualism, Utilitarianism in the latter part of the century was at a temporary disadvantage. Hegelian philosophy, waiting at hand to replace it, had now the opportunity to do so. But before this could be done those things which made it difficult for Englishmen to adopt it must first be removed from Hegelianism. This was the task of T. H. Green.

The Hegelian in Green

It is obvious how very much Hegelianism Green's writings contain. Green wholeheartedly believed in the existence of Hegel's Divine Spirit or Reason. This to him was "the vital truth which Hegel had to teach." He believed that this Divine Spirit or Reason was constantly pushing forward to its goal, which was perfect realisation. History, therefore, for Green as for Hegel, was a constant progress which embodies the "eternal consciousness." He believed that the Divine Spirit reaching its goal was full Reality, that what men call the "ideal" is more real than is actual life. In words that Hegel might have written, he declared: "To anyone who understands a process of development, the result being developed is the reality." He insisted, as Hegel did, that when man holds fast to the ideal his grasp of reality is strongest. He maintained with Hegel that all institutions, communities, associations were embodiments of the Divine Spirit. He accepted Hegel's view that every new embodiment of this Divine Spirit was a fuller embodiment than the one preceding it. Each step taken by the Spirit on its march through the world was more real than the one before. The association was more real than the family, the State was more real than the association. He believed that men also were at least partial embodiments of this Divine Spirit. While not minimising human frailty and human passions any more than did Hegel, believing as did Hegel that in great men, the agents of history, they were "overruled" for good so that he can write that while Cæsar may have been actuated by desire for power and glory he, nevertheless, founded the Empire which brought to the world the blessing of Roman Law, he held firmly to the idea, as did Hegel, that the Divine Spirit in him constituted man's real self. With Hegel, Green accepted the view that the State was the latest and fullest existing embodiment of the Divine Spirit, an embodiment of the greatest possible significance to man since it helped him to increase in himself that measure of the Divine Spirit which he already possessed. Without the State in fact, Green believed, man is not really man at all. Only in the State can he fully express himself, can his nature be developed to its fullest capacity. Hence he must clearly look upon the State, not as an evil made necessary because of his own inherent viciousness, but as a good made indispensable because of his own inherent virtue; not as a chaining of the Devil, but as a releasing of the God within him. The political life of man, Green concludes in words which almost paraphrase Hegel's, is "a revelation of the Divine Idea."

It is clear, too, that in Green, as in Hegel, there is a very full realisation of the majesty and might of the State. The State, Green insists, is the only source of actual rights. "Ideal rights," he says, "may be conceived which are not in the State; only when they are in it do they become rights."

Green's State, like Hegel's, is a community of communities, but again like Hegel's there is no question but that it is supreme over all the communities it contains. "The members of the State derive the rights which they have as members of other associations from the State, and have no rights against it," he declares. And, like Hegel's, Green's State differs from all the associations within it in that in it alone the General Will is fully realised.

Like Hegel, Green is very concerned with the problem of Freedom, and his view of Freedom bears a strong resemblance to Hegel's. For both, man is most free when he most completely identifies himself with the Divine Spirit. Freedom, Green says, is not being left alone to do what one likes, since all depends on what one likes to do. Man is free only when he is following his "true" good, and his "true" good is also "social" good since it can only be achieved when the good of others is also realised. Freedom, then, Green writes, "is a positive power or capacity of doing or enjoying something worth doing or enjoying and that, too, something we do or enjoy in common with others." Or more simply, Freedom is "the liberation of all the powers of men for the social good." But men are capable of pursuing social good only because of the Divine Spirit that is in them. Therefore Freedom is identification of oneself with the Divine Spirit. Since Green agrees that the Divine Spirit finds its highest embodiment in the State, it is obvious how close is his approach to the Hegelian thesis that true liberty is realised in the State.

Finally, Green's view of the importance of Society is very similar to Hegel's. "Without society no person," he writes epigrammatically. He believed with Hegel that each community develops its own standard of morality which moulds the moral outlook of its citizens. Hence an action which would be moral for a Chinese would be immoral for an Englishman. The implication that what is right seems clear, that the individual should be more influenced by the moral code of his community than by any purely abstract code. At all events, Green says, it is for the community and not for the individual conscience to declare what acts should be committed. So long as the moral consciousness of the community was not offended man had the natural right "to drive at any pace through the streets, to build houses without any reference to sanitary conditions, to keep his children at home or send them to work analphabetic," and only when it became offended did man lose that natural right. There is here almost as full a realisation of the importance of the community as anything to be found in Hegel. This helps Green to see, as Hegel does, that no reform will endure which ignores national sentiments, character, and institutions. But it also carries him far towards Hegel's views. It is significant, for instance, that when Green speaks of the obligations of the citizen, these are not to other actual citizens but to some "real" entity called Society. It is difficult to avoid the conclusion that there is a very great deal of Hegelian mysticism in Green's thinking about Society.

In these views of his on History, on Man, Society and the State, Green is not of course influenced solely by Hegel. His Hegelianism is intermingled with a good deal of Aristotelianism, as might have been expected of an Oxford scholar bred on the classics. Nevertheless, his is a sufficiently stiff dose of Hegelianism, and almost certainly it would have proved too unpalatable for Englishmen to swallow had it not been diluted by a very strong measure of English common sense, had Green, similar in so many things to Hegel, not differed from him radically in so many more.

The Individualist in Green

In his lectures on the *English Commonwealth*, Green quoted the remark of Vane the regicide: "The people of England have been long asleep. I doubt they will be hungry when they awake"; and he added: "If they should yet awake and be hungry, they will find their food in the ideas which, with much blindness and weakness, he vainly offered them, cleared and ripened by a philosophy of which he did not dream." Here we have, as it were, the two streams that came together in Green. The one is Hegelianism—the philosophy of which Vane did not dream. The other is Radical Individualism, which could find so much to admire in Vane and the English Puritans. In spite of his Hegelianism, Green remained a Radical and an Individualist. It is typical of him that he was a friend of Chartism and an opponent of that "national honour" in whose name so many crimes have been committed. On being asked as an undergraduate to join a University Rifle Corps against Chartism, he replied that he would "like to learn the use of the arm in order that he might desert to the people if it came to such a pass." He thought that Palmerston had done "about as much harm as it is possible for an individual Englishman to do" —until, that is, Disraeli came along, and then he wasn't sure. It was because of his Radicalism, because he was at least as much an Individualist as he was an Hegelian, that Englishmen listened to his teaching.

For all his belief that the State was the embodiment of the Divine Spirit, he never regarded the State as an end in itself. It was a means to an end, and that end was the full moral development of the individuals who compose it. He believed passionately with Kant that every man has a worth and a dignity which forbids his exploitation for any purposes whatever. "The life of the nation," he insisted, "has no real existence except as the life of the individuals composing it." "To speak of any progress or improvement or development of a nation or society or mankind except as relative to some greater worth of persons," he wrote, "is to use words without meaning." It is typical of him that he regards the function of the State as being negative, not positive. It is not to make men moral, since morality consists in "the disinterested performance of self-imposed duties," it is to remove the obstacles which prevent men becoming moral.

It is true, of course, that in order to remove obstacles the State must interfere to such an extent that what appears negative in form soon seems most positive in content. "To any Athenian slave, who might be used to gratify a master's lust," he wrote, "it would have been a mockery to speak of the State as a realisation of freedom; and perhaps it would not be much less to speak of it as such to an untaught and underfed denizen of a London yard with gin-shops on the right hand and on the left." It was for the State to see that the mental and physical malnutrition, together with the gin-shops, were removed. "To uphold the sanctity of contract," he said, "is doubtless a prime business of government, but it is no less its business to provide against contracts being made which from the helplessness of one of the parties to them, instead of being a security for freedom, become an instrument of disguised oppression." In acknowledging that as its business, the State was assuming no inconsiderable powers of intervention. Green's indignation at the moral degradation which for so long Society had so easily accepted shines through his words: "We content ourselves with enacting that no man shall be used by other men as a means against his will, but we leave it to be pretty much a matter of chance whether or not he shall be qualified to fulfil any social function, to contribute anything to the common good, and to do so freely." Indeed, he would gladly have echoed Carlyle's "that one man should die ignorant who has the capacity of knowledge, that I call a tragedy, though it should happen, as by some computations it does, a thousand times a minute." If the State was to intervene to prevent that tragedy, to ensure that everyone should be qualified to contribute something to the common good, its intervention was likely to be steady, constant, and far-reaching, and its purpose would clearly be positive.

The negative form in which Green speaks of the State as the remover of obstacles is nevertheless significant. It is a reminder that in the final analysis what matters most in life must remain within the province of the individual—the development of his moral nature—"the fulfilment of a moral capacity without which

man would not be man." It is a reminder, too, that the limits
of State action are, after all, very strictly defined; indeed, far
more strictly defined than ever they can be by Utilitarianism.
The State can do everything which will help, but it must do
nothing which will hinder the free development of moral personality. "The true ground of objection to 'paternal government' is not that it violates the *laisser-faire* principle and con-
ceives that its office is to make people good, to promote morality," he adds, "but that it rests on a misconception of morality.
The real function of government being to maintain conditions
of life in which morality shall be possible, and morality con-
sisting in the disinterested performance of self-imposed duties,"
paternal government "does its best to make it impossible by
narrowing the room for the self-imposition of duties and for the
play of disinterested motives."

There can thus be no question that for Green the State is
not an end in itself, but is only a means to the development of
men. And as though to leave not the shadow of doubt about
it, Green is never tired of insisting that institutions exist for
men not men for institutions. They are important for the effect
they have on their members. "The value of the institutions of
civil life," he emphasises, "lies in their operation as giving
reality to the capacities of will and reason and enabling them
to be really exercised."

After his insistence on the importance of individual men and
women, it is hardly surprising to find that in spite of the aura
of mysticism which surrounds his conception of Society, the
State for Green is not something other and greater than the
sum of the wills of its citizens. He does not see in it, as Rousseau
did, "Un moi commun," a common me.

It is true that he believes in the existence of the General Will.
Indeed, he is convinced that this General Will is the real basis
of the State. Legal Sovereignty, he agrees with Austin, must
reside in the supreme authority within the State, in that body
which recognises no power above itself. But behind this legal
Sovereign is the General Will, and this General Will, not force
or fear, is what really determines the habitual obedience of a
people. Men habitually obey only those institutions which, perhaps unconsciously, they feel represent the General Will. And
this is true irrespective of the form of government the State may
possess, since even an absolute monarchy must inspire loyalty

and voluntary submission in its subjects. "There's on earth a yet auguster thing, Veiled though it be than Parliament or King," Green quotes. This is the General Will, the true Sovereign of the community.

Green thinks, then, sufficiently highly of the General Will. But his is no metaphysical or vague definition of it. He writes of "that impalpable congeries of the hopes and fears of a people, bound together by common interests and sympathy, which we call the General Will." He calls it "the common consciousness of a common good"; "a sense of possessing common interests, a desire for common interests on the part of a people." It is obvious that for him the General Will is the will for the State, not the will of the State. His General Will is certainly not that in whose name so many crimes have been perpetrated, which has proved such an excellent stick, not only with which to beat minorities, as Dean Inge saw, but with which to bludgeon whole communities into obedience, that it has become almost the accredited villain of modern political thought.

Believing that will not force is the true basis of the State, yet knowing that there are States in which force not will is preponderant, Green has to admit, although he has already told us that the State is the latest and fullest embodiment of the Divine Spirit, that "actual States at best fulfil but partially their ideal function." And he is prepared to draw from the vital distinction between the State in idea and the State in fact conclusions which Hegel can never admit. Hence while Green rejects Rousseau's view that the General Will is entirely in abeyance in all existing States, he also rejects Hegel's view that the laws in existing States are synonymous with the General Will. The State, therefore, as it exists is not necessarily a completer embodiment of the Divine Spirit than the individual. The ideal State would be, of course, but there may be a great difference between the actual and the ideal State. Green thus cannot be accused of sacrificing the individual to the State, as Hegel can. There is a very important difference between his and Hegel's idea of Freedom, similar as at first they might seem. For Hegel, Freedom is the voluntary identification of self with the laws of the State. For Green, Freedom is the right of a man to make the best of himself. This may mean voluntary identification of self with the laws of the State. If the State is a good State, if it is adequately fulfilling its function, it will mean this. But it might not mean this. It might even mean that the individual, albeit in fear and trembling, will be compelled to go up against the State —a possibility which Hegel could never but which Green readily admits.

Nowhere does Green more obviously differ from Hegel than in this belief that the individual may be justified in disobeying the State. It is true that Green does nothing to make the path of the resister easy. He is not concerned to build broad highways for would-be resisters, for of all broad highways they would, he believed, lead quickest to the everlasting bonfire. Rather he insists there can never be any right to disobey the State, for the State alone is the source of rights. He is emphatic that resistance can never be justified merely because legislation runs against personal inclinations. "There can be no right to disobey or evade any particular law on the ground that it interferes with any freedom of action, any right of managing his children" or "doing what he will with his own," Green says. "If upon new conditions arising or upon elements of social good being taken account of which had been overlooked before, if in any of these ways or otherwise the reference to social well-being suggests the necessity of further regulation of the individual's liberty to do as he pleases, he can plead no right against this regulation, for every right he has possessed has been dependent upon the social judgment of its compatibility with general well-being." He warns men that in resisting the State they should always be aware that they will probably be wrong and the State almost certainly right, for the State will be speaking with the wisdom of the ages, and that may be presumed to be greater than the wisdom of individual men. He tells them that they should always know that resistance may be utterly disastrous, since it may tempt men to unleash the bonds of that mighty demon Anarchy. He commands them, wherever they have the fortune to enjoy constitutional government, to put up with objectionable laws until they can repeal them constitutionally, for the common good will suffer far more from resistance than from conformity to even a bad law for the time that must elapse before it can be changed. Even where the blessings of constitutional rule are unknown men should, he says, feel justified in disobeying the State only when certain conditions obtain. If the legality of the command objected to is doubtful, if there are no means of agitating for its repeal, if the whole system of government is so bad, because so perverted by private interests, that temporary anarchy is better than its continuance, or if anarchy is unlikely to follow resistance, then only should the State be disobeyed.

But when all warnings are uttered, Green will ultimately agree that there are occasions when man, if he is to be true to himself and at whatever cost, must refuse to give obedience to the State. Knowing all that can be urged against it, Green says, if you must resist you must, and the choice can be no one's but yours. You will never have the right to resist, but you may be right in resisting. And if you are, it will be your duty to resist—and the poorer citizen you if you don't. Your resistance, of course, can be justified only on social grounds, on the ideal of the common good, because in existing circumstances your full moral development would be impossible. But if you are convinced of all this you must act. Normally your resistance should be based on popular and widespread discontent. But you may dispense even with this since your action is not to be determined according to the Chinese saying: "Where there are many persons their prestige is great." Yours may be the Daniel's part to dare to stand alone, for where popular sentiment is apathetic it may be your duty to act in the interests of the common good.

Not content with admitting that Luther's "Ich kann nichts anders" (I can do no other) is a cry which if need be every man worthy of the name must be prepared to raise against the State, Green goes on to re-enunciate something like a doctrine of Natural Rights on behalf of individuals within the State. Utilitarians and Idealists had joined in attacking the idea of Natural Rights as rhetorical nonsense and unreal, a view which, as far as those rights were concerned which Locke had thought were man's in the State of Nature, Green would have unhesitatingly accepted. But he believes that men may have certain claims which ought to be recognised as rights, even if in fact they are not. Such claims are those which must be granted if man is to fulfil his moral nature, and such claims Green calls Natural Rights. Since these Natural Rights "arise out of and are necessary for the fulfilment of man's moral capacity," they are not based on the claims of an earlier against a later state of Society, but are rather an appeal from a less developed to a more mature Society. They are therefore "ahead of, not behind, political development."

But how are we to tell what these Natural Rights are? We are not to listen to "some remote philosopher's view of it." We must take into account the common good that is actually recognised by Society, for our idea of the good life for all, on which we must base the Natural Rights we wish to put forward, must depend not on our own idea of good alone, but on what we believe our fellow citizens will recognise to be for the common good. We "must be able to point to some public interest, generally recognised as such, which is involved in the exercise of the power claimed as a right, to show that it is not the general well-being, even as conceived by our fellow citizens, but some special interest of a class that is concerned in preventing the exercise of the power claimed."

The confusion of Green's utterances on Natural Rights is to be regretted. "Rights," he tells us, "are made by recognition. There is no right but thinking makes it so." Yet he also tells us that there are Rights which ought to be recognised—which seems to imply that Rights are not made by recognition. Perhaps we must conclude that he should not have spoken of Natural Rights since he can only mean unrecognised powers, which according to his definition are not Rights at all. There seems, moreover, some incompatibility in what he says about the determination of Rights. In determining Rights, he says, it is only what Society thinks that matters. Yet he adds that only what is necessary for the individual's full moral development is important. Man's full moral development is possible only in Society, yet what Society wants may not always coincide with what is necessary for man's full moral development. And finally, if we agree that all Green is saying is that the appeal from the State as it is to the State as it ought to be is the appeal to the State as it might reasonably be expected to be, remembering that its citizens are neither devils nor gods but men in a world of men, a difficulty still remains. Apart from the indication that the remote philosopher would not be the best of guides, we are left unaided to answer the question: Who is to be the judge of what might reasonably be expected? It cannot, then, be denied that what Green has to tell us about Natural Rights is lacking in that crystal clarity which is to be desired in all philosophers. But neither can what he says be regarded as anything but a strengthening of the individual against the State. There is no confusion, no lack of clarity, no lack of firmness in his conclusion that "there may be cases in which the public interest is best served by a violation of some actual law." In this and its attendant view that the judgment of conscience is morally the court of last resort, Green stands poles apart from Hegel. Green's view here is a necessary and logical consequence of the distinction which he makes between the *de jure* sovereign, which is Rousseau's sovereign, residing solely in the General Will and which, unlike Rousseau, he believes is to be found to some degree in most States, and the *de facto* sovereign, which is the remnant of laws in every State which are not the product of the General Will but which proceed from the particular will of some ruler who depends on force and who procures obedience through fear. For the implication of this distinction is the rejection of Hegel's view that the willing of a common good acquires moral significance only within the State, the rejection of Hegel's view that "civil society" has no moral significance until it comes under the control of the State, and the return to the earlier view of Locke and the Natural Law philosophers that Society itself is moral and embodies a system of rational justice not because of the State's power but because of the developing moral conscience of its members. Hence in spite of his Hegelianism, Green reverts to the old English tradition of individualism, in which the importance of the individual's moral conscience is understood and the State's authority suspect. His is the faith which to Hegel would have been the heresy of heresies, that in the final analysis there exists within the community an ethical system which is independent of the State and which gives the individual a standard whereby to criticise the State itself. How this leads him to conclusions that would have been anathema to Hegel, his views on associations and on International Relations will make still further clear.

In Green's State as in Hegel's the supremacy of the State over the associations it contains is unquestioned. But there is a significant difference between them in the reasons for it and the nature and exercise of it. For Hegel, associations are important because they embody the State instinct which is co-operative, not the principle of "bourgeois society" which is competitive. In so far as they do this they prepare men for that voluntary obedience which they must give to the State. "The more there is of the more, the less there is of the less," the old Spanish proverb says. Since the whole value of associations lies in the fact that they

develop the State instinct in man, they can never assert themselves against the State. For Green, however, associations are important because they fulfil the individual. They existed before
the State came into being, and have their own system of rights
which arise from their very nature as associations. The State
must be supreme over them because it must co-ordinate and
adjust them. But it must also preserve them. "A State," he says,
"presupposes other forms of community, with the rights that
arise out of them, and only exists as sustaining, securing and
completing them." Thus, while for Hegel if associations do not
result in the State, they are no true associations; for Green if
the State does not preserve associations, it is no true State. In
both Hegel and Green the fact of the State's supremacy is
unquestioned. But in the one the exercise of the supremacy of
the State is unlimited because of its own nature and the nature
of associations. In the other the exercise of the State's supremacy
is limited by its own nature and the nature of associations.

And if Green's State must preserve the rights of the lesser
communities within it, it must respect the rights of the larger
community outside it. Just as Green believes that there can be
an ethical system within the community independent of the
State, so he thinks that even in the absence of a super-State
there can be a common General Will of humanity, "the common consciousness of mankind," from which can be formulated
an ethical code whereby to judge the morality of the State's
behaviour to its neighbours. In existing circumstances he knows
that this cannot be complete, nor its sanctions absolutely
effective. But he is sure that such a code exists and that it can
be still further developed. As consciousness of common interest
had in the process of time led to the General Will fashioning
within the State an ever more complete ethical system, so outside the State it would in time lead to the more complete formulation of international ethics. An international ethical code is, he
believes, the obvious extension of the ethical system accepted
within the State. Both spring from a common source—man's
desire as a moral being to fulfil himself.

It is obvious how emphatically Green rejects the Hegelian
thesis that such an international code is impossible, that the
State can never seek to base its external actions on morality because it is itself the sole source of morality and what it does in
its own interests is the whole of morality. Four of Hegel's propo-

sitions, in particular, Green takes exception to: to the proposition that war is not evil, that it is a necessary consequence of the existence of States, that no higher form of Society than the State can ever be conceived, and that International Law is a contradiction in terms.

War, he asserts, is always an evil which violates man's right to life. There may, he admits, be circumstances in which peace is a still greater evil, where war is the only means of maintaining conditions necessary to the moral development of men. But such circumstances, he is convinced, will be very rare, and where they exist they are the result of some greater evil that has taken place in times past. The Italian War of Liberation was an evil made necessary by the still greater evil of former Austrian occupation. Even where it is hard to tell where guilt lies, Green says with that humility which is one of the rarest virtues of political philosophers, that is "only a reason for more general self-reproach, for a more humbling sense (as the preachers say) of complicity in the radical (but conquerable because moral) evil of mankind which renders such a means of maintaining political freedom necessary." Of those "who from time to time talk of the need of a great war to bring unselfish impulses into play," he comments: "They give us reason to suspect that they are too selfish themselves to recognise the unselfish activity that is going on all around them." And as for the argument that war is necessary as providing opportunities for noble endeavour, he writes: "Till all methods have been exhausted by which nature can be brought into the service of man, till society is so organised that everyone's capabilities have free scope for their development, there is no need to resort to war for a field in which patriotism may display itself."

He roundly denies that "the wrong which results to human society from conflicts between States can be condoned on the ground that it is a necessary incident of the existence of States." The State, he said, is "an institution in which all the capacities that give rise to rights have free play given to them, and the more perfectly each State attains this object, the easier it is for others to do so." Or again, "no action in its own interest of a State which fulfilled its idea could conflict with any true interest or right of general society." Thus he concludes: "It is not the State as such, but this or that particular State, which by no means fulfils its purpose, and might perhaps be swept away and superseded by another with advantage to the ends for which the true State exists, that needs to defend its interest by action injurious to those outside it."

Finally, Green is willing to admit the possibility of the State's supersession by other and perhaps higher forms of Society. "It is easy," he writes, "to conceive a better system than that of the great States of modern Europe with their national jealousies, rival armies, and hostile tariffs." And while acknowledging how far mankind is from realising "the dream of an international court with authority resting on the consent of individual States," he believes "that there is nothing in the intrinsic nature of a system of independent States incompatible with it, but that on the contrary every advance in the organisation of mankind in States in the sense explained is a step towards it." Much as he owes to Hegel, Green could hardly have more effectively marked the gulf that lies between them.

Though his preference for popular control and participation in government is admitted, it has nevertheless been claimed that the seeds of authoritarianism are to be detected in Green's writings. It has been said that he did not claim that good government must be popular government, that he admitted that Dictatorship might act according to the General Will, that as his sole criterion was the common good this could be as well provided for by an authoritarian as by a constitutional government.

There seems some evidence for this view. Whether in the absence of public control private interests could be kept from ousting public good, whether good citizenship was possible without active participation in politics, these, for instance, seemed to Green "questions of circumstances which do not permit of an unqualified answer." Green is too good an Hegelian not to see the importance of historical differences between States, too humble and at the same time too wise to think that all is dross that is not Liberalism.

But if Hegelianism makes him aware that he ought not to give an unqualified answer to the questions he raises, individualism in fact compels him to give one. He says of the Reform Act of 1867: "We who were reformers from the beginning always said that the enfranchisement of the people was an end in itself. We said, and we were much derided for saying so, that only citizenship makes the moral man; that only citizenship gives that self-respect which is the true basis of respect for others, and without which there is no lasting social order or real morality." Instinctive loyalty is too little to demand from citizens. They must be "intelligent patriots," longing to serve their country. "The citizens of the Roman Empire," he wrote, "were loyal subjects, the admirable maintenance of private rights made them that; but they were not intelligent patriots, and chiefly because they were not the Empire fell." Only active interest in the service of the State can make intelligent patriots, and only participation in the work of the State can produce that active interest.

We cannot doubt where Green stands. We must not in listening to the grudging admission forget the triumphant assertion. Green, though all his instincts urge him to, will not deny that there may be good government which is not self-government. But he loudly proclaims his conviction that the best government can only be self-government. Un-Hegelian in his refusal to consider the State an end in itself, as something other and greater than the sum of the individuals who are its citizens, as necessarily a completer embodiment of the Spirit than the individual, un-Hegelian in his insistence that the individual may have the duty to act against the State, that the State must preserve the rights of the lesser communities within it and respect the rights of the greater community of which it is itself part, Green is no less un-Hegelian in this, that for the passive voluntary identification of self with an authoritarian State which Hegel demands, he substitutes an active participation in a democratic State which his individualism requires. Green, the individualist, who judges State, Society, General Will by their worth for the development of individual morality and individual character, who so notably and so nobly dedicated himself to social and political service in the City of Oxford, would not have been true to himself had he done less—and would certainly have made much less of an appeal than he did to Englishmen.

His Achievement

"If it be individualism to see in every political movement the fate of human beings and in every controversy over institutions the weal or woe of fellow citizens, then there are few more declared individualists in political philosophy than T. H. Green," writes Maccunn. Yet there can be no doubt that T. H. Green belongs to the Idealist school of political philosophers. He rejects the Mechanistic theory of the State as being too artificial, and as overlooking the importance of the historical growth and development of communities. He rejects the Force theory of the State, since he is convinced that will not force is the true basis of political obligation. He accepts the Organic theory of the State, even though, as has been seen, only with many qualifications. He regards the State as natural since man is necessarily a social animal. He sees Freedom not as the absence of restraint but as a process of self-development by freely obeying laws and customs which are seen to embody a rational scheme of Justice within the Community. He believes the State to be essentially good, because it is an indispensable guide enabling men to understand their own moral obligations, calling upon the best in them and providing them with a code of duties in discharging which they can find true freedom.

He is, then, we must admit, an Idealist, but an Idealist who can be hailed as an Individualist. Perhaps that is why we must further agree that he is the most easy of Idealists to criticise—though we might add in so many ways the most difficult to disagree with. We may say that his theory that institutions are the embodiment of reason is dangerous since it may so easily lead to the view that whatever is is right. We may believe that his theory of Sovereignty, combining as it does the ideas of Austin and of Rousseau, is unsatisfactory. Sovereignty, he says, is supreme power, but it is only supreme power when supported by the General Will. Hobhouse's criticism is called for: "In so far as it is will, it is not general, and in so far as it is general, it is not will." We may find singularly unconvincing his theory that in great men the bad is "overruled" for good—seeing in it an uncomfortable reminder of the truth of Frederick the Great's assertion that however bad the means used to attain an end may be there will always be found some philosopher to whitewash them. We may consider his whole approach much too rational. He neglects the subconscious factors that influence men's actions in States, just as in his theory of Punishment he appears to forget their emotions. His picture of man as almost pure consciousness is as unreal as the Utilitarian's picture of man the pleasure-seeker or the classical economist's picture of economic man. We may think his economic views are inadequate and unsatisfactory since he is content with demanding land reform while he sees no danger in concentration of capital. And recent events suggest that Mrs. Partington attempting to sweep back the waves with her mop was a supreme pessimist compared with those who believe, as he was tempted to and as Article XI of the League of Nations maintained, that world public opinion will suffice to stop the excesses of power. We have seen the difficulties into which his theory of Natural Rights lead him. It might seem that he continually takes away with one hand what he gives with the other, a trick that would be readily seen through were it not for the fact that like the juggler he successfully manages to keep everything in the air anyhow. When he agrees that the judgment of conscience is morally the court of last appeal, yet insists that the individual can never have a right against the community but only a duty to improve the community, this must appear an elaborate attempt to have it both ways. It must also incidentally be a strong reminder of the difficulties under which all believers in the organic State labour of making adequate provision for the operation of the individual conscience. And if practically we find Green's views not unsatisfactory, logically we can hardly regard them as very convincing.

But however much we are impelled to criticise him, so many of his conclusions are convincing and satisfactory, even if more so than the logical process whereby he arrives at them. Benthamism had built on selfishness and had ignored man's capacity for sacrifice. In spite of appearances, it had made no adequate provision for the limiting of the State's authority. Against all probability, it had asserted the identity of the interests of the individual and of the group, but in any case it was convinced that a true theory of politics could be based on interest alone. Green called on the best that was in man. He showed that when man gave of his best there could be no conflict between his true interests and the interests of the true State. He taught men to see that faith in their own moral development and faith in their fellow-men mattered far more to them than any particular interest they might have. In his distinction between outward acts and inward will, between what is better done even from the wrong motive and what is only valuable because of its motive, he gave men a far sounder criterion whereby to judge State action than did Mill with his doctrine of self-and-other-regarding actions. In doing so he gave the individual a far more effective protection against the undue exercise of the State's power than anything with which Utilitarianism could provide him. Idealism had sacrificed the individual to the State, had made the State an end in itself and the sole source of morality, had emphasised the antithesis between the State and its neighbours, seeing morality in *raison d'état* and virtue in war. Green teaches men that the individual need not be sacrificed to the State, which is neither an end in itself nor the sole source of morality. And he shows them that it is not true to say of States, as the Corinthians said of the Athenians, "to describe their character in a word, one might truly say that they were born into the world to take no rest themselves and to give none to others." The sole law between States is not the law of the jungle, war is evil, and an immoral action remains an immoral action even if committed by the State. Correcting and supplementing both Utilitarianism and Idealism, Green gives men a common-sense criterion which they can apply to States. Every State, he shows them, can be judged by its practical content here and now. It will be a good State if it contains the largest possible number of happy, moral human beings.

So far Green has endeavoured to give what he has to say a universal application. Yet we cannot be unaware that his good State and his good citizens are recognisably English. It is very revealing that he hopes "for a time when the phrase [the education of a gentleman] will have lost its meaning, because the sort of education which alone makes the gentleman in any sense will be within the reach of all. As it was the aspiration of Moses that all the Lord's people should be prophets, so, with all seriousness and reverence, we may hope and pray for a condition of English society in which all honest citizens will recognise themselves and be recognised by each other as gentlemen." His whole approach is demonstrably English, even to the warning against the remote philosopher. No German who had survived that far could have read further in Green. And any Frenchman who had arrived with Green at the point where he discusses a right that ought to be a Right but wasn't a Right and couldn't be a Right, must have closed the book and gone sadly away convinced, as he had always suspected, that the English fog found its fitting counterpart in what the English in their conceit called their minds. Even the view that Natural Right implies an appeal from the State as it is to the State as it might reasonably be expected to be, becomes less opaque when addressed to Englishmen who do in fact ask their State to justify itself continually, but who, perhaps by way of reaction to the violence of their earlier history, and perhaps because of the protection of their mother, the sea, have for many years shown themselves remarkably reasonable in their politics without necessarily taking the trouble, or even possessing the capacity, to define what they mean by reasonableness.

Here, then, is Green's achievement, that he gave Englishmen something more satisfying than Benthamism at a price they were prepared to pay, that he left Liberalism a faith instead of an interest, that he made Individualism moral and social and Idealism civilised and safe. Englishmen at least will consider that achievement no inconsiderable one.

CHAPTER IV

THE STATE AS CLASS
(MARX, LENIN, STALIN)

KARL MARX, 1818–1883

"PHILOSOPHERS have sought to interpret the world: what matters, however, is to change it," Marx declared. Judged by the standard he himself would have applied, Marx must be regarded as one of the most important, because most influential, political philosophers who have ever lived. He did, indeed, offer an interpretation of the world, but much more important from his point of view he can claim to have fashioned one of the great formative forces of history. Recognition came slowly to him in his own life-time. His *Communist Manifesto*, published in 1848, began to exercise an appreciable influence only after the founding of the First International in 1864. But thereafter his stature grew and grew and his influence reached out to the four corners of the earth, until today millions in Europe and in Asia accept his teaching as revelation and look upon him as the God of the New Age. Their voices acclaiming his godhead and venerating his disciples swell into the most menacing roar that civilisation as it has been developed in the West has ever heard.

The Appeal

His, then, has been a shattering impact on the world. Men continue to die gladly in answer to his appeal. Wherein lies his secret?

The age in which he was writing was one of great physical and technical achievement. Marx is almost lyrical in his enthusiasm for its technical perfection. "The bourgeoisie," he writes in the *Communist Manifesto*, "has been the first to show what man's activity can bring about. It has accomplished wonders far surpassing Egyptian pyramids, Roman aqueducts and Gothic cathedrals. . . . The bourgeoisie . . . draws all nations into civilisation. . . . It has created enormous cities . . . and thus rescued a considerable part of the population from the idiocy of rural life . . . and, during its rule of scarce 100 years, has created more massive and more colossal productive forces than have all preceding generations together. Subjection of nature's forces to man, machinery, application of chemistry to industry and agriculture, steam-navigation, railways, electric telegraphs, clearing of whole continents for cultivation, canalisation of rivers, whole populations conjured out of the ground—what earlier century had even a presentiment that such productive forces slumbered in the lap of social labour?"

It was an age that was becoming increasingly rationalist and materialist, an age which at once valued technical achievement and confidently anticipated that such achievement would become bigger and better. Max Beerbohm's cartoon in which he portrays a stout, prosperous, complacent Victorian gentleman contemplating a future in which he sees a stouter, more prosperous, more complacent edition of himself is typical of it. It was an age in which the products of technical achievement were very unevenly spread, an age of growing wealth for many and, so it seemed, of increasing misery for more. It was an age in which religion was no longer exercising its former appeal, and the world had grown colder in consequence. It was an age in which civilisation was not as impressive as technical achievement. Greek slavery, Marx maintained, at least produced an aristocracy of marvellous taste, a culture which still thrills the world. Industrial slavery, on the contrary, could claim for itself no more impressive purpose than "to transform a few vulgar and half-educated upstarts into 'eminent cotton spinners,' 'extensive sausage makers' and 'influential blacking dealers.' " It was an age that was repulsive in its banality, warping in its effect on the mind, destructive of many of man's finer feelings. "God says 'Take what you want from the world and pay for it,' " runs the Spanish proverb. Marx saw the achievement of bourgeois civilisation and saw also the cost. It has left intact, he wrote, "no other bond between man and man but naked self-interest, but callous 'cash-payment.' It has drowned the sacred awe of pious ecstasy, of chivalrous enthusiasm, of bourgeois sensibility, in the ice-cold water of egoistic calculation. It has dissolved personal dignity into exchange value . . . torn off the veil of feeling and affection from family relationships and reduced them to purely financial connections." Seeing the enormous growth of capitalism, Marx values it correctly. Aware of the transformation of things that it has produced, he is not blind to the transformation of men that it has entailed.

An age, then, of achievement and suffering, of strident scientific assurance and fading religious faith, of apparent fulfilment and of a great and growing emptiness, an age of which it could be said as Milton said of his time, "the hungry sheep look up and are not fed"—this was the age in which Marx lived. It was because he was able to fill that emptiness that he has gone striding the world like a giant to this day.

Marx was not, of course, the first Socialist writer of the 19th century. There was a rich crop of Socialist ideas before he wrote; its very abundance bearing witness to the spiritual emptiness of the age. St. Simon and Guizot were spreading the idea of the class war; Proudhon the notion that property is theft; Fourier the conception of the middle classes as commercial despots; Sismondi the view of the inevitability of crises, booms, and slumps; Owen the faith that the new factory era would be one of co-operation instead of competition. Marx was bitterly contemptuous of such men—"Utopian" Socialists he called them in scorn because they attacked the wrongs in the Capitalist system, not the system itself, and because they could never say how their Utopias could be either attained or maintained. They conjured up visions of beautiful roses, but, preparing no soil for the rose trees, left them to feed merely on beauty. Marx, who was the most bitter, indeed scurrilous of disputants, was not in the habit of being just to his opponents. Much more can be said for the Utopian Socialists than he allowed. They voiced those irrational longings of the empty soul from which so much of the driving force of Socialism comes. They provided him with many a useful brick and tool. They popularised the idea of a socialist society. They elaborated the labour theory of value. But they failed where he succeeded because they did not see that two requisites of Socialism as a serious political factor were a doctrine which maintains that real social forces are making for Socialism and a permanent contact with a source of power which can be harnessed for revolutionary socialist activity. They failed, too, because they were unable to present their ideas with anything approaching Marx's religious fervour.

Marx succeeded because he was such an explosive compound of Hebrew prophet and scientific propounder of political and economic theory. It is Marx the Hebrew prophet who is so filled with a religious conviction of the rottenness of Western civilisation that he makes denunciation the keynote of the *Communist Manifesto* and of *Das Capital*. It is Marx the scientific propounder of political and economic theory who produces alike a theory of party tactics and a philosophical theory of the inevitable course of social development. Sometimes the two elements in him, Hebrew prophet and social scientist, support each other. It is not fanciful to suggest that the Jewish belief in the opposition between the chosen people and the Gentiles strengthens his belief in the opposition between the proletariat and the bourgeoisie, that the firm Jewish faith in the inexorable divine judgment on Gentiles increases his confidence in the inexorable judgment of Dialectical Materialism on Capitalism, that the Jewish certainty of the ultimate restoration of the chosen people in the Messianic Kingdom confirms his certainty of the eventual achievement of the classless society. Sometimes the two elements in him contradict each other, and discrepancy between the moral point of view of the prophet and the scientific point of view of the social scientist becomes plain. As prophet he is filled with fury at the wickedness of those who have acted in a way that as scientist he maintains was indispensable for the progress of the race.

But illogicality is not always a source of weakness, and though we would be surprised if Darwin overflowed with compassion for the animals and plants which had been eliminated in the struggle for life, it is different with Marx. His compassion and his moral indignation are vital to his success. He filled the emptiness of his age because he gave to his teaching both the force of religious conviction and the certainty of apparently scientific proof. To many to whom the old faiths could make no appeal, his terrestrial paradise of Socialism meant a new ray of light, a new meaning of life. To those who followed him he was indeed the prophet of a new religion, holding out to men at once a system of ultimate ends embodying a meaning of life and forming absolute standards by which action should be judged, a path of salvation for the chosen to tread, and paradise on earth as the victor's crown. To this day the Marxist's characteristic attitude towards opponents, who are regarded as being not only in error but in sin, bears the authentic stamp of full-blooded religions.

But preaching alone would never have won Marx the success that has been his. Something other than religious fervour was demanded by his rationalistic and materialistic age which would not tolerate any creed that had no scientific or pseudo-scientific pretensions. It was because his message was also a most masterly analysis of the social processes, because he claimed to be revealing the laws of historical development, because he proclaimed that socialistic deliverance from the ills of the world was a certainty amenable to rational proof, that he became so wildly successful. Preaching alone would have appealed only to the few, analysis of the development of man in society to still fewer. But a combination of the two, preaching that could claim to be analysis, analysis that carried with it a religious devotion to man's deepest needs, generated an enthusiasm and won a passionate allegiance that spread widely the conviction of eventual victory.

The Message

What was his message?

It is a revolutionary call to the working-class. "The workers have nothing to lose but their chains. They have a world to win. Workers of the world, unite!" It is a call for the working-class to follow the leadership, though not to accept the dictatorship, of the Communist Party, the vanguard of the proletariat. It is a call for the working-class to adopt certain tactics, highly flexible in kind and changing with changing circumstances, but consistent in their revolutionary purpose. "The thing to do now," Marx wrote to Lasalle, "is to instil poison wherever possible." Thus it is laid down in the *Communist Manifesto* that Communists must make use of all antagonisms between the bourgeoisie of different countries and between different bourgeois groups within every country. Thus the *Communist Manifesto* has no interest in reform but only in revolution. Yet for purposes of propaganda it is ready to simulate an interest in immediate reforms that it does not feel—as Communists have done from that day to this. Thus Communists ever since have understood that the only consistency which has any meaning for them is consistent devotion to the cause of Proletarian Revolution. In the words of Yaroslavsky: "What coincides with the interest of the Proletarian Revolution is ethical." It is wrong to believe that Communists accept the necessity of defending any form of capitalist government against any other form. Surprised indignation, therefore, at the attitude of the Communists towards the Social Democrats in the Weimar Republic when the Nazis were on the attack is as out of place as it is at the Communist attitude towards the last war prior to the German attack on Russia. In both cases the Communists were mistaken, though they will not admit it. But they were not inconsistent. The true Marxist is inconsistent only if, in the opinion of his leaders, he acts in such a way as to delay or prevent successful revolution. Marxism is, furthermore, a call for the working-class to follow a certain strategy—to strike home and rise in revolt only in revolutionary situations. Marx had as little patience as Lenin and Stalin with revolutions which have no hope of success.

Of his call to the working-class to act, we need say no more than that good action for him is action appropriate to the circumstances, and that, as he is never tired of insisting, circumstances change and new circumstances of course demand new study. Marxism, however, is much more than this clarion call to the working-class. It is also a means of knowing exactly, as a result of detailed study of a particular kind of the stresses and strains in existing societies, what are revolutionary situations. And it is an assurance of the ultimate victory of the working-class. What Marx offers here as a guide to action and as a promise of success is a theory of Dialectical Materialism, a theory of Historical Materialism, and an economic analysis that taken together can fairly claim to be the greatest and most compelling statement of Scientific Socialism ever made.

Dialectical Materialism

Nowhere unfortunately, does Marx tell us what he means by "materialism." But at least he makes it plain that his materialism is dialectical not mechanical. In mechanical materialism evolution is the path taken by material things under the pressure of their environment. In dialectical materialism, evolution is the development of matter from within, environment helping or hindering, but neither originating the evolutionary process nor capable of preventing it from reaching its inevitable goal. Matter, to the dialectical materialist, is active not passive, and moves by an inner necessity of its nature. Therefore dialectical materialism is more interested in motion than in matter, in a vital energy within matter inevitably driving it towards perfect human society just as Hegel's demi-urge drove forward to the perfect realisation of Spirit. As Engels said: "The dialectical method grasps things and their images, ideas, essentially in their sequence, their movement, their birth and death."

This motion, to the dialectical materialist who follows Hegel very closely here, is made possible by the conflict of opposites. Every stage of history which falls short of perfection carries within itself the seeds of its own destruction. Each stage reached in the march to the classless society, the thesis, calls into being its opposite or antithesis, and from the clash between the two a new synthesis emerges in which what was true in both thesis and antithesis is preserved and which serves as a starting-point for the whole process again until the classless society has been achieved.

"Contradiction," then, as Hegel says, "is the very moving principle of the world." But for the Marxist as for the Hegelian, it works in a peculiar way. The change it produces takes place gradually, imperceptibly, until a certain point is reached beyond which it becomes sudden so that each synthesis is brought about very abruptly. Water becomes ice, Feudalism Capitalism, Capitalism Socialism, as a result of a sudden qualitative change.

How closely Marx follows Hegel here is obvious. For Hegel the universal substance is Spirit; for Marx it is Matter. Both Spirit and Matter need to develop themselves and both do so by means of an inner dialectic. For Hegel the inevitable goal is the Idea fully conscious of itself; for Marx the inevitable goal is the classless society, perfectly organised for production, sufficient for itself. Neither Hegel nor Marx proves that the goal which they state to be inevitable is indeed so. Both begin with the assumption that it is and in both historical analysis serves to illustrate but not to prove the initial act of faith. In both the dialectic retains a strong element of mysticism. It is not too much to say that the influence on Marxists of the Hegelian triad of thesis, antithesis, and synthesis, is that of a religious myth. Not only does it greatly simplify social tensions, it symbolises the continual growth and protest of what can be regarded as the young forces of life against those that are old and grey, and it gives assurance of victory as the final outcome of the struggle. Lenin was justified in saying how impossible it is to understand Marx without having studied Hegel. The only important differences between them are that Marx applied the dialectic to the future and indulged in much pseudo-scientific fortune-telling which Hegel would have been the first to condemn, and that, of course, he completely rejected Hegel's philosophic idealism. As he wrote in the preface to the second edition of *Das Capital*: "In Hegel's writings, dialectic stands on its head. You must turn it right way up again if you want to discover the rational kernel that is hidden away within the wrappings of mystification."

Not the least of the difficulties that confront the student of dialectical materialism is that Marx and Engels never worked out their ideas about it. Nowhere do they treat it in detail, though it is of course assumed in all their writings. They are clear only in their expressions of dislike for what has usually been called materialism. Thus the opening sentence of Marx's Theses on Feuerbach reads: "The chief defect of all hitherto existing materialism." Thus, too, Engels spoke of the typical materialists of his day as "vulgarising pedders" and "cobweb-spinning flea-crackers"—definitions lacking in clarity but not in contempt. Clarity might have resulted had Marx chosen a different name for what he clearly regards as a philosophy very different from that normally known as materialist.

But clarity is not always desirable. It might have made impossible such effective epigrams as: "It is not the consciousness of men that determines their existence, but, on the contrary, their social existence determines their consciousness." Marx believes that society is governed by inexorable laws. Thus he writes in the preface to *Das Capital* of "tendencies which work out with an iron necessity towards an inevitable goal." Thus he said that a country which was more highly industrialised than others "simply presents those others with a picture of their own future." Yet this is hardly compatible with his theory of knowledge which insists that knowledge is indissolubly bound up with action and that its function is to change the world. Moreover the third of his theses on Feuerbach runs: "The materialistic doctrine that men are the products of circumstances and education, and that changed men are therefore the products of other circumstances and a changed education, forgets that circumstances are changed by men and that the educator must himself be educated." Later in life he again maintains: "Man makes his own history," even though "he does not do so out of conditions chosen by himself," and he believed that those higher departments, such as law and philosophy, of the superstructure of society, which is itself determined by the productive forces of the substructure, are always seeking to free themselves from their tether in economic interest and to evolve a professional group at least partly independent of class bias.

It seems clear that he had the idea that man could become the master of his own destiny—though he persuaded many that he meant the exact opposite, that history is wholly predetermined. Engels later admitted that he and Marx had overstated the extent to which economic causes could be found for political and legal institutions. In a letter to Bloch written in 1890, a letter which he found so satisfactory that he repeated the gist of it to Starkenburg four years later, he said: "Marx and I are partly responsible for the fact that at times our disciples have laid more weight upon the economic factor than belongs to it. We were compelled to emphasise its central character in opposition to our opponents, who denied it, and there wasn't always time, place and occasion to do justice to the other factors in the reciprocal interactions of the historical process."

Yet in that letter Engels maintains that the economic situation is "in the last instance the determining factor of history," is "finally decisive." This is far from being as satisfactory as Engels found it, since it is so clearly an attempt to have it both ways. The problem remains. If man is really master of his destiny, that can only be through the use he makes of his mind. But if mind is only superstructure, it is itself determined by the productive forces of the substructure, the operation of which is determined by the dialectic. If there is really interaction between them, then the whole thesis falls to the ground since we cannot now be dealing with a purely economic factor but with one which has been in part determined by non-economic factors, and it cannot, accordingly, be said that the economic factor must always be decisive. Marx, in fact, was wedded to two ideas, to the idea that productive forces develop automatically, and to the idea that in some way man's mind develops them. It may therefore be thought that obscurity is advantageous to polygamists even of the intellectual variety, and that if Marx had really attempted to work out the connection between mind and material forces, he would have had to abandon his theory.

Historical Materialism

Historical materialism is the application of the principles of

dialectical materialism to the development of society. Before out-
lining it, it is as well to deal with an immediate difficulty. The
name, though Marx used it, does not convey accurately what is
meant. It is, in fact, an economic interpretation of history,
according to which all the mass phenomena of history are determined by economic conditions. This view has no necessary connection with materialism, with which Buckle's belief that climate
is decisive in the history of man or Freud's conviction that sex
is the determining factor, are as compatible as Marx's contention
that economic causes are fundamental.

The theory begins with the "simple truth, which is the clue
to the meaning of history, that man must eat to live." His very
survival depends upon the success with which he can produce
what he wants from Nature. Production is therefore the most
important of all human activities. Men in association produce
more than men in isolation, and Society is thus the result of an
attempt to secure the necessities of life. But Society has never
accomplished that to the satisfaction of all its members, and has,
in consequence, always been subject to internal stresses and
strains. Hence man, not realising that unsatisfied needs are
merely the result of defective modes of production, has always
imagined another world in which those needs will be met, and
religion, which is no more than the shadow cast by a defective
economic system—"the sob of the oppressed creature, the heart
of a heartless world, the spirit of conditions utterly unspiritual"
—and which will pass away with the defects that have produced
it, has been widespread. It is "the opium of the people," not in
the sense that it is a drug administered to the exploited by the
exploiters, but that in a society where no one's needs are fully
met religion is the resort of all.

Man's attempts in recorded history to secure life's necessities
can be grouped into four main stages. There is the primitive
communist or "Asiatic," in which the forms of production are
slight and communally owned. There are the ancient, the
feudal, the capitalist, in all of which the class which controls
the forces of production dominates the rest, thus perpetuating
tension and conflict. In all stages of human life the forms or
conditions of production determine the structure of society. Thus
"the hand-mill gives you society with the feudal lord; the steam-
mill society with the industrial capitalist." The structure of
society will in its turn breed attitudes, actions, and civilisations.

Therefore "all the social, political and intellectual relations, all religious and legal systems, all the theoretical outlooks which emerge in the course of history, are derived from the material conditions of life."

We must, then, distinguish between the foundations or the substructure—the productive forces—and the superstructure—religion, morals, politics. As Marx writes in *The 18th Brumaire*: "Upon the several forms of property, upon the social conditions of existence, a whole superstructure is reared of various and peculiarly shaped feelings, illusions, habits of thought and conceptions of life. The whole class produces and shapes these out of its material foundation and out of the corresponding social conditions." This is not to say that men, consciously or unconsciously, act only from economic motives. It is only to say that while other motives exist they are always subordinate to the economic factor and in the long run ineffective. Nor is it to declare that religions, metaphysics, schools of art, ethical ideas, literary tastes, and productions are either reducible to economic motives or of no importance. It is only to uncover the economic conditions which shape them and to which they owe their rise and fall. Generalising and popularising, it may be said that the Theory of Historical Materialism holds that our daily work forms our minds, that it is our position within the productive forces which determines our point of view and the particular sides of things that we see.

The forms of production which underlie society, the theory further maintains, change according to necessities inherent in them so as to produce their successors merely by their own working. The system, for instance, characterised by the "hand-mill" creates an economic and social situation in which the adoption of the mechanical method of milling becomes a practical necessity. The "steam-mill" in turn creates new social functions, new groups, new outlooks, which in time outgrow their own frame. The factories which are necessary to solve the economic problems of the 18th century create the conditions of 19th-century problems. These self-developing forms of production are, as it were, the propeller which accounts first for economic and then for social change, a propeller which requires no external impetus.

It follows, then, that until the stage of perfect production is reached, all societies will be transitory. It follows, too, that each stage is a step nearer perfection. Every society, Marx says, is confronted with problems which it must face and solve—or collapse. But the possibility of collapse is never considered, though no great knowledge of history is needed to convince one that civilisations can and do collapse. Indeed, in his *Critique of Political Economy* Marx even says: "Mankind always takes up only such problems as it can solve." In the most literal sense of the word, Marxism can certainly claim to be progressive. Each stage, however bad it may seem, is a necessary stage on the way to the classless society. Marx said of Feudalism: "It is the bad side which calls into being the movement which makes history, in that it brings the struggle to a head. If, at the time of the supremacy of feudalism, the economists in their enthusiasm for knightly virtues for the beautiful harmony between rights and duties, for the patriarchal life of the towns, for the flourishing home industries in the country, for the development of industry organised in corporations, companies and guilds, in a word, for everything which forms the finer side of feudalism, had set themselves the problem of eliminating everything which could throw a shadow on the picture—serfdom, privileges, anarchy— where would it all have ended? They would have destroyed every element which called forth strife, they would have nipped in the bud the development of the middle class. They would have set themselves the absurd problem of blotting out history." No stage will end until it has become a fetter on, rather than a spur to, the forces of production. Men cannot therefore short-circuit history and "overleap the natural phases of evolution." Finally, the productive forces inherent in any society develop completely before a change takes place, and the change itself will be sudden as when water turns into steam. In that sudden revolutionary change the entire structure of society will be eventually transformed, until the new society in its turn is overthrown and remoulded.

Marxism, then, is an optimistic doctrine of inevitable progress and of the ultimate triumph of man. "Man has only to know himself, to measure all conditions of life against himself, to judge them by his own character, to organise the world according to the demands of his own nature in a truly human way, and he will have solved all the riddles of our age," is Engel's proud claim. But so far man has appeared in Marx's picture only as a Chinese painter of the old school would present him— as a small, insignificant figure sitting at the foot of a rock or of a tree, dwarfed by the immensity of nature around him. The underlying forces of production, of which he and his skill are admittedly a part, are the explanation of the major historical transitions. Has he no more important role in the historical process of which he is part?

He has, for men are the agents through which the organisation of the world is adjusted to the changing needs of the powers of production. In maintaining that, Marx is not thinking of men as individuals. The great importance he attaches to production leads naturally to his view that man as an individual has little significance. Production is a collective act, and it is the collective, therefore, not the individual that is the unit for Marx. In all social structures until the classless society has been reached the collective is the social class which, if conditions of life determine people's thinking and behaviour, must be composed of those whose conditions of life are similar.

As soon as mankind emerges from the primitive communist state, it is seen that at every stage of society a particular class gets control and exploits the rest. That it does so is no matter of chance, but is the result of the inexorable law of history. The class which exercises ownership of the means of production will dominate the rest. When, for instance, the most important factor in the forces of production is agricultural, land-owners will be the ruling class. The dominant class alone has freedom, and to preserve this must act the part of oppressors. They therefore create an executive and repressive instrument by the use of which they hope to maintain their position and which is called the State. Force is, then, the *raison d'être* of the State, repression its characteristic. As Marx expressed it in *Das Capital*: "After every revolution marking a progressive phase in the class struggle, the purely repressive character of the State power stands out in bolder relief." As the conditions of production change, the existing State ceases to meet the requirements of the new exploiting class. The feudal state, based on status, is not an effective instrument for capitalists, and is therefore replaced by the capitalist state based on contract. The collapse of the old order and the arrival of the new State, with its moral and political beliefs and its property relations suitable to the interests of the new dominant class, is inevitable, but it will not happen automatically at the very moment when economic conditions justify it. What will happen automatically is that a revolutionary situation will be produced, and within that revolutionary situation the struggle between the new challenging and the old challenged class will take place. The history of society is the history of class war. The idea of class war was not of course new. St. Simon and Guizot had both made use of it. What is, however, original in Marx is the union of this idea with Hegel's dialectic. The rise and domination of each class, Marx teaches, is as necessary as are the various phenomena of history which, in Hegel's view, were needed by the Spirit on its way to its goal. Applying the dialectic, it follows that each dominant class necessarily develops its opposite, and from the clash between the two, baron and serf, freeman and slave, burgess and journeyman, oppressor and oppressed, the new ruling class emerges. This class war at last reaches its simplest phase when the capitalist is face to face with the proletariat. Capitalism, the thesis, calls into being its anti-thesis, organised labour, and from the resultant clash the final synthesis of the classless society will result, when "pre-history ends and history begins."

This idyllic state will, however, be preceded by a transitional period known as Socialism, in which the dictatorship of the proletariat will gradually socialise natural resources and stamp out the last remnants of capitalism. In this period goods will still be distributed, not according to need but according to work performed. The dictatorship of the proletariat will be as much repressive as was the dictatorship of all preceding dominant classes. The State continues to be the repressive organ of the class controlling the means of production, but instead of the minority oppressing the majority the majority will oppress the small group of former exploiters. The workers' State will thus be far more democratic than the bourgeois parliamentary democracies. They, indeed, were a sham and a contradiction in terms, since democracy cannot exist in any society which is divided, as it is under capitalism, into two irreconcilably antagonistic groups. Marx must appear as a very unconvincing champion of democracy. He was a great autocrat, convinced of the infallibility of his views. He could never have said as did Cromwell: "I beseech ye in the bowels of Christ, think it possible that ye be mistaken." Belief in infallibility is not the hall-mark of the democrat, nor is the view, so typical of him, that only the collective mattered, not the individual who could never have rights against it. But since he believed that revolutions were possible

only in the fullness of time when the proletariat would be both
the great majority and capable of taking over what was best in
capitalist, bourgeois, parliamentary democracy, he took for
granted that, as Engels said, democracy would be "the specific
form of the dictatorship of the proletariat."

Under the loving care of the dictatorship of the proletariat,
Socialism will blossom into Communism. But of that Marx
tells us little, regarding it as "Utopian" to speculate on the
new society that was the goal of man's desiring. Two things,
however, we can say of this golden age. Society will be organised
then and goods distributed on the principle "from each according to his ability, to each according to his need." And of course
there will no longer be a State. That instrument of class
oppression will have come to the end of its long march through
history, for there will be no more classes.

It is much to be regretted that Marx and Engels are so vague
and even confused in what they say of the State "withering
away." The highly interesting doctrine of the "withering away"
of the State is elaborated by Engels from Marx's tentative expressions. In 1874 Engels declared that the State, "as a result of the
social revolution of the future, would vanish," because all public
functions would simply be changed from political into administrative ones. What this is supposed to imply is far from clear.
In 1877 he writes that by converting the means of production
into State property the proletariat would abolish the State as
State. This same seizure of the means of production would "at
once be its last independent act as a State." This, if no less great
a tax on our credulity, is at least more definite, as it tells us
when to expect the State to wither away. In 1882 Engels adds
that when the State seizes the means of production there will
take place "the leap of humanity out of the realm of necessity
into the realm of freedom." The prospect becomes still more
appealing, and the date remains no less definite. But two years
later there is an unfortunate retreat. The whole machinery of
the State, Engels says, will be relegated to the museum of an-
tiquities, along with the bronze axe and the spinning wheel.
This relegation, however, will no longer take place when the
means of production have been nationalised, but evidently at a
much later time. In 1891 he speaks of the victorious proletariat
"paring down the worst aspects of the State, until a new generation grown up in the new, free social conditions, is capable of

putting aside the whole paraphernalia of State." This is in his preface to the new edition of Marx's *Civil War in France*, in which Marx wrote that the working-class "will have to go through long struggles, a whole series of historical processes which will completely transform men and circumstances alike." Engels, it is obvious, has transposed this idea which Marx intended to apply to the period before the revolution to the post-revolutionary era. "In Marx," said Lenin, "you will find no trace of Utopianism in the sense of inventing the 'new' society and constructing it out of fancies." In general this is true, but it can hardly be doubted that the idea of the State withering away belongs to the realm of fantasy and is as Utopian as anything that Marx condemned in others.

"What I did that was new," Marx claimed, "was to prove (1) that the existence of classes is only bound up with the particular, historic phases in the development of production; (2) that the class struggle necessarily leads to the dictatorship of the proletariat; (3) that this dictatorship itself only constitutes the transition to the abolition of all classes and to a classless society." Here, then, is Marx's theory of Historical Materialism, not a sovereign formula to be mechanically applied, but a working hypothesis, a method of investigation which will help us to understand the pattern of the past and to predict the path of the future. In *Das Capital* he shows how he intended it to be applied, and in *Das Capital* also he supported it with an economic analysis of capitalist exploitation of Surplus Value.

His Economic Analysis

Marx's famous theory of Surplus Value is an extension of Ricardo's theory according to which the value of every commodity is proportional to the quantity of labour contained in it, provided this labour is in accordance with the existing standard of efficiency of production. Labour power equals the brain, muscle, and nerve of the labourer. Being itself a commodity, it must command a price proportional to the number of labour hours that entered into its production. This will be the number of labour hours required to house and feed the labourer and to bring up his family. This is the value of his services, for which he receives corresponding wages. But labour is unique among commodities because in being used up it creates more value. The employer therefore, once he has acquired the labourer's stock of potential services, can make him work more hours than would be required to produce that stock. The value thus created over and above what the labourer is paid for, Marx calls Surplus Value, and he regards it as the source of all profit.

If his theory of Surplus Value is an attempt to explain prices it soon runs into difficulties. For if, as Marx says, Surplus Value is produced by the consumption of labour power, an industry in which capital is invested in labour would be more profitable than one in which capital is invested in machinery—which is absurd. In Volume III of *Das Capital,* Marx tries to deal with this difficulty. Competition between capitalists for more profitable investments, he says, tends to equalise returns on invested capital. There is, as a matter of fact, no justification for the assumption that there is a uniform rate of profit in a capitalist economy at any given period, but even if there was, Marx is now explaining price as equalling the cost of production plus the average return on all the capital invested. This is clearly not the same as his first definition of price, according to which the price of a commodity is determined by the labour power put into it.

But perhaps it is fairer to Marx, who intensely disliked economics and whose chapters devoted to economic theory are the dullest in *Das Capital,* to regard his theory of Surplus Value not so much as a theory of price but rather as a theory of the Just Price. For all his apparent concentration on what is, it is in what ought to be that his main interest lies. In spite of the failure of his involved attempts to explain away the inherent absurdities of the notion of Surplus Value, he can still make use of that idea to show that the initiative, skill, intelligence of the workers bring them no reward since they are turned solely to the advantage of the capitalist who portrays them as his own enterprise, foresight, providence, and organising ability. He can still use the theory of Surplus Value to show that a competitive system in which labour power is regarded as a commodity is self-destructive, and that, as Engels wrote, the only salvation is Socialism, "which will emancipate human labour-power from its position as a commodity." As a theory of price, the theory of Surplus Value is rubbish; as an appeal that it is degrading to treat labour as a commodity, it is powerful. "It is impossible," as Max Beer said, "to set aside the view that Marx's theory of value has rather the significance of a political and social slogan than of an economic truth." We can agree with him that "unique as an investigator of the laws of the proletarian movement, eminent and even a great pioneer as a sociologist, Marx is, in respect of economic theory, predominantly an agitator."

Marx's theory of Surplus Value is merely the introduction to something that interested him far more, an examination not of capitalism as it is but of capitalism as it was becoming. Using nature in the Aristotelian sense of what a thing will become when fully developed, we may say that it is with the nature of capitalism that Marx is primarily dealing, and that his main concern is to show that its nature is self-destruction. Capitalism, according to him, is doubly doomed—doomed by the general law of capital accumulation and centralisation which begins to operate automatically as soon as capitalists appropriate Surplus Value; doomed also by its own internal contradictions. According to the law of capitalist accumulation there occurs "the concentration of already formed capitals, the destruction of their individual independence, the expropriation of capitalist by capitalist, the transformation of many small capitals into a few large ones." This accumulation of capital is unavoidable, not because the capitalist "shares with the miser the passion for wealth as wealth," but because, "what in the miser is a mere idiosyncrasy is, in the capitalist, the effect of the social mechanism of which he is but one of the wheels." "To accumulate," Marx says, "is to conquer the world of social wealth, to increase the mass of human beings exploited by him, and thus to extend both the direct and the indirect sway of the capitalist." To fail to accumulate is itself to be thrust into the ranks of the exploited masses. Competition, the growth of credit, the development of a joint-stock system, technical improvements involving high initial capital cost, all speed up the accumulation and the centralisation of capital. But "poverty grows as the accumulation of capital grows." For technical improvement lessens the immediate demand for labour, creates a pool of unemployed which keeps down wages, and the lot of the workers becomes harder and harder to bear until "they have nothing to lose but their chains." Moreover, the development of capitalism simplifies the class struggle, since it leaves only two classes, the property owners and the wage-earners, embattled against each other. Thus by increasing the poverty of the great majority and by simplifying the class struggle, the law of capitalist accumulation leads capitalism to the final and inevitable clash with the proletariat that can have no other ending than the triumph of the oppressed.

As though to make assurance doubly sure, Marx demonstrates that capitalism must destroy itself by its own internal contradictions. It is too wasteful of men. Under the pressure of competition it becomes "a squanderer not only of flesh and blood, but also of nerve and brain." This waste must eventually cause a breakdown of the mechanism of capitalism, which cannot work without men. Of even greater importance, it creates abundance and fails to cope with it. Capitalism can never resolve the fundamental contradiction that competition both makes inevitable the greatest increase in the production of goods and by rationalisation of production methods and consequent lowering of wages reduces the market for these goods, thus destroying the possibility of existence for the over-developed enterprises it has itself called into being. It completely fails to deal with the crises it thus itself brings on. "And how does the bourgeoisie get over these crises? On the one hand by enforced destruction of a mass of productive forces, on the other by the conquest of new markets and by a more thorough exploitation of the old ones. That is to say, by paving the way for more extensive and more destructive crises, and by diminishing the means whereby crises are prevented." Crises become bigger and bigger until they endanger the whole community. Then, when it is demonstrated beyond all doubt that capitalism cannot provide security "for its slaves even within the confines of their slavish existence," the day of reckoning is at hand. The ringing tones of the Hebrew prophet announce it: "Along with the constantly diminishing number of the magnates of capital, who usurp and monopolise all advantages of this process of transformation, grows the mass of misery, oppression, slavery, degradation, exploitation; but with this, too, grows the revolt of the working-class, a class increasing in numbers and disciplined, united, organised by the very mechanism of the process of Capitalist production itself. The monopoly of Capitalism becomes a fetter on the mode of production which has sprung up and flourished along with it and under it. Centralisation of the means of production and socialisation of labour at last reach a point where they become incompatible with their capitalist husk. This bursts asunder. The knell of capitalist private property sounds. The expropriators are expropriated."

Marx's economic analysis has thus achieved its purpose, which is to afford scientific proof of Historical Materialism and to make good the claim of the *Communist Manifesto*: "The theoretical conclusions of the Communists are in no way based on ideas or principles that have been invented or discovered by this or that would-be universal reformer. They merely express, in general terms, actual relations springing from an existing class struggle, from an historical movement going on under our very eyes." Sustained by the triple assurance of Dialectical Materialism, of Historical Materialism and of an economic analysis of the nature of capitalism, the Marxist can march confidently on, firm in the faith that the trampling of proletarian feet is already echoing across the promised land.

An Appraisal of Marxism

Through years of bitter poverty, Marx applied himself to the task of constructing scientific socialism, and the magnitude of his achievement cannot be denied by even his most unsympathetic critic. He uncovered vital truths, and he foresaw important developments that were hidden from his contemporaries. He realised, as they did not, what was the relationship between the trade-cycle and over-production and unemployment. He saw that machine industry would grow too big to be confined within national frontiers. He knew that the volume of trade is no true test of national well-being. He was aware of the evil results that can follow from making men mere minders of machines, and he was right in believing that, by way of compensation, concentrating people in large factories or mines would produce in them a strong psychological feeling of unity. He saw that industrialisation must necessarily involve great changes in social relationships. In showing that economic factors had been overlooked by historians, he opened up new possibilities in historical writing. It can certainly be agreed that his idea of the interdependence of political and legal institutions with the prevailing economic system is one of the most fruitful of 19th-century conceptions. Perhaps it can even be admitted that because of this he was the most important social philosopher of the whole 19th century. There has been no more powerful attack on complacency and squalor than his, and when we read, for instance, in Townsend: "It seems to be a law of nature that the poor should be to a certain degree improvident that there may be always some to fulfil the most servile, the most sordid, and the most ignoble offices in the community. The stock of human happiness is thereby much increased, whilst the more delicate are not only relieved from drudgery, but are left at liberty without interruption to pursue those callings which are suited to their various dispositions," perhaps we can add, and none more necessary.

There is thus much that is true and worth-while in Marx, but much also that must be criticised. There is the unresolved dilemma in his conception of materialism. It can be agreed that his is no crude fatalistic materialism. But there is no denying the fact that the idea of economic forces operating independently of man's will is of the essence of his teaching. Where he deals with the forces of production, or the stages of history or of social consciousness, the language he uses is the language of determinism. Where he deals with men or particular events, he speaks of deliberate intent and conscious direction. He has it both ways, surreptitiously as it were, though he will not allow us to have it both ways more openly by claiming that both material and non-material factors are of the utmost importance in man's development. His curious evasion of the possibility of failure that lead Engels to the absurd contention that if Napoleon had never lived someone else would have appeared to do his work for him is an illustration of the strength of determinism in his teaching. It is no accident that he excludes the element of chance, though no very wide knowledge of history is needed to convince most of us of the truth of Voltaire's remark : "The older one becomes, the more clearly one sees that King Hazard fashions three-fourths of the events in this miserable world."

Interesting as Marx's theory of classes is, examination even of Western civilisation will not support the view that economic position always determines social eminence. It is, indeed, frequently the very reverse, and in few countries is business achievement even today the only or the best avenue to social distinction. Marx, too, is wrong in his static conception of classes. Classes are not fixed and rigidly maintained blocks. There is constant movement from class to class, so much so that perhaps the most salient features of social classes is the incessant rise and fall of individual families from one to another. No doubt this fact is truer of some countries than others, so that Sorel could write : "The English are distinguished by an extraordinary lack of understanding of the class war." But it is certainly not true only of Great Britain.

Marx believed that he had "scientifically proved" that the development of capitalism would leave facing each other in irreconcilable opposition two and only two classes. That has not been so. He did not allow for the emergence of a new class of managers and skilled technical advisers. As he could only judge by past experience, he is not to be greatly blamed for this. But he claimed to be able to foretell the future of capitalism and it seems evident that he has failed to do so. The forecasts based on his economic analysis of Surplus Value have similarly proved wide of the mark. He declared that working men must become ever poorer until the day of final reckoning. But real wages today are higher than they were a century ago, not lower as they should now be according to Marx. He said that capital would be concentrated in fewer and fewer hands. The development of trusts seems to confirm this, but only superficially. Small businesses persist because new enterprises are constantly arising and because there is a point at which the disadvantages of size outweigh the advantages of centralisation. In fact, the ownership of capital is being more evenly spread throughout the community than at any previous period. Marx did not foresee the possibilities of the Trade Union Movement and of the Social Service State. Engels lived long enough to have some inkling of the future. "The British working-class," he wrote in disgust, "is actually becoming more and more bourgeois, and it seems that this most bourgeois of all nations wants to bring matters to such a pass as to have a bourgeois aristocracy and a bourgeois proletariat side by side with the bourgeoisie." To be mistaken seems to be the fate of economists, of whom the *New Yorker* once said: "These fellows have the whole thing down to an inexact science." But Marx's mistakes here are important. He was convinced that the classless society was coming because he believed that the next phase of history would witness the revolutionary clash of two completely opposed classes. As these have not emerged, the classless society would still appear to be shimmering dejectedly on far-away horizons.

Nor should Marx's serious historical faults be overlooked. There is no justification for his division of history into four main periods. The dialectic seems to demand it, and therefore it is arbitrarily done, centuries difficult to fit into the division being conveniently forgotten in the process. Marx cannot be blamed for not knowing what has only been learned since his death—that modern anthropology would not substantiate his description of primitive communism. But there is no excuse for his view of the ancient world. The great achievements of the age of the Antonines were well known when he was writing. It was nonsense to say of such an age that Christianity was the expression of the frustrated hopes of the downtrodden proletariat. It was even greater nonsense to speak of a movement from the low level of such an age to a higher "feudal" level—merely to suit the requirements of an imaginary dialectic. A philosophy of history which is based on the experience of a hundred years and neglects the teaching of the previous thousand would not, Acton warns us, be very satisfactory. We may apply his remark to Marx, adding the reflection that Marx has never asked himself why the development of capitalism should have occurred only in Western Europe. If only material factors shape history, this development of capitalism should be true of all civilisations all over the world. That it is not true of other civilisations should teach us that important as are the material factors that Marx stressed, other factors influencing man's development are to be neglected only at our peril.

Marx was wrong in ignoring the psychological aspects of politics. Though his is an explanation of the State in terms of force, nowhere does he give us any adequate treatment of the problem of power. Nowhere in his work is there the realisation that men desire power for the satisfaction of their pride and self-respect and that for some men power must be regarded as an end in itself. One must go further and say that nowhere does he show any real appreciation of the defects in human nature. His most readable pages are those in which he allows a deep compassion and a righteous wrath to call forth the rolling thunder of the prophet. Yet he hardly seems aware of man's selfishness in any immediate sense. Lenin once said: "The great socialists, in foreseeing the arrival of the classless society, presupposed a person not like the present man in the street." That naïve admission that human nature is ignored by Marx is perhaps the most convincing proof that great man as he was he yet knew not all things.

Yet it cannot be denied that the true and the false together in him constitute one of the most tremendously compelling forces that modern history has seen. Sometimes in alliance with, sometimes in opposition to, that other great force of the 19th century, Nationalism, it has girdled the earth. For the power of his message, for the inspiration of his teaching, and for his effect upon future developments, Marx can be sure of his place in any collection of the world's great masters of political thought.

VLADIMIR LENIN, 1870–1924

His Task

It is not uncommon in the history of faiths to find that commentaries on the original doctrine soon make their appearance, and commentaries on the commentaries, until in course of time fundamental parts of the faith are altered almost beyond recognition. This has been true of Marxism, much of the inner meaning of which has been radically changed by one of its most fanatical, dogmatic, and apparently orthodox disciples who happened to be also one of the greatest political geniuses of modern history. Yet Lenin was not a great theorist. The real Marxian scholar among Russian revolutionaries was Plekhanov. Nevertheless, Lenin's writings are formidably numerous, for he assumed the task, as Stalin tells us in his *Foundations of Leninism*, of bringing Marx up to date, of restating the faith and rescuing the true revolutionary Marxism which had been buried by the opportunists and revisionists of the Second International, and of adapting Marxism to Russia. In accomplishing it, Lenin set the feet of Marxists upon that Stalinist road which the great majority of those who have not been liquidated seem to have been content to tread hitherto.

Marx had taught that the development of capitalism and its concentration in the hands of the few would leave two classes embattled against each other—the possessors of capital and the proletariat. Intermediate classes would be pressed down into the proletariat, and the class struggle would grow ever more intense. His prophecies, as Bernstein in the 1880's had no difficulty in showing, had proved singularly inept. The lower middle classes had not been crushed out of existence: they had grown stronger. The class struggle had not become more pronounced: it had become so much less obvious that in 1914 socialist parties all over Europe saw their interests no longer in the advocacy of class war but in the active support of national war. Where prophecies were so clearly wrong, it might reasonably be expected that the analysis which gave rise to them would come to be seen as mistaken. Lenin therefore hastened to the defence of Marxism, bringing it up to date in the latest stage of capitalism, and, by making use of his Theory of Imperialism, explaining away developments which were the very reverse of those which Marx had foreseen.

His Theory of Imperialism

In his *Imperialism: the Highest Stage of Capitalism,* Lenin maintained that the lower middle classes and the skilled workmen of advanced industrial countries were saved from the increasing misery which Marx had foretold for them, and therefore forbore to prosecute the class war with vigour, only because of the colonial territories which their countries dominated. Their relationship to colonial peoples was the relationship between capitalists and proletariat. They, who in the absence of empire would have been the proletariat, were now the capitalists, and the genuine proletariat, sunk ever deeper in their misery and degradation, were the wretched, exploited inhabitants of colonial lands. This stage of Imperialism, Lenin asserted, was in no sense a contradiction of Marx's teaching but a fulfilment of it, even though Marx himself had not sufficiently foreseen it. As capitalism develops, Lenin says, units of industrial production grow bigger and combine in trusts and cartels to produce monopoly capitalism. The same process takes place in the financial world. Banks combine and become masters of capital that the industrialists use so that monopoly capitalism is also finance capitalism. Monopoly-finance capitalism is aggressively expansionist. Its characteristic export is capital, and its consequences are threefold. It results in the exploitation of colonial peoples, whom it subjects to the capitalist law of increasing misery and whose liberty it destroys. It produces war between the nations, since it substitutes international competition for competition inside the nation, and in the clash of combines and Powers seeking markets and territory war becomes inevitable. And ultimately it brings about the end of capitalism and the emergence of the new order, since with the arming and military training of the workers wars which begin as national wars will end as class wars. Marx therefore, says Lenin, was not wrong. He had merely paid insufficient attention to one stage, and that the penultimate stage, of his own argument. That argument, however, was essentially correct, and the faithful could believe that all would come about as he had foretold.

Lenin's Theory of Imperialism was a neat answer to criticisms made against Marx, but it was fundamentally dishonest in a way that Marx himself had indeed specifically condemned. Marx said on one occasion: "It is a distorting speculation to declare a later historical development to have been the cause of a precedent event or development." The consequences of a process cannot precede the process itself. Yet this is exactly what Lenin makes them do. When discussing economic institutions, he had to choose a late opening date for the period of imperialism. He could not put the dominance of industrial combinations earlier than the first decade of the 20th century. But when discussing the political consequences of industrial and financial trustification, he had to choose an early opening date for the period of imperialism which was in its heyday far earlier than the first decade of the 20th century. The partitioning of the New World, for instance, was complete much before the end of the 19th century. The results, in fact, seem to be there long before the cause—an anomaly confirmed by contemplation of Great Britain which had the largest empire in the world and which was never dominated by finance capitalism as Lenin defines it. Lenin was aware of the awkwardness of making the political consequences of an economic process precede the process itself, and he sought to relieve embarrassment as cardsharpers have frequently done—by shuffling the cards. He used an early or a late date as the beginning of the period of imperialism to suit the changing needs of his argument.

Nor is that the only sleight of hand of which he is guilty. If the real international is not the Communist but the Capitalist through the development of international cartels, why should that not lead—as Kautsky believed that it might—to an international sharing of markets, to an internationalisation of political institutions which would reflect the economic internationalisation of interlocking combines, as an alternative to war? Lenin, of course, will have none of this. He charges Kautsky with not seeing that the partitioning of world markets is proportionate to power, to the power of sovereign states and of the economies which arise within them. Here he is smoothly sliding the ace from his sleeve into his hand. He is smuggling in a political factor—the power of sovereign States—which governs economic evolution and is not governed by it. In so doing he is contradicting his assertion that monopoly capitalism governs the politics of the imperialist age and is saying that the politics of the imperialist age govern the development of monopoly capitalism. That is both true and non-Marxist. His view is a credit to his realism, though not to his honesty and least of all to his Marxism. It is Kautsky the attacked, not Lenin the attacker, who abides in this exchange by Marxian rules.

There remains a further ambiguity in Lenin's Theory of Imperialism. History has so strikingly refuted it. Lenin argued that investing capitalists pushed their governments into dangerous diplomatic adventures and maintained that this was the root cause of war in the age of imperialism. More frequently the very opposite has happened. It was, for instance, the governments of Italy and of Russia who pushed their financiers into situations which made war against Turkey and Japan extremely probable. And at the time they did so they were importers of capital, not exporters as, according to Lenin, expansionist States should be. Financiers may have pushed Great Britain towards the Boer War, but other interests, interests of power believed to be threatened by Kruger's flirtation with Germany, took her into that war.

In other ways Lenin's facts were wrong. He said that the export of capital did not "develop formidable proportions until the beginning of the 20th century," and that the greater part of British capital was invested in the British colonies. He was wrong on both counts. He insisted that there was an inseparable connection between the export of capital and empire. The Swiss surpassed all other nations in their holding of foreign investments per head of the population, yet there is no Swiss Empire. He held that the possession of empire allowed a labour aristocracy in the mother countries to enjoy a high standard of living by exploiting colonial workers. Yet Sweden and Denmark, which had no empire, maintained a standard of living higher than that of France and Belgium, which had. He contended that impoverishment and servitude accompany capital when it is sent abroad. That of course sometimes happens, but by no means as a rule. For a long time America, Canada, Australia, New Zealand headed the list of capital-importing countries, and they are not notorious either for poverty or subjection. Real poverty is to be sought where capital imports are low—in Haiti, British West Africa, India, China. Indeed, as Professor Staley has conclusively shown, the correlation between the movement of capital and poverty seems to be the direct opposite of what Lenin declared it to be. His Theory of Imperialism, in fact, in so far as it is a defence of Marxism, is both dishonest and untrue; in so far as it is true it is not a defence but an effective renunciation of the teachings of the master.

His Restatement of Dialectical Materialism and of Revolutionary Marxism

It was his task, Lenin tells us in *State and Revolution*, "to resuscitate the real teachings of Marx." He sought to do this in two ways, firstly by reaffirming the fundamental faiths of dialectical materialism which he believed were being undermined by the contemporary attempts, as for instance in *Studies in the Philosophy of Marxism*, to restate them in terms of the new physics, and secondly by insisting that progress towards Socialism could only be revolutionary, not evolutionary as Bernstein and the revisionists maintained.

In *Materialism and Empirio-Criticism*, Lenin examines at length the nature of materialism and the dialectic, and considers the relationship between Marxism and science. It is the measure of his stature as a Marxist theorist that far from containing any significant contribution to Marxism, it is in fact a dreadfully dull, repetitive, dogmatic, and superficial survey, chiefly of note for its crude notion of materialism, hardly different from the materialism of Feuerbach which Marx attacked. There is nothing here of Marx's subtle view, admittedly never clearly worked out, that after all the human spirit will be able to master its animal nature, that each of the higher departments of the superstructure, such as law and philosophy, will seek to evolve a professional group which shall be at least partly independent of class bias and whose work stands in the most indirect and obscure of relationships to economic forces. There is only here the strictest letter of economic determinism, according to which everything is to be directly explained by existing economic systems.

In *State and Revolution*, Lenin deals much more ably with those who sought to make Marxism evolutionary. The vigour and speed of *State and Revolution* is in most significant contrast with the dreary repetitions of *Materialism and Empirio-Criticism*.

For action, not theory, was his forte. He was one of the greatest revolutionary strategists of all time, and nothing is more typical of him than his unequivocal insistence on the necessity of revolution—and than his violent denunciation, expressed in the beautiful language that is one of the minor joys of the Communist heaven, of those unblushing, impotent, insincere, dishonest, cynical, opportunist, vulgar people who opposed him.

In later life Marx himself had thought it possible that in the most advanced and favoured industrial communities, such as Great Britain and the United States of America, and perhaps also Holland, socialism might be achieved gradually, without revolution. Engels, too, in his preface to the new edition of Marx's *Class Struggles in France*—published in 1895—has discovered that street-fighting inevitably involves certain inconveniences, and is of the opinion that, after all, the faithful need not necessarily feel committed to it. It is not, therefore, surprising if socialists who believed that Marx was wrong about the lower middle classes being crushed out of existence, and who thought it certain that many potential sympathisers were being kept away merely by their fear and dislike of revolutionary violence which in theory Marxists extolled, wished to revise Marx's teachings on revolution. They seized on what Marx had said about the State "withering away," and held it to justify their conclusion that universal suffrage and increasing partnership in industry meant that socialism could be attained even without revolution. It was obviously unnecessary to go to the unpleasant lengths of forcibly abolishing a capitalist state which seemed to be withering away rather quickly.

Lenin, who held in its extreme form the doctrine that the whole of history is the result of the collision of opposing forces who believed that the very act of collision was both unavoidable and right, saw in these ideas of Bernstein and the revisionist an unpardonable sin against the light. He insisted that the "withering away" referred to the "remains of the proletarian State system after the socialist revolution." It could not apply to the State which exists before that revolution. By very definition the pre-Socialist State is a "special repressive force" wielded by the possessing class. It will never of itself "wither away" and can only be abolished—by revolution.

It is obvious here that in spite of Stalin's insistence, in his first lecture on the "Foundations of Leninism" delivered a

Sverdlov University in 1924, that the view is incorrect that Lenin revived the early revolutionary teaching of Marx as against his later moderation, Lenin was in fact reverting to an early, more revolutionary Marx. He points out that in the period of imperialism the peaceful transitions to socialism which Marx thought might be possible can no longer be expected, and he is particularly impressed with the only number of the German-French year-books which Marx published, in which he advocates "merciless criticism of everything in existence," above all "criticism with weapons." Restatement of materialist philosophy was for Lenin a work of necessity for which he was not naturally suited; restatement of revolutionary faith was a labour of love by one than whom none better could be found.

His Adaptation of Marxism to Russia

It was Lenin's third great task to adapt Marxism to Russia. As a Russian of the Russians who need yield place to no one in Russian history in his instinctive understanding of Russian realities, and as a revolutionary strategist of genius, he realised that in certain circumstances revolution was possible in Russia. Those circumstances were Tsarist defeat in war and the existence to take advantage of it of a resolute, highly disciplined group of professional revolutionaries, limited in number, wielding ruthless terror, and impervious to the voice of reason or the dictates of humanity. His interpretation of Marx convinced him that war was inevitable. His knowledge of Russia convinced him that Russian defeat was inevitable. Therefore it was for him to create the party which would carry the revolution through to its successful conclusion.

But in doing this he had to overcome a difficulty far greater than that implied by the existence of the Russian secret police—a difficulty arising from Marx's own teaching. Russian revolutionaries had accepted Marxism, seeing in it a revolutionary gospel of unsurpassable force that was at the same time a compound of economic theory, philosophy, and history exactly suited to their taste. But Marx must have rejected Russian revolutionaries, since the social and economic structure of Russia failed to fulfil any one of the conditions which he regarded as essential for the success, and even for the emergence, of his type of socialism. True Marxists among Russian revolutionaries, such as Plekhanov, knew this and accepted the thesis that serious socialism can spring only from full-fledged capitalism. Therefore they could not believe that there might be those short-cuts to revolution which Lenin's analysis of the given situation led him to think possible. For Marx had taught that there could be no such short-cuts since revolutionary movements must arise spontaneously and cannot outrun the underlying industrial and economic conditions which give rise to them. No society perishes before all the forces of production which it contains are developed. Therefore the bourgeois revolution must be completed before the proletarian revolution could be begun.

It could be argued that this was not very adequate as a fighting creed, as Gottschalk, Head of the Communist League, had argued when he demanded of Marx: "Why should we, men of the proletariat, spill our blood for this? Must we really plunge deliberately into the purgatory of a decrepit capitalist domination in order to avoid a medieval hell, as you, Mr. Preacher, proclaim to us, in order to attain from there the nebulous heaven of your Communist creed?" But it was difficult to deny that this was what Marx had taught. At most, Marx had claimed, his teaching could only "shorten and lessen the birth pangs" of the new order. It could not help a society to "overleap the natural phases of evolution." Consequently force, as Engels devoted three chapters of his book *Anti-Dühring* to showing, can only supplement a revolutionary situation which cannot exist until the proletariat are revolutionary and until they are sufficiently developed to establish a socialist order which would include everything of permanent value in capitalism.

Nor could genuine Marxists like Plekhanov accept the method which Lenin's analysis of the situation led him to think necessary—the creation of the narrow, disciplined, undemocratic party. They could of course admit the truth of the contention that unwise publicity today might mean Siberia for revolutionaries tomorrow. But they were not convinced when Lenin said to them: "Think it over a little and you will realise that 'broad democracy' in party organisations, amidst the darkness of the autocracy and the domination of the gendarmes, is nothing more than a useless and harmful toy." They feared that this was a convenient excuse, and they believed that if democracy was denied in the party there could be little hope that the masses would receive the education in it which they held to be "a necessary condition of socialism."

Lenin, it is true, was much more interested in making men carry out his policy than he was in justifying it theoretically. Yet as a Marxist, and perhaps also as a Russian, he felt the need of advancing some theoretical justification of it. How was he to do so?

Marx had been both more verbose and more logical than most men. But he had not worked out all the problems raised by his doctrine of the relationships of man to the material world. He left in happy obscurity the respective roles in revolutionary policy of the spontaneous action of the masses, which is dependent on the objective material situation, and of the conscious leadership which is based on an understanding of the technique of revolution. On the one hand he insists, as Lenin did, on detailed analyses of particular situations to discover the actual location of political and economic strengths and strains—as his own studies of the Paris Commune and those of Engels on the Peasants' Revolt make clear. On the other hand he maintains that revolutions are possible only in the fullness of time, when material conditions have made the proletariat ready to assume power. However, beyond the warning that both conscious leadership and the spontaneous action of the masses are necessary, Marx is silent as to how the balance between the two should be maintained.

His Idea of the Party

Lenin adapts Marxism to Russia by seizing upon one side of Marx's teaching, what he has to say about conscious leadership, and, in spite of his warning, ignoring the other, his views on the spontaneous action of the masses. His is almost a classic case of winning the tug-of-war by letting go of the rope. Even so, he does not make the best case he could have made. The very crudeness of the materialism he has advanced in his *Materialism and Empirio-Criticism* makes it impossible for him to argue that his idea of the revolutionary role of the party is a legitimate deduction from Marx's idea of the superstructure evolving professional groups not obviously dependent on their classes. Though even if he had adopted that line of argument, he would have found it difficult to evade Marx's insistence that the Communist Party should be the vanguard but never the masters of the workers. As it is, Lenin produces a new, non-Marxian theory of the revolutionary function of intellectuals. Emancipation, he maintains, is to be the work of a band of intellectuals officering the rabble, not, as Marxist dogma has it, the work of the proletariat itself. The workers, he says, do not spontaneously become socialists, but only trade unionists, and revolutionary ideology must in consequence be brought to them by middle-class intellectuals.

Several implications follow from Lenin's idea of the Party and from the justification he puts forward for it. The first is that "ideas" and not the "material conditions of production" are the effective causes of revolution—the very reverse in fact of Marx's teaching. The second is that force can be far more effective than Marx and Engels will allow. The third is that the revolution will always be violent, whereas for Marx the force that the revolutionaries will command is likely to be so overwhelming that the violence will be limited. Yet even now when it seems so clear that Lenin was adopting an essentially un-Marxian position, he still tries to reconcile it with orthodox Marxism. He could not claim to be preparing the party to bring about the bourgeois revolution, since he was preparing it in such a way, and justifying it in such a manner, as to make impossible any but his own version of the socialist revolution. Yet he opposed Trotsky's argument that the socialist revolution could develop at once from the bourgeois revolution. It was inspired opportunism, not theoretical conviction, as he admitted, that made him change his position and carry through the second revolution in Russia in 1917. Yet his action then was not only consistent with his own theory, but strictly speaking was the only action that would have been. So that it can be said that Lenin's relegation to "the archives of 'Bolshevik' pre-revolutionary antiques" of the idea that a time of preparation must elapse between the bourgeois and the proletarian revolutions is also one of the implications which follow from his doctrine of the role and the solidity of the Party even though he himself had not so understood it.

The Dictatorship of the Proletariat

That doctrine has yet another implication of the greatest importance. It necessitates a new version of Marx's teaching on the dictatorship of the proletariat. For Marx the State is an institution whereby one class oppresses the others. It is in this sense that, after the revolution which abolishes capitalism, he speaks of the dictatorship of the proletariat just as before that revolution he would have spoken of the dictatorship of the middle classes. Far from implying by it the establishment of a one-party dictatorship State, Marx never doubts that his dictatorship of the proletariat will be the most truly democratic State that the world has seen. He writes in the *Communist Manifesto*: "The first step in the revolution by the working class is the raising of the proletariat to the position of ruling class and to establish democracy." Engels is even more emphatic. He writes in 1891: "If anything is certain, it is that our party and the working class can only come to power under the form of the democratic republic. This is, indeed, the specific form for the dictatorship of the proletariat, as has already been shown by the great French Revolution."

Engels was referring there to the Paris Commune of 1870. What he and Marx approved in the Commune was the fact that it was formed by universal suffrage, that its officials were elective, responsible, and revocable—characteristics that are those also of democracy in many capitalist States. But if Lenin was right and Marx wrong in saying that the workers do not "develop" a revolutionary consciousness but have to be told, it must follow that if a revolution comes before they have been adequately instructed they will not be able to take control, nor would they know what to do if they were. Therefore the small body of informed, disciplined revolutionaries must themselves seize power and hold and use it as their superior knowledge and revolutionary consciousness dictates. The dictatorship of the proletariat must become a dictatorship over the proletariat. Trotsky was right, though by no means without responsibility for the very thing he criticises, when he described Lenin's idea of the Party as "the replacement of the dictatorship of the proletariat by a dictatorship over the proletariat, of the political rule of the class by organisational rule over the class." Lenin admitted as much when, in his commentaries on Marx's *The Civil War in France*, and *Critique of the Gotha Programme of 1875*, he makes the dictatorship of the proletariat become the dictatorship of a one-party State.

Yet he is as reluctant to accept this fully as he was to admit that the socialist could at once follow the bourgeois revolution. It is amusing to notice how, the greater and more important his deviations are from Marx, the more insistently he tries to reconcile his position with that of Marx. Trotsky makes no bones about admitting that a minority cannot come into power democratically. That is what he meant when he said: "The real kernel of the class revolution has come into irreconcilable conflict with its democratic shell." Radek, too, was honest in saying: "The Soviet Government is no democracy, it is the form of the government of the workers." "Democracy," he added so that there should be no mistaking his meaning, "is the domination by capital, a side-scene of the domination by capital." But Lenin still maintained Marx's doctrine that the transformation of the proletariat into the ruling class is equivalent to the establishment of democracy. In *State and Revolution* he writes: "We all know that the political form of the 'state' at that time [after the Revolution] is complete democracy." He was led into the most violent of mental contortions by his attempt to square the circle, to make the dictatorship of the proletariat a democracy since Marx and Engels will have it so. Thus he tells us that the proletarian State is "the most complete democracy"; that is, that democracy is possible only within a State. Then he writes that "full democracy" is possible only when this State has ceased to exist. Finally he informs us that "full democracy" will be realised only in order to disappear. He says only after the State has ceased to exist "will democracy itself begin to wither away"; that is, there will be a period when the Communist society will be no State but will still be a democracy—in spite of the fact that he has already said that "democracy is also a State" and that "consequently democracy will also disappear when the State disappears." Lenin was adept at hair-splitting and in sheltering when necessary behind a dense fog of words. But not even Lenin can cover up the absurdity of these contradictions.

There may, however, be real significance in Lenin's attempt to portray the dictatorship of the proletariat as democracy. His was a complex character, and part of him undoubtedly wanted it to be so. Two months after the Revolution he could, for instance, write: "Every rank-and-file worker and peasant who is able to read and write, who can judge people and has practical experience, can do organisational work." And there is no reason for thinking that he did not believe what he wrote in *State and Revolution*, surprising as it is in one who had spent himself so much in dealing with problems of organisation and of power. He wrote: "The exploiters are naturally unable to suppress the people without a very complex machine for performing this task; but the people can suppress the exploiters even with a very simple 'machine,' almost without a machine, without a special apparatus, by the simple organisation of the armed workers." He was, moreover, willing to allow a good deal of freedom of discussion within the Party. He accepted defeat by Bukharin and the Left Bolsheviks on the vital issue of German peace terms in February 1918. He wrote in his essay on Religion: "A political party cannot examine its members to see if there are any contradictions between their philosophy and the Party programme." As far as the Party was concerned, he preserved, too, the human touch that seems so absent in the present monolithic Russian State—surprisingly enough since the letter to Gorki in which he wrote: "It would not matter a jot if three-quarters of the human race perished; the important thing was that the remaining quarter should be Communists," does not suggest that humanity was one of his most eminent characteristics. Thus he prevented the severe punishment which his colleagues intended to visit upon the polyandrous Kollontai when she neglected her revolutionary duties to go off to the Crimea with a handsome young naval officer, saying merely that the couple absent without leave should be sentenced to spend five years together. And he disliked the new Soviet bureaucracy almost as much as he had disliked the old Tsarist autocracy. In considerable bitterness he called the Soviet Republic "a Work-State with bureaucratic excrescences," and at the end of 1922 he admitted: "We have taken over the old State apparatus."

His regrets were doubtless genuine, but the development he regretted was the logical result of his own deviations from Marxism. Since power abdicates only under the stress of counterpower, as he so well knew, it was as vain to expect, as he did, that the disciplined, undemocratic, minority Party which he had called into being as the master of the people would blossom forth into a democratic leadership of the people, as it was to hope, as again he did, that after a revolution carried through by such a Party the State would gradually wither away. His own most significant actions were dictatorial through and through. His famous revolutionary slogan, "All power to the Soviets," for instance, was a denial, not an assertion of democratic stirrings. It meant nothing more than "All power to the Party through the Soviets." He always insisted on the "narrow" as against the "open" Party, opposing every scheme which threatened its monopoly. And in his doctrine of "democratic centralism" he insists on the subordination of lower to higher party organs, even using this principle at the 10th Party Congress in 1921 to force unanimity on the Party. Trotsky was right when he said of democratic centralism: "The apparatus of the party substitutes itself for the party, the Central Committee substitutes itself for the apparatus, and finally the dictator substitutes himself for the Central Committee." The violent denunciations of Lenin's *The Proletarian Revolution and the Renegade Kautsky* remind one of nothing so much as the preacher's note: "Argument weak here. Shout!" Kautsky asked how the rule could pass from the "vanguard of the oppressed" to the exploited majority of yesterday. Lenin had no convincing answer for him. Nor had Stalin. Marx's statement that a socialist society can be established only in a highly civilised and industrialised country remains unrefuted —in spite of Lenin's adaptation of Marxism to Russia. Yet, even if his is a bastard Marxism, no one will minimise the significance of what he bequeathed to Russia and to the world.

JOSEPH VISSARIONOVITCH (DJUGASHVILI) STALIN, 1879–1953

As Marxist Scholar

Before the rising of the 7th November 1917, which determined the destinies of Russia and involved an abrupt departure from accepted Marxist thought, Lenin consulted his holy books much as Cromwell did before taking his fateful decision to purge the Long Parliament. Lenin's searching of the Marxist scriptures to justify an action which he had already determined to take, and which was in fact contrary to Marx's own teaching, is typical of the way in which Communist theory has become the obedient handmaiden of Communist practice. As Communist practice, like the practice of most of us, is very largely determined by day-to-day considerations which frequently change very rapidly, it follows that Communist theory often boxes the compass with a rapidity that is disconcerting to those who are not skilled navigators on Communist seas, and that is a sufficient cause of embarrassment for anyone who wishes to synthesise and interpret it. If it be any comfort, it can be borne in mind that the difficulty of keeping step in the quickly revolving dance is undoubtedly much more embarrassing for Russian writers. Changes in the Party line are frequently a matter of disconcerting, violent, and even fatal surprise for those who are ill-advised enough to proclaim today what they would have been punished for not maintaining yesterday.

Until the late twenties, moreover, when events were arranged and history rewritten to suit an autocrat's wishes, Stalin's reputation as a Marxist scholar was deservedly poor. His essay, *Marxism and the Nationalities*, suggested and supervised by Lenin, certainly increased his prestige in the Party. But the general view of him still remained that of Ryazanov who interrupted him when he was engaging in a theoretical argument: "Stop it, Koba. Don't make a fool of yourself. Everybody knows that theory is not exactly your field." With Stalin the worst elements of Communist theorising are exaggerated—the hair-splitting, for which Lenin is so largely responsible, goes drearily on, and massed illogicalities parade up and down, constituting in their very number the big battalions to whom fearful men give the crown of victory. The dialectical contradictions which as thesis and antithesis are supposed to issue in a higher synthesis become more obviously absolute opposites, which are resolved only by the outright victory of one of them. Thus Stalin gives as an example of the dialectic: "Lenin's attitude towards the right of nations to self-determination, including separation." "Lenin," he says, "sometimes expressed the principle of national self-determination in a simple formula: 'Separation for amalgamation.' Just think—separation for amalgamation. It smacks even of the paradoxical." Yet when all the verbiage is cleared away all that he means is that oppressed peoples wanting to separate from Russia should be forcibly amalgamated with her —Georgia and the Ukraine yesterday; Latvia, Lithuania, Estonia today. Instead of the clash of thesis and antithesis producing some new synthesis, all that has happened here is that the antithesis "amalgamation" has completely swallowed the thesis "separation." Thus Stalin informs the 16th Party Congress in June 1930: "We are for the withering away of the State. And yet we also believe in the proletarian dictatorship which represents the strongest and mightiest form of state power that has existed up to now. To keep on developing state power in order to prepare the conditions for the withering away of state power—that is the Marxist formula. Is it 'contradictory'? Yes, 'contradictory.' But the contradiction is vital and wholly reflects the Marxian dialectic. Whoever has not understood this feature of the contradictions belonging to our transitional time, who- ever has not understood this dialectic of historical processes, that person is dead to Marxism." Yet here again the contradiction is straightforward and absolute and to call it dialectical and claim for it a higher logic is to deprive language and thought of its meaning. In fact, in Stalinist theory it can safely be claimed that if a conclusion follows logically from its premises, it must be all right; while if it seems to contradict them, it is dialectical and so must still be all right. Such mental contortions are of as little interest as value. Legend has it that Confucius returning from an interview with Lao-tze, unimpressed by his profound specu- lations, said of him: "Who shall follow the footprints of the dragon in the air?" It would indeed be as unprofitable to study in detail the many convolutions of Stalinist theory—involved, rapidly changing, disingenuous as it is—as Confucius believed it would be to follow the flights of Lao-tze.

It is, however, worth while to consider two of the emendations Stalin made to Lenin's teaching—his doctrine of Socialism in One Country and his views on revolution. Both have played an important part in the development of contemporary Russia.

Socialism in One Country

In his *Problems of Leninism*, written in the autumn of 1924, Stalin first concluded that it was possible to establish socialism in one country even if the world remained capitalist. Russia was strong enough to pick herself up by her own boot-strings. Her efforts alone would suffice for the complete organisation of a socialist economy since a proletarian government, controlling industry and credit and supported by the great mass of the people, could develop, as no other government could, her vast spaces and great potential wealth. This belief in Socialism in One Country, soon to become the party shibboleth, was none of Lenin's teaching. Lenin, and indeed Trotsky, looked upon Russia as a powerful proletarian fortress which could be made still stronger by further socialist advance and which could resist protracted capitalist siege. But Lenin, who thought of socialist society in essentially international terms, had never declared that the embattled fortress could stand so indefinite a siege as to make possible the full development of socialism within it, while Trotsky had grimly foretold that, unless helped by international revolution, socialism even in Russia must fail. Not only was Stalin's new doctrine of Socialism in One Country a departure from Lenin's thought, but it was a departure not long contemplated and hastily made. Early in 1924 Stalin could still write: "For the final victory of socialism, for the organisation of socialist production, the efforts of one country, particularly of a peasant country like Russia, are insufficient." It was a departure hastily made to serve an immediate purpose, to provide Stalin with a weapon to be used against Trotsky in the struggle for power that took place between them after Lenin's death.

In that struggle Trotsky's theory of "permanent revolution" found many adherents. According to that theory, put forward as early as 1906, the anti-feudal or bourgeois revolution, which could be expected to break out in Russia, would become almost immediately an anti-capitalist and socialist revolution. Contrary, therefore, to accepted Marxist views, backward Russia and not the progressive Western countries would be the first to march along the road to socialism. But she could not hope to get very far along that road unaided. However, her influence and example would be such that revolution having begun in Russia would spill over into Europe. In this way the advanced Western countries, having been helped by Russia, would in their turn help her to achieve socialism. Therefore not Socialism in One Country but Socialism in One World must be the object of all true revolutionaries. It was to defeat this theory, which had at least the merit of foretelling the course which events actually took in the two revolutions in Russia in 1917, that Stalin hit upon his doctrine of Socialism in One Country. And a potent weapon he found it, for together with his subtle manœuvring and his clear-sighted appreciation of the realities of power, it gave him victory.

As would be expected of a hasty development decided upon for an immediate purpose, Stalin's ideas on Socialism in One Country were not well thought out. He put forward no serious answer to the criticisms levelled against it that the peasants would resist the collectivisation it implied, that if standards of living remained lower in Russia than in capitalist countries, socialism must fail even in Russia; that in an economy of scarcity which an isolated Russian economy in its present backward condition must necessarily be, glaring material inequalities between social groups were bound to arise. Nor was his acceptance of the new doctrine unconditional. He insisted that the victory of socialism in Russia could never be secure so long as the surrounding capitalist powers threatened her. And he continued to parade his belief in the nearness of world revolution. What he gives with one hand he thus at least partly takes back with the other. And, perhaps strangest of all, there seems on the surface little difference between his views and those he was attacking. In both views there is acceptance of the necessity of pressing ahead with plans for socialist reconstruction. In both there is admission that socialism could not be achieved for a very long time. In both there is agreement that hostile capitalism might wreck what socialist development has already been accomplished. And in both there is the hope that world revolution might come to the help of hard-pressed Russia. Apparently the only point in dispute is whether the job which all admit must be tackled and which all agree will be long, arduous, and dangerous, can be completed or not. That such an issue could arouse much interest, let alone unloose great passions, might seem as curious as that medieval schoolmen should be concerned with the absorbing question : "How many angels can dance on the point of a needle?"

Yet the differences which seem so slight are vital, and in spite of all its ambiguities the doctrine of Socialism in One Country is of great importance. It was the recognition of the fact that Russia was a force in her own right, not just a springboard for world revolution as Trotsky considered her. And the Stalin who regarded Russia as an end in itself was much more likely to win her support than the Trotsky who viewed her merely as a means to an end. To the old Bolshevik who agreed with Trotsky, Western Europe was the real centre of the world, and Russia a backward community on the edge of outer darkness which might, nevertheless, help Europe but which must in its turn await the saving strength of Europe. To Stalin, Russia was the centre of the world. It was her destiny to become the centre of a new civilisation superior to that of capitalist Europe. Isolated and backward though she was, she nevertheless possessed the truth that would save not only herself but the whole of struggling mankind. Socialism in One Country was the 20th-century version of Moscow the Third Rome, the dream of 19th-century Slavophils. It was the marriage of Russian revolution with Russian history. From that marriage was born the force which carried Stalin to supreme power. And perhaps the truest view of the purges that followed upon it is that they were the terrible revenge taken by Russian history on revolutionaries who had dared to deny her.

The Totalitarian State

The direct result of the adoption of Stalin's policy of Socialism in One Country was the growth in Russia of a totalitarian State acknowledging not so much the dictatorship of a Party as of an individual, working through a huge bureaucracy and dedicated to the use of force, a Moloch to whom the majority of Lenin's original companions have been sacrificed.

The growth of Stalin's dictatorship can be seen in the changing nature of the Party. The Communist Party, while Lenin lived, enjoyed a considerable measure of freedom of discussion and even of action. It debated, at great length and with greater virulence, the policy to be adopted towards the German peace terms offered at Brest-Litovsk. Then, when a weak Russia was involved in a life-and-death crisis, a group of Communist leaders—Radek, Kollontai, Orinsky—published a daily paper in Moscow expressly to defeat Lenin's policy. Then, too, considerable discretion was left to Trotsky in his negotiations with the Germans. Trotsky's pre-revolution quarrels with Lenin, indeed, seemed no bar to their intimate collaboration after it. Lenin, who loved theoretical disputations, could conduct the fiercest of polemics with Bukharin and yet remain friendly with him. *Pravda*, the organ of the Party, ran a special discussion page to which Trotsky, Kamenev, and Zinoviev never hesitated to contribute articles highly critical of adopted policy.

There was no such Party freedom when Stalin became supreme. Then no one dare proclaim himself an "oppositionist" and ask for the right to criticise the policies of the Government. On the contrary "the principle of hierarchical discipline", accepted in 1925, bound every level of the Party to present the level beneath it with a unanimous mandate, made of the Party rank and file mere cogs in the machine of government and of the Party itself little more than an uncritical instrument of centralised administration. It is indeed hardly surprising that reporting to and consulting the Party became formalities about which Stalin did not concern himself unduly. In the difficult years of war and turmoil from 1918 to 1925 Party Congresses met annually. Since Stalin became all-powerful the 15th Party Congress met in 1927 after a two years' interval, the 16th in 1930, the 17th in 1934, the 18th in 1939 and the 19th in 1952.

The growth of the dictatorship can be seen in the disappearance of possible sources of resistance in both town and country. In the town the trade unions have lost all freedom. The annual conventions of the Miners' Federation, of the Textile Workers, of the Trades Union Congress, have not met since 1932. Since January 1936 there has been no more collective bargaining in the U.S.S.R., so that after a visit there in 1946 Morgan Phillips, Secretary of the Labour Party, reported: "In Russia there is no collective bargaining as the Trade Unions know it in Great Britain. I am not sure that the workers' organisations can be regarded as 'trade unions' in the British sense that they are free agents to speak and act as their members demand irrespective of Government stricture. The very fact that strikes are illegal seems to dispose of any pretence to freedom of action as we know it." In the country the peasants have been dragooned into collective and co-operative farms, one reason for which has undoubtedly been the increased control over them which the State can thus exercise. Everywhere it has become obvious that, in spite of its grandiose title, the Union of Soviet Socialist Republics, the Soviet has no independent existence in Russia today. Stalin admitted as much in 1933 when he said: "From the standpoint of Leninism the collective economies, and the Soviets as well, are, taken as a form of organisation, a weapon and nothing but a weapon." As Buber so finely commented: "One cannot in the nature of things expect a little tree that has been turned into a club to put forth leaves."

Before Stalin's death the dictatorship even revealed peculiarities which characterised the Fascist and Nazi dictatorships—such as the habit of conducting huge plebiscites at which overwhelmingly favourable votes were recorded, and the habit of expressing faith in the regime by indulging in a nauseating worship of the leader. Thus we read of elections at which Communist candidates polled 99·4 per cent of the total votes cast. Their record in the 1946 elections was still more impressive. They polled 99·8 per cent of the votes—a revolutionary advance of ·4 per cent, all the more remarkable as the electorate had been increased by several millions, inhabitants of annexed territories, whom the Soviet press had very recently called authentic reactionaries, bourgeois, and Nazis. This is indeed an outstanding achievement since with the birth-rate and the death-rate in mind such high percentages warrant the conclusion that good Soviet citizens postpone both arrivals and departures so as not to interfere with electoral arrangements. Perhaps the only discouraging feature about figures so high was the extremely small margin left for further revolutionary advance. Fortunately such a reflection is one that need occur only to bourgeois minds. In the elections of December 1947 Stalin, who stood for a Moscow constituency, polled 131 per cent of the votes. Higher mathematics of this sort offer such a scope for unlimited advance as is not dreamed of in our philosophy. Thus we read, too, of the extraordinary adulation of Stalin. His name, for instance, appeared 101 times on the title page of *Pravda* for the 17th December 1950. It appeared 45 times on the first page of the *Medical Worker* of the 28th December 1950. Perhaps, indeed, we should speak of the deification rather than the adulation of Stalin. Here is an extract from *Pravda* of the 28th August 1936:

> "*O Great Stalin, O Leader of the Peoples,*
> *Thou who didst give birth to man,*
> *Thou who didst make fertile the earth,*
> *Thou who didst rejuvenate the Centuries,*
> *Thou who givest blossom to the spring,*
> *Thou who movest the chords of harmony;*
> *Thou splendour of my spring, O Thou*
> *Sun reflected in a million hearts.*"

Prose is no less fervent: "Stalin, I say to the universe. Just Stalin, and I need say no more. Everything is included in that tremendous name. Everything: the party, the country, the town, love, immortality—everything." And the following gem is not to be ignored: "I write books. I am an author. All thanks to thee, O great educator Stalin. I love a young woman with a renewed love and I shall perpetuate myself in my children all thanks to thee, O great educator Stalin. I shall be eternally happy and joyous, all thanks to thee, O great educator Stalin. Everything belongs to thee, chief of our great country. And when the woman I love presents me with a child, the first word it shall utter will be: Stalin."

The Stalin dictatorship has had its international reflection, too. As early as 1924 the French Communist Souvarine was expelled from the Third International of World Communist Parties, or Comintern—the first to be excluded because of lack of submission to Stalin. Thenceforward the Comintern increasingly reflected the Stalin line. Its 6th Congress in 1928 was the last at which any variety of opinion was allowed. Today its successor, the Cominform, is merely a rubber stamp of the Kremlin.

However much many convinced Communists must have disliked it, the development of this bureaucratic, monolithic, Byzantine autocracy that Stalin perfected, an autocracy incidentally which is the only form of government the Russians have tolerated, was necessary because if socialism was to be established in Russia, the State must be made powerful enough to do it. The doctrine of Socialism in One Country was thus a doctrine of force as the mother, not the midwife, of the new society. This 20th-century strong totalitarian belief in force is perhaps the greatest difference between Stalinism and the traditional Marxian outlook. Lenin had departed far from Marx's view that force could play only a subordinate role compared with the basic economic and social processes. Stalin left it behind altogether.

Stalin made other changes, too, in Marx's teaching. He virtually abandoned the classical Marxian theory of the State, according to which the State is merely the repressive instrument of a dominant class which will disappear when classes are abolished. It is typical of him that in the 1936 Constitution to which he gave his name the terms "State" and "citizen" have been brought back and a bi-cameral Parliament on the 19th-century model set up, whereas in Lenin's Constitution of 1921 the word "State" has disappeared as being bourgeois and is replaced by the word "Soviet," while "citizen" has become "proletarian," "peasant," and "soldier." Stalin still paid lip-service to the belief that the State will "wither away," but that miraculous event he postponed to the Greek Kalends. Engels had once believed that this would happen as soon as the means of production were nationalised and all class differences ended. This, said Stalin, speaking on the 1936 Constitution, had already been accomplished in Russia, which was now a socialist, classless society free from exploitation. But there was still no sign of the State withering away. In a report to the 18th Party Congress on the 10th March 1939, he explained why this was so. The State could

not wither away, he said, because of "capitalist encirclement."
The admission that the State remained necessary because of the
internal situation was avoided by linking internal trouble with
capitalist encirclement and speaking of those purged as capitalist agents. In putting forward this view, Stalin had to correct
not only Marx and Engels but also Lenin. Even for Stalin, public
correction of Lenin was not without its embarrassments. But he
managed it neatly by declaring that Lenin had intended to
enunciate the new doctrine in a second volume of his *State and
Revolution*. "Death, however, prevented him from carrying this
task into execution. But what Lenin did not manage to do
should be done by his disciples." "Will our State," he went on,
"remain in the period of Communism also? Yes, it will, unless
the capitalist encirclement is liquidated and unless the danger
of foreign military attack has disappeared. Naturally, of course,
the forms of our State will again change in conformity with
the changes in the situation at home and abroad. No, it will not
remain, and will atrophy if the capitalist encirclement is liquidated and a Socialist encirclement takes its place." It is, then,
only the world Socialist State which will wither away. Since
such a State is ardently hoped for but not yet expected, the
Stalin State goes on developing its power, stoutly maintaining
the while that any who declare that this is a curious preliminary
to it emulating the Snark and softly and silently vanishing away
and never being heard of again are blind to the dialectics of
Marxism.

Two further consequences of the policy of Socialism in One
Country are worth noting. One is the strong condemnation of
the idea of "equality in the sphere of requirements and individual life" as a "piece of reactionary petty bourgeois absurdity
worthy of a primitive set of ascetics, but not of a Socialist society
organised on Marxist lines" which is contained in Stalin's
address to the 17th Party Congress in 1934. "It is only Leftist
blockheads," he added for good measure, "who idealise the poor
as the eternal bulwark of Bolshevism." Unequal returns, as he
saw, were necessary to encourage the skill and efficiency without which the industrialisation which was essential to the success of the policy of Socialism in One Country could not be carried through. There was support for his view in Marx's saying
that even in a classless society pay at first would be according to
labour and not needs. Yet a strong strand of equalitarianism

runs through Marxism, typical of which is the practice on which Lenin insisted that no member of the Party should receive more than the wages of a skilled workman. And it is difficult to resist the conclusion that the differentiation of wages which was necessitated by the needs of industrialisation was carried by Stalin to lengths incompatible with the spirit if not the letter of Marxism.

The other result worthy of note is the strong growth of Russian nationalism which can hardly be regarded as a development of Marxian views. It is first clearly seen in a speech which Stalin gave to business executives in February 1931. The cold Communist clichés which he used on that occasion warmed and sprang to life only when he began to speak of the purely Russian motives for his policy. "We do not want to be beaten. No, we don't want to. Old Russia was ceaselessly beaten for her backwardness. She was beaten by the Mongol Khans, she was beaten by the Turkish Beys, she was beaten by Swedish feudal lords, she was beaten by Polish-Lithuanian Pans, she was beaten by Anglo-French capitalists, she was beaten by Japanese barons, she was beaten by all—for her backwardness. For military backwardness, for cultural backwardness, for political backwardness, for industrial backwardness, for agricultural backwardness. She was beaten because to beat her was profitable and went unpunished. You remember the words of the pre-revolutionary poet: 'Thou art poor and thou art plentiful, thou art mighty and thou art helpless, Mother Russia.' We are 50 or 100 years behind the advanced countries. We must make good this lag in 10 years. Either we do it or they crush us." Stalin here portrayed Russia as the victim, whereas it had been Bolshevik practice to depict others as her victims. That practice, as in Pokrovsky's histories, was now frowned upon and his books banned. The development of Russian nationalism is seen in the wartime appeal "Your Motherland needs you," and in the resuscitation of old Russian heroes, like Dimitri Donskoi, Peter the Great, Suvarov. It is seen also, despite some post-war toning down, in Stalin's announcement, as an amateur philologist in the summer of 1950, of the doctrine of the superiority of the Great Russians over all the other nationalities of the U.S.S.R. It is seen, above all, in the close parallel between Soviet Imperialism and Tzarist Imperialism which has startled the world since 1945.

Stalin and Revolution

The policy of Socialism in One Country has brought Russia far from the teaching of Karl Marx. Yet it would be wrong to conclude that Russia today is no more than Tzarism writ large. She retains a genuine interest in revolution, as we will see as we turn to Stalin's views on the subject. In his *Dialectical and Historical Materialism* Stalin wrote: "Dialectics does not regard the process of development as a simple process of growth, where quantitative changes do not lead to qualitative changes, but as a development which passes from insignificant and imperceptible quantitative changes to open, fundamental changes, to qualitative changes; a development in which the qualitative changes occur not gradually, but rapidly and abruptly, taking the form of a leap from one state to another." The practical consequences he deduces from this are as follows: "If the passing of slow quantitative changes into rapid and abrupt qualitative changes is a law of development, then it is clear that revolutions made by oppressed classes are a quite natural and inevitable phenomenon." The change from capitalism to socialism, he believed he has proved, can be achieved only by a qualitative change, by revolution. There is no reason to regard this as merely lip service to a once-held faith, revealing no interest let alone portending no action. Admittedly from time to time, as international exigencies dictated, Stalin declared that the socialist and capitalist worlds could exist peaceably together. But his actions never suggested that he really believed in that possibility. There is no evidence to show that he ever compromised on essentials or that he failed to hold firm the revolutionary faith that he proclaimed so loudly at the 7th Congress of the Third International in 1935, when he said: "The Congress will have a great historic importance. It must open up broad revolutionary perspectives to the millions of workers of the West, of the East, of America, and of the colonial and semi-colonial countries; it must mark the beginning of an era of war and of revolutions."

On the contrary, he was very much concerned with the doctrine of revolution he inherited from Lenin. In his *Foundations of Leninism* he used Lenin's "theory of the uneven development of Capitalism," according to which in the period of world imperialism, the rivalries of the Powers and the basic problems and contradictions of capitalism reach, as it were as the result of forcibly feeding the colonial and semi-colonial countries, different degrees of acuteness in different parts of the world so that revolution might break out, in some "weak link" of the imperialist chain while capitalism remained strong elsewhere, to prove that any country could become ready for socialism. Since he accepted wholeheartedly Lenin's idea of the revolutionary function of the small, highly disciplined, ruthless Party, he was led to the conclusion that not only was revolution possible but that it ought to take place. If it did not, that could only be because it had been betrayed—hence not only the vilification of socialist leaders but the purging of communist leaders the world over. He was also confirmed in his readiness to see revolutionary situations where such did not necessarily exist—hence his instructions to the German Communist Party in 1931–2 to attack the Social Democrats, which in effect meant assisting the Nazis in destroying the Weimar Republic.

Only in one way might it seem that he denied his belief in the inevitability and necessity of revolution—when he envisaged in 1924 the possibility, which then seemed "extremely hypothetical" but which after 1945 became a matter of lively interest to communists in Eastern Europe, of a peaceful transition to socialism in certain capitalist countries which might become subject to what he called a "socialist encirclement." It has been argued that in saying this Stalin was not breaking with traditional Marxist theory since Marx himself conceded the possibility of a peaceful development of socialism in certain advanced countries. In fact, the breach is complete, since the peaceful transition to socialism in countries subject to socialist encirclement would obviously be made possible only by external force—by the strength of the Red Army, not by the internal force, which alone Marx would have recognised as legitimate, that was the result of the full working out of social and economic processes. Stalin's belief in revolution was a belief in force. His belief in the possibility of a peaceful transition to socialism through socialist encirclement was also a belief in force. The differences were differences of degree not of kind.

But how, it may be asked, could Stalin's doctrine of Socialism in One Country be reconciled with his interest in revolution and in the use of force in countries outside the U.S.S.R.? The answer to that is not easy, and many will be of the opinion that Stalin would have got further with the one if he had forgotten his interest in the other. However, he clung to both, reconciling them by thinking of world revolution only in the interests of Russia. He never wrote off the possibility of world revolution, but only the possibility of that revolution being other than a Russian world revolution. World revolution, for Stalin, and in the absence of proof to the contrary we must add for his successors, is to follow from Russia's strength, not from Russia's example, and as such it will inevitably follow the Russian pattern. When it comes, it will usher in the Russian century. Until it comes, its looming shadow will be one of the most potent influences preparing the way for that century. Meanwhile for millions the U.S.S.R. remains the true home of a crusading faith, and what the world is facing in Russia today is not merely Russian Imperialism but Russian Imperialism allied to revolutionary faith. That compound of Imperialism and Faith, as always in history, is capable of generating enormous force. The Russia that Stalin fashioned is indeed a tremendous monument to power.

Stalin and Lenin

Would Lenin have rejoiced in Stalin's achievement? Perhaps not. He would not have liked the bureaucracy, the inequality, the nationalism, the deification of the leader and of course he became increasingly critical of Stalin's conduct.

Yet Stalin's Russia is not a betrayal but a fulfilment of Lenin's Russia. The main characteristics of that Russia are the logical result of Lenin's basic assumptions. Rosa Luxemburg had no difficulty in showing the bureaucratic tendencies inherent in Lenin's conception of the small party of professional revolutionaries. He himself had maintained that "Soviet Socialist Democracy is in no way inconsistent with the rule and dictatorship of one person; the will of a class is at times best realised by a dictator, who sometimes will accomplish more by himself and is frequently more needed." And as Bertrand Russell saw, his conception of Bolshevism was internally aristocratic and externally militant, and from the concentration of power for which he was striving "the same evils would flow as from the concentration of wealth." Lenin could not have long prevented the development either of inequality or of nationalism. As early as 1920 Russell could write: "Nationalism is natural and instinctive; through pride in the revolution it grows again even in the breasts of Communists." He saw it in the Polish war. When Trotsky called for "Three cheers for our brave fellows at the front," he noted, "the audience responded as a London audience would have responded in the autumn of 1914." He even appreciated that "the reconstruction of Asiatic Russia has revived what is essentially an imperialist way of feeling." We must surely conclude that it was Lenin indeed who had made possible Stalin's Russia.

Khruschev and the Relaxing of the Dictatorship

Since Stalin's death, however, considerable changes have taken place in that Russia. At the 20th Congress of the Communist Party of the U.S.S.R. his dictatorship was violently denounced. In a lengthy and savage speech Khruschev claimed that Stalin was himself responsible for the event which ushered in the great purges of the mid-1930's, the assassination of Kirov, Governor of Leningrad, in 1934. He accused Stalin of having fabricated charges of treason against Marshal Tukhachevsky and seven other leaders of the Red Army in 1937 and then having them executed without trial, of having murdered 5,000 innocent officers and hundreds of Old Bolsheviks, including more than half of the delegates of the 17th Congress of the Communist Party of the U.S.S.R., and 70 per cent. of the members of the Central Committee elected by that Congress. He declared that Stalin had liquidated so many thousands of industrial managers and technicians that the Soviet economy was almost paralysed and called him a master of mass repressions and terror, a monster who would destroy colleagues of long standing if he imagined their glances to be at all shifty. "We never knew," he said, "when we entered Stalin's presence, whether we would come out alive." In short, if the "cult of personality" was never so highly developed as in Stalin's Russia, it has never been so noisily repudiated as in contemporary Russia.

A still more convincing proof of the relaxing of dictatorial power than the attack on Stalin has been the marked weakening of the secret police, now publicly denounced for their unconstitutional use of torture to extract confessions. Almost as striking evidence of the reality of change in the U.S.S.R. is the fact that the struggle for power is becoming much less red in tooth and claw. Beria, indeed, was executed for what was said to be his attempt to seize control. Yet Malenkov, Molotov, Kaganovich, Bulganin, when they clashed with Khruschev, were removed from high office, but not from all political activity, still less from life.

But if it canot be doubted that Stalin's dictatorship has been considerably relaxed in contemporary Russia, neither can it be doubted that Russia today has seen the consolidation of the rule of the Communist Party. The challenges to that rule that seemed to be developing from the Red Army and from the Bureaucracy at the time of Beria's death have been triumphantly removed. Whatever relaxation may be visible in Russia today no criticism of the Communist Party, its position in the country and its mono-poly of power has yet been allowed. Nor has there been any sign in Russia of lessening dedication to Communist ends. This, Khruschev has told us, is only likely to happen when shrimps learn to whistle, an accomplishment in the acquisition of which they are expected to be some little while. This continued dedi-cation of the U.S.S.R. to Communist ends of course implies con-tinued acceptance of unremitting struggle with the world of capitalism and continued faith in ultimate and complete victory over that world.

But though this is so, Khruschev's Russia has produced one change in Soviet thinking of the greatest importance. It has admitted that in an age of nuclear power war as a means of conducting struggle is to be avoided. Struggle there is still to be, but armed struggle as a means of promoting Socialism makes no sense. It may well be that in this admission lies the greatest con-tribution of Khruschev to the development of Marxist-Leninist thought.

The non-Marxist will be impressed with the confusion of thought that rejects total war on the one hand and that insists on total victory on the other. To him it must seem that the correct conclusion to be drawn from conditions which make total war unacceptable is that total victory and total defeat are now totally things of the past. But the Marxist who believes that he cannot without destroying himself attack capitalism in arms, also be-lieves that there exists a way in which with perfect safety to himself capitalism can be made to destroy itself. Lenin taught that it was only the possession by the highly industrialised coun-tries of colonies that made it possible for their workers to avoid the increasing misery which Marx had foretold for them, only imperial rule that prevented capitalism's slaves from rising in their wrath to destroy it. If this is true, as every Communist believes, then if capitalist countries are deprived of colonies, their working men will soon feel the pinch and themselves destroy capitalism. And by the faithful the troubles in Belgium that followed withdrawal from the Congo were seen as proving the truth of this thesis. Hence Khruschev's rejection of war as a means of advancing Socialism has not yet resulted in any greater Soviet readiness to admit the possibility of the indefinite continued existence of non-Marxist countries. It is permissible to believe that the realities of the nuclear world will one day force that admission. But whatever the changes that have taken place in the U.S.S.R. since Stalin's death we are not yet entitled to conclude that that day has already dawned.

Mao-Tse-Tung

In the post-war years a third great communist leader emerged, Mao-Tse-Tung. He brought to China the universal orthodoxy of Marxism to replace that of Confucianism and so interpreted it as to seek to make China again, even at the expense of conflict with the U.S.S.R., what she had always claimed to be, the Middle Kingdom, the sole source of civilisation and light. In doing this he removed two typical pieces of Marxist nonsense and so exaggerated a third as to reveal it for the glaring absurdity it is. He admitted that even under communism tensions, the "Non-antagonistic contradictions" would exist. He acknowledged that the state would be needed to deal with them and so would not wither away. He nevertheless believed it possible to perfect men by perfecting their environment. The Commune, he thought, would "create an entirely new kind of man in an entirely new kind of society" and when that failed he looked to the Cultural Revolution to achieve the same end and to the idea of permanent revolution, a perpetual bath, as it were, that would constantly wash away the grit of imperfection and leave men in a Garden of Eden in which apples and serpents would have no place. Struggling to attain the unattainable, he has in the process destroyed much of the costly achievement of his régime. And if that sacrifice rids communism of its absurd belief in human perfectability the world may yet have cause to thank him. Though it is more likely to be as a Stalin whom his people can reject as well as honour than as a Marx or a Lenin, the great founding fathers of the faith, that the communist of tomorrow will look upon him.

CHAPTER V

CONCLUSION

WE have seen in the preceding chapters something of the organic and of the mechanistic theory of the State as it has been held by some of the great masters of political thought. It may seem so obvious to the English that the State exists for man that they regard it as proof positive of German wrong-headedness if not of German original sin that the Germans have held to the opposite view that man exists for the State. Yet the masters who have preached the organic doctrine of the State have been neither patently wrongheaded nor obviously greater exemplars of original sin than the rest of us. And unless we are to believe that manifest stupidity is the sovereign recipe for survival, we cannot conclude that a view that has been accepted throughout the ages has nothing to be said for it. On the contrary, we must acknowledge that both the organic and the mechanistic views of the State have their strength and weakness.

It cannot be denied that the organic view has the great merit of corresponding to our experience of life at least in this that it acknowledges that there is a warring within man's members so that too often he does what he would not and what he would that he does not, and it appreciates that when he acts according to his better self he can most truly be called man. It recognises the different me in a way that mechanistic theory too frequently does not. And more than mechanistic theory it recognises the existence of the social me. It knows that the individual is never an isolated atom, but is formed to a very large extent by the society in which he lives. Mechanistic theory has sometimes ignored man's social character, and in it the State has not infrequently been hostile to those lesser liberties of associations which organic theory has been very ready to admit are like cells which go to form the whole living organism of the State. Insistence on the political effects of environment in its broadest sense, on the consequences of antecedent events, on the great importance of political organisation and the close interdependence of citizens and the State, on the general truth that policies must be bad if they disregard national character, environment, and history, and that the end of the State must be kept in view and recognised as something still more important than the temporary satisfaction of the possibly fluctuating demands of the present generation, all may be no more than a commonplace statement of the general causal interrelation of things, but it is a statement to be found much more in the upholders of the organic than the mechanistic view of the State. And more than mechanistic theory, organic theory encourages both the best and the social me, for in it the State, the greatest of man's creations, is used to help him to achieve the greatest development of which he is capable. Because it encourages the best and the social me it is a much more satisfactory explanation of the urge of public duty than anything that Utilitarians, for instance, can rise to. And even though too often in those who have insisted on the unity of ethics and politics, ethics would seem to have become political rather than politics ethical, the value of the view that the State is an ethical institution with a moral end must be admitted. Moreover, organic theory is a weighty reminder that the view of liberty as being left to do what one likes is inadequate, that freedom to be worth while must be positively and not negatively defined. In giving us that reminder it presents us with a facet of the truth that extreme individualism could never glimpse. If for no other reason than that it has redressed the balance weighed down by extreme individualism, organic theory is important.

If the organic theory of the State had not been impressive, it would hardly have survived so long. Its weaknesses, indeed its dangers, are, however, striking. In any theory in which the State is real and the individual an abstraction, the danger of the reality engulfing the abstraction is a great one. Organic theory shows that too great an amalgamation of individual and State is as dangerous an ideal as too great emancipation of individual will. In it man, overshadowed by the State, too frequently becomes less than man. He is treated as no more than a conduit pipe for the divine energy, as a passive creature for whom things must be done, not as a being who finds fulfilment in positive activity. In it, naturally, the individual can never take up a stand for conscience' sake against the State, since if he did he would be denying the superior reality of the State. Conscientious objectors, for instance, would never be tolerated in any State which regarded itself as organic. Such a State can never make a distinction between the good man and the good citizen, for goodness in such a State consists only in serving the State. It follows that in organic theory the citizen can have no rights against the State, that that theory leaves man no safeguard for liberty. It will allow no distinction to be made between society and the State, so convinced is it that man is absorbed in his relation to the political community. Hence not even society can act as a cushion between man and the State. In fact, however much it may seek to define liberty in a positive sense, it reduces liberty to obedience to the State. In all this it defeats itself. For it can never sufficiently appreciate that individual variation, unlikeness, effort is as necessary for the welfare of mankind as collective activity and mutual support. It tries to give social life an ethical character. But it does not see that individuals must continually re-create whatever spirituality there is in the social whole. Moreover, it regards the State as the only conceivable entity. Organic theory has been aware more than a great deal of mechanistic theory of the existence and importance of associations, but it never allows them a full and free growth. It has never been aware of the possibilities of a larger entity than the State. In organic theory the finality of the State is a shibboleth. And since it is the sole source of morality, organic theorists have rarely resisted the tendency to be bellicose in its interests. When Hobhouse said of Hegel's *Philosophy of Right*: "In the bombing of London I had just witnessed the visible and tangible outcome of a false and wicked doctrine, the foundations of which lay, as I believe, in the book before me. . . . Hegel himself carried the proof sheets of his first work to the printer through streets crowded with fugitives from the field of Jena. With that work began the most penetrating and subtle of all the intellectual influences which have sapped the rational humanitarianism of the 18th and 19th centuries, and in the Hegelian theory of the god-state all that I had witnessed lay implicit," he was overstating the case. But there was some truth in what he said. We may think that such a view of the State would have been dangerous, anyhow. In days when the new tribalism appeals, when the primitive gods and the customs of the folk have been called upon, as in Germany, Italy, Japan, and Russia, to give warmth and comradeship and protection in a world made cold by capitalist practice and classical liberal ideas, such a theory is doubly dangerous. The call of the Nazis: "Ein Reich, Ein Volk, Ein

Führer"; the outburst of Hitler: "I need men for judges who are deeply convinced that law ought not to guarantee the interests of the individual against those of the State; that their duty is to see to it that above all Germany does not suffer"; the cry of Mussolini: "For Fascism the State is an absolute, in whose presence individuals and groups are the relative," show clearly the connection between Nazism, Fascism, and the organic theory of the State. We can reflect, for good measure, that the organic theory is necessarily undemocratic, since the toes cannot dictate to the brain and since there is no representative government in the individual organism. Moreover, in organic theory equality is openly regarded as a delusion. For men fulfil different functions, and those functions are not equally important for the maintenance of the whole. Hence they are to be treated as equal only to the extent to which the State itself decides that its interests require them to be equal. When, in addition, we remind ourselves that States have never in all history been as strong as they are today, we may well doubt if a doctrine whose tendency is inevitably to make them stronger is really desirable in the 20th century.

The mechanistic theory of the State is strong where the organic theory is weak, weak where the organic theory is strong. Its teaching, that the individual is real and the State only a device, that there is no such thing as a common good of the State which is something other than the good of all citizens, is a very powerful and timely insistence that the State can justify itself only in so far as it exists for the individuals who compose it. The great merit, indeed, of the mechanistic theory lies in its safeguarding of the individual. It recognises, of course, that individuals differ in natural capacity and therefore in what they have to offer to the State. But it will not agree that the State has the right to sacrifice them in consequence. It separates State and society, so that society can on occasion act as a support to the individual in his relationship to the State. It agrees that men may have to resist the State on grounds of conscience, knowing the anarchism latent in such an admission, but believing it less dangerous than the assertion of perpetually superior morality by the State. Mechanistic theory, moreover, lends itself very well to the creation of democratic institutions, thereby providing further safeguards for the individual. It can reasonably be claimed, too, to be a better inoculation against the new tribalism, and to be perhaps a little bit less of a menace to peace than organic theory. At least it does not make the strong State unnecessarily stronger by giving it an almost religious devotion. And it is not committed, as is organic theory, to the view that the State is the final end of man's evolution. It regards it merely as a device that has proved indispensable in the past and that can give way to something else should something else prove indispensable in the future.

But like the organic theory, the mechanistic theory of the State is of course very much open to criticism. There is nothing spiritual about a machine, nothing that calls out the best in a man. It is difficult to deny either that the State can or that it should do this. Perhaps it is not an accident that States which regard themselves as machines seem on the whole more concerned with material than with spiritual values. Mechanistic theory does not take account of the individual's wish to be something better than he is. At least it does not consider that this is something in which the State should have an interest or something which the State can do anything about. There is certainly truth in the view that in mechanistic theories of the State an adequate account of justice is possible only by surreptitiously substituting the rational spiritual being for the isolated natural being on whom the theory rests, so that the fundamental contradiction of, for instance, Locke and Adam Smith is that they work with natural units and treat them like rational units, thereby demonstrating the inadequacy of the philosophic movement that they represent. Indeed, it is never easy in mechanistic theories to understand the alchemy whereby private interests are turned into public duties. It may be added, too, that mechanistic theory has rarely had a sufficient appreciation of the importance of society in developing the citizen. Further, if there are dangers in describing freedom as the pursuit of rational action, there is aridity in defining it as the absence of restraint, and the frequency with which mechanistic theories do this is significant. And if organic theory lends itself so readily to the new tribalism, it may be that mechanistic theory has done something to bring about that new tribalism by lending itself so readily to the view which Ford expressed: "We now know that anything which is economically right is also morally right. There can be no conflict between good economics and good morals." Anyhow, it may be maintained that mechanistic theory is simply unreal, that it does not correspond to our experience. The citizen, says Bradley, "sees the State every day in its practice refute every other doctrine, and do with the moral approval of all what the explicit theory of hardly anyone will morally justify. He sees instincts are better than so-called 'principles.' He sees in the hour of need what are called 'rights' laughed at, 'freedom,' the liberty to do what one pleases, trampled on, the claims of the individual trampled under foot, and theories burst like cobwebs. And he sees, as of old, the heart of a nation rise high and beat in the breast of each one of her citizens, till her safety and her honour are dearer to each than life, till to those who live her shame and sorrow, if such is allotted, outweigh their loss, and death seems a little thing to those who go for her to a common and nameless grave." Some of the above criticisms might be met by the reply that society is a living growth, an organism, and that this living organism, society, creates for its own convenience the machine that we call the State. But not all the above criticisms, and certainly not the last, could be refuted in this way.

"The discovery of wisdom is the surpassing good," Philo wrote. "When this is found all the people will sing." It will be apparent that all wisdom is not with either the organic or the mechanistic view of the State, and that mankind as yet has but learned to croak. Nevertheless, all who think of these things will be partisans, although it will be a matter of little profit and conceivably of great harm if they allow themselves to think, in their conviction that the one view is the better, that all who hold the other are fools or knaves. Both views, it must be admitted, can be held by men who are neither. Moreover, it must be conceded that they correspond to existing States. Great Britain and America are clearly examples of the mechanistic State, as Italy and Germany yesterday and Russia today, with its State worship and subordination of the individual to the State, are examples of the organic State. Further, it must be agreed, the differences between the organic and the mechanistic theories of the State, and therefore between the States which embody these theories, are fundamental. Much as we might long for one world in which there will be a single moral and political system, we have to admit that such a world does not yet exist and has little prospect of existing in the immediate future. The world in which we live is a world of States with such different moral beliefs that no compromise in principle is possible between them. And the question we must ask, given differences which are genuine, fundamental, irreducible, and incapable of compromise and given the embodiment of these fundamentally opposed points of views in first-class Powers, is : Can such different views peacefully co-exist? Is the world committed to a series of ideological wars, tempered perhaps by tiredness, but leading inevitably to the last battle of the Gods that Norse mythology foretold?

Kant did not believe that such radically different views could live peacefully together. Accepting the sovereignty of each State and rejecting the idea of a world State, he thought that international peace was possible only when all States were ruled on something like the same internal principles. Lenin, in another context, agreed with him. "We are living," he said, "not merely in a State, but in a system of States, and the co-existence of the Soviet Republic side by side with imperialist States for a long time is unthinkable. One or the other must triumph in the end." The experience of our own lifetime, too, must make us wonder if Kant and Lenin were not right. The 20th century has become known as the century of violence because of the devastating wars that have already taken place in it between organic and mechanistic States, the last of which has left in a yet stronger and more menacing position the last remaining great organic State. Furthermore that State has shown that it is at the moment in the grip of a force compound of the expansive imperialistic zest of a strong and growing State and of a proselytising faith. That force wherever it has shown itself, as for instance in France at the time of the Revolution, has come to be recognised as one of the most explosive in history, big with tribulation for other peoples. Russia, in effect, says today what Boissy d'Anglas triumphantly said in France during the Revolution : "There is only one good way to administer a country, and if we have found it why should other people not benefit by it?" Therefore the words which Pitt applied to the French : "They will not accept under the name of Liberty any model of government but that which is conformable to their own opinions and ideas, and all men must learn from the mouth of their cannon the propagation of their system in every part of the world" can be legitimately applied to the Russians now. And we have learned in bitterness in the last few years that no genuine agreement between the Russian and the Western world has proved possible. Clearly, then, it would be stupid to believe that there is no evidence whatever for the view of Lord Russell that "we are now again in an epoch of wars of religion, but a religion is now called an ideology," and dangerous to be sure that such an epoch will not demand blood as it did in the 16th and 17th centuries.

But though it would be madness to forget that only with mutual exhaustion, the spreading of the ideas of the Politiques to whom the new religion of the State mattered more than the old religion of the Church, and the development of Rationalism to which all religions were equally false and all fanaticism folly, did the epoch of religious wars come to an end, it is unnecessary to believe that there is any historical law according to which what has once demanded blood will always continue to do so. History does not repeat itself, if only because men can read its elementary lessons and determine not to repeat mistakes. To avoid the sin of hybris let it be said at once that they are unlikely to run out of mistakes to make in either the present or the future. But there may be a limit to the price which even fanaticism is prepared to pay to achieve its object; in an atomic age the price to be paid would certainly be high. Indeed, the very price which all must pay if those who deny the possibility of the peaceful co-existence of the organic and mechanistic theories embodied in their respective States are right is such that it can itself be used as an argument to prove them wrong. For if it becomes plain beyond all doubt that to follow the path of proselytising faith will be to damage national interests, consciously, deliberately, and devastatingly, even the most Messianic of peoples might be expected to recoil. After all, men have learned to get along together even though their views are as irreconcilable as those of Catholics and Protestants, True Believers, and Infidels. There is much truth in the dissenting opinion of Justice Holmes in the famous case of Abrams *v*. the U.S.: "Persecution for the expression of opinions seems to me perfectly logical. If you have no doubt of your premises or your power and want a certain result with all your heart, you naturally express your wishes in law and sweep away all opposition. But when men have realised that time has upset many fighting faiths, they may come to believe even more than they believe in the very foundations of their own conduct that the ultimate good is better reached by free trade in ideas—that the best test of truth is the power of thought to get itself accepted in the competition of the market, and that truth is the only ground upon which their wishes can be safely carried out." If men can indeed remember that time has upset many fighting faiths, they must also reflect upon the impossibility, or at least the very great difficulty, of exporting either the organic or the mechanistic view of the State. The West, for instance, has found in Germany and Japan how difficult it is to convert a people who believed in the organic theory of the State to the mechanistic theory. Hitler's New Order similarly showed the difficulty of converting a people who believed in the mechanistic theory of the State to the organic. And Soviet Russia today reveals the contradiction that was to be found in Napoleonic France—the assertion of the external rights of National Sovereignty and the denial of the same rights to others. Those, too, who are understandably oppressed by the persistence and virulence of a communism that seems impervious to argument might recall with comfort the words of Herbert Spencer: "A wave of opinion, reaching a certain height, cannot be stopped by evidence, but has gradually to spend itself." Remembering all this, men may find in it yet another reason for believing that situations will not always be so strained and that both views of the State can exist peacefully side by side.

Upon those who believe that they can, a very great responsibility rests. They must make their view prevail that however valuable Crusaders may be their rightful place is not in the Foreign Offices of the world. They must never forget the cost of Crusades nor allow others to forget it either. They must beware of the common danger so well illustrated by the Vice-Chancellor of Cambridge University in his opposition to the scheme of the Eastern Counties Railway "to run excursion trains to Cambridge on the Lord's Day with the object of attracting foreigners and undesirable characters to the University of Cambridge on that sacred day . . . the Vice-Chancellor of the University of Cambridge wishes to point out to the Directors of the Eastern Counties Railway that such a proceeding would be as displeasing to Almighty God as it is to the Vice-Chancellor of the University of Cambridge"—of acting as the assured but unaccredited agents of God. They must expect less from politics, refusing to believe that God speaks invariably in the Cabinet in London, the White House in Washington, or the Kremlin in Moscow. And they must pay more attention to politics, taking care not to allow those situations to develop that would encourage the devotees of ideological conflict. In this way they may act as the new Politiques leading the way from an era of ideological conflict into one wherein practical adjustment of interests is possible. If this does not happen, there will be without question a new predicament of mankind, calling for a new political philosophy to resolve it. But it would not profit us to speculate about the ideas of the post atomic-war world.

INDEX